LIMITLESS SKY

Life Lessons from the Himalayas

David Charles Manners

RIDER

LONDON · SYDNEY · AUCKLAND · JOHANNESBURG

1 3 5 7 9 10 8 6 4 2

First published in 2014 by Rider, an imprint of Ebury Publishing

Ebury Publishing is a Random House Group company

Text copyright © 2014 by David Charles Manners

David Charles Manners has asserted his right to be identified
as the author of this Work in accordance with the Copyright,
Designs and Patents Act 1988.

The Random House Group Limited Reg. No. 954009

Addresses for companies within the Random House Group
can be found at: www.randomhouse.co.uk

A CIP catalogue record for this book is
available from the British Library

The Random House Group Limited supports The Forest Stewardship
Council® (FSC®), the leading international forest-certification organisation.
Our books carrying the FSC label are printed on FSC®-certified paper.
FSC is the only forest certification scheme supported by the leading
environmental organisations, including Greenpeace.
Our paper procurement policy can be found at:
www.randomhouse.co.uk/environment

Typeset by SX Composing DTP, Rayleigh, Essex
Printed in Great Britain by Clays Ltd, St Ives plc

ISBN 9781846044458

Copies are available at special rates for bulk orders. Contact the sales
development team on 020 7840 8487 for more information.

To buy books by your favourite authors and register for offers, visit:
www.randomhouse.co.uk

David Charles Manners is the co-founder of Sarvashubhamkara, a charity that works in north India with socially ostracised individuals and communities, most of whom bear the stigma of leprosy. He is also a representative for Diversity Role Models, a charity that works with British schools to eradicate homophobic bullying. His first book, *In the Shadow of Crows*, received international acclaim. For over twenty years, he has lived between the Sussex Downs in Britain and the foothills of the Bengal and Garhwal Himalayas.

*To the memory of Penny Povey,
from whose joy for life and unreserved
generosity of heart I continue to learn.*

Listen with open ears.
Approach the world with an unfettered mind.
Learn wisdom.

Kushal Magar: *In the Shadow of Crows*

CONTENTS

AUTHOR'S NOTE

Limitless Sky describes real people and events. Time has been condensed to maintain the narrative, whilst personal names, places and details connected to those portrayed have been changed to protect their true identities. May this account do them justice and offer the reader ideas for new ways to live and love more fully, joyfully and wisely.

INTRODUCTION

To those who are in darkness,
this is the light that dispels it.
Tripura Rahasya

I n the foothills of the Bengal Himalaya, snow-capped
peaks hover like static clouds above forests of cinnamon,
cardamom and dense bamboo. Villages balance on
wooden stilts along ridges stained poinsettia scarlet and
datura white.

Each new dawn is marked by rites at shrines to deities
of cave and spring. And when day is done, dusk descends to
the quarrel of crows, the keen of jackals and the rhythmic
'journeying' of shamans' drums.

These foothills were once the mountain homeland of
none but the Lepcha, a distinctive tribe with a language,
countenance and culture of their own. Today, they share
their native landscape with Bhutia and Bhutanese who
have breached their borders; Bengalis and Mawaris from
the Plains who now monopolise all commerce; and Indian
infantry posted to protect against expansionist ambitions of
the neighbouring Chinese.

The Lepcha also share their fertile soil with Tibetans who
fled the Great Leap Forwards bearing gilded bodhisattvas and
arcane texts; the remnants of an Anglo-Indian community
that still gathers beneath decaying Victorian gothic to sing

salvation for their hybrid souls; and with Nepalis, whose language and culture have come to dominate the region since they escaped the tyranny of Gurkha kings and took to plucking British tea.

It is in the heights and valleys of these busy foothills that a remarkable approach to life survives, characterised by rejection of any rigid creed, hierarchy, priesthood or dogma, its gentle wisdom imparted through progressive initiations to protect against misuse. Those who choose its skilful path are challenged to reconsider who and what they believe themselves to be. And this, that they might learn to live and love not only fully, fearlessly, joyfully, wisely and without condition, but also without detriment to themselves or others.

In the Nepali-speaking Bengal Himalaya – where I underwent a series of initiations over several years – these practical, transformative teachings are referred to as Thuture Veda, the Spoken Knowledge; or Purna Marga, the Path of Wholeness, Abundance, Contentment.

However, whether practised in the lowland millet meadows that merge into rice paddies, or the hillside jungles that temper into forests of dark deodar, this tantric path to wisdom is more commonly called Paramparaa: 'that which leads forwards, mediates, restores order', 'that which is our best future' – the Tradition.

PART ONE

I

There is no fate, no destiny.
Our own choices determine the course of our lives
For ours is a universe of infinite possibilities.
Bindra

'Do you know what you want?'

I blinked back at the serene stranger sitting at the scarlet doors of his little wooden temple.

I watched his smile furrow sun-parched skin, exposing a clutter of tea-stained teeth.

I watched the bright intensity of his eyes explore me in unsettling detail, as though dissolving my defences to render me transparent.

Yet still I could not find an answer to his question.

I had journeyed through India alone, from Gujarati fields and Rajasthani deserts, through Himachali hill-stations and across the immensity of the Plains, to reach the eastern foothills of the Himalaya. In fulfilment of a promise once made to my grandmother, I had found the place where the lives of two childhood heroes had been rumoured to converge: the very hilltop town where my 'Hindoo' Great-Uncle Oscar had taken a tribal princess as his wife, and where their progeny had been dandled on the lap of poet-

1

philosopher Rabindranath Tagore. For here, gathered in verandah-fronted bungalows as though just waiting to be found, I had come upon a clan of Anglo-Indian cousin-brothers and cousin-sisters, cousin-uncles and cousin-aunts, all of whom had, until that moment, been consigned to little more than domestic legend.

Yet whilst I knew the facts, the real reason why I now found myself sitting on this chilly hillside beneath dense cinchona trees, silver river far below and snow-topped Kanchenjunga high above, was still unclear.

It had all begun when my newly discovered cousin Samuel and I had braved the busy marketplace at Kalimpong, the old hill-station's ramshackle heart, piled high with vegetables and spices, bloody meat and stinking fish. I bent to scour broken prayer-wheels, strings of coloured beads and manuscripts laid out across a blanket on the ground. Beneath the clutter, I found a wormy wooden plaque inscribed with angular calligraphy and asked its price. The pedlar shook his head, insisting he could not let me leave with anything so beetle-tooled and damaged. He attempted to direct my attention instead to a cardboard box of shiny new trinkets, but my heart was set upon the broken board.

The old man had smiled.

'He says you have an unfettered mind,' Samuel translated. 'And now he wants me to take you to somewhere in the mountains I've never even heard of, called Lapu-*basti*, the village of Lapu. He seems to think someone is waiting for you there.'

With all the reckless courage of our youth, Samuel and I had grinned at one another, our sign that we would accept the hawker's peculiar quest without hesitation. We had both been eager for any opportunity that might hint at new adventure. I noticed, however, that on returning home Samuel told his mother neither the true origin nor purpose of our madcap expedition as she busied herself in the kitchen with the wrapping of our travel-tuck and a merciless interrogation.

Just four days apart in age, although a good foot's difference in height and a broad continent apart in colouring and culture, Samuel and I had forged a loyal friendship on first meeting. Together we had found an effortless familiarity that already defied the limits of mere genetic ties, or even the casual mateship so often easily shared between young men. Samuel's unflagging zest for life, his mischievous wit, instinctive kindness and fearless affection had immediately won my admiration. Even through his rare mix of Anglo-Swedish, Lepcha, Tibetan and Nepalese blood, we still recognised in each other traits of both character and appearance that confirmed our bond of blood.

Samuel and I had begun our climb at daybreak. By the time all vegetable *pakhoras*, fresh tomato chutney, boiled eggs, pancake-like *puri* and pungent *churpi* yak's cheese were consumed, the sun had already passed its zenith. We had travelled far, from humid jungle up to chilly pine, down monsoon-shattered roads to temperate oak and maple.

We had eventually arrived at a remote scattering of cottages and step-cut fields, where a woman herding goats and trailing chickens directed us down the lower hillside to Lapu-*basti*. Yet still I did not know why we had come.

The path was perilous in its steepness, but as we stepped out from the dark of forest trees, the entire Kanchenjunga range was revealed before us. And, for a very real moment, the tick of time had paused.

To our right, we caught sight of a pair of wooden buildings tucked into the hillside: one a single-roomed hut, the other a rustic temple. Both were surrounded by carefully tended flowers. Both were topped by quiet crows.

The man sat so motionless that neither of us had seen him in the shade of the temple canopy. Shoulders wrapped in a woollen shawl, legs crossed and tightly bound in white *suruwal* trousers. Feet flat, bare and black.

'*Dayagari aunuhos. Ma asa gardaitye*,' he had announced in cheerful greeting. 'Please come. I have been expecting you.'

Samuel turned to me with alarm. 'David-*dajoo*, I don't understand why we're here,' he whispered, deferentially calling me his 'elder brother'. 'This man's a *jhankri*!'

'A what?' I hissed, unsettled by my normally dauntless cousin's sudden apprehension.

'Here, we like to say the goddess first formed humankind from earth and fire, wind and stone, leaf and water. But then she suffered to see our self-inflicted troubles – you know, like jealousy and anger. So she took a handful of purest snow from the mountain Pundim Chyu, and formed the first *jhankri* to oversee our welfare.'

He glanced back towards the man and dropped his voice yet further.

'Well, *dajoo*, this is a *jhankri* – a word that means both "few and far between", because they're very rare, and "one who peeps in and out", because of their remarkable insights into the true nature of things.'

I was intrigued.

'Just look at the *marensi mala* around his neck!' Samuel exclaimed. 'Little skulls carved from old men's bones. And see the flute pipe in his lap? Know what that's made from?'

I peered at its knobbly length, shrugged and innocently suggested, 'Bamboo?'

'No, no!' Samuel grimaced. 'It's bone from a dead man's forearm!'

I looked back into the face of the placid figure on the temple steps. He smiled and nodded that we were welcome to approach.

'Be careful, *dajoo*,' Samuel insisted. 'The *jhankri* have great power . . .'

And so it was that I had stepped forwards alone to bow my head courteously in *pranam*.

II

A scattered mind is the cause of pain.
Tripura Rahasya

'*Namaskar hajur*! *Ma* David *huñ*,' I announced in introduction, bravely experimenting with my newly minted Nepali.

'*Namaskar bhai*,' the *jhankri* replied warmly, addressing me as 'younger brother'. '*Ma* Kushal Magar *huñ*.'

The affability of our introductions seemed to prompt Samuel to take his place beside me. He offered his own respectful *pranam*, then turned to explain in a pantomime half-whisper that among the Nepali-speakers of the eastern Himalaya *jhankris* undertook the role of healers, advisors, reconcilers and teachers – a varied vocation performed through a skilful blend of symbol, word, chant, drum, dance and trance.

The consequence of this responsibility is such that these highly respected *jhankri* men and *jhankrini* women not only live relatively solitary, liminal lives, but possess physical stamina, mental stability and intellect to a remarkable degree.

They are also of both a perceptive and receptive disposition, and considered bearers of such primal knowledge that they are referred to as *prakrtacharins*: those who live in accordance with the fundamental form, the source – with nature.

In the face of such arcane erudition, I wavered for a moment. What madness had seized Cousin Samuel and me to follow instructions from a hawker in the town bazaar and undertake our journey to this quiet stranger, before whose gaze I now found myself so acutely exposed?

Only the *jhankri*'s kindly smile suspended my anxiety.

'Come, sit,' he offered in invitation, unexpectedly revealing an effortless English.

I had taken my place beside him on the temple steps, but found myself unsure of the cultural formalities now expected of me. I knew in these hills never to pat a child on the head, nor point my feet at company. I knew never to lick or point my fingers, blow my nose in public, and certainly never to spill or step on rice. However, as to the more subtle social niceties, I was at a loss.

Instead, I purposefully avoided his eyes by seeking out the mountain peaks that gleamed where clouds might have been expected.

'So you have travelled far across the Seven Rivers,' the *jhankri* said, drawing me to look at him. 'But tell me, brother, do you know what you want?'

I blinked back in silence.

Was he asking what I wanted from this meeting, or from my life? Was he asking what I wanted of him, or of myself?

'You may not yet know why you are here,' he responded, as though to my unvoiced doubts, 'but again I must ask: do you know what you want?'

I had been raised in a culture that told me I wanted a mortgage on a comfortable house, generous bank credit, sunny holidays, a well-waxed car, and the promise of an easy retirement of all-inclusive cruises and decent dentistry. I had been brought up being told I wanted a dependable and patient wife with whom to decline into dotage, children to justify my existence by perpetuating my genes, and an extended family bound by that tricky mix of guilt and duty with whom to endure Christmas.

'Do you know what you want?' the *jhankri* pressed. 'For it is in this that all else begins.'

Perhaps it was the clarity of mountain air I breathed that now exposed an overwhelming truth to me. What I had been told I wanted, I did not want. What I wanted in its place, I did not know.

'Brother, life is limitless,' the *jhankri* declared, leaning in to set his hand against my heart, 'but only half lived when undertaken without intention. A wise man does nothing without purpose, without first understanding his reasons and its consequence. He does nothing without dedicating each deed of every day with mindful intent.'

I glanced back to Samuel, expecting him to beckon me away to the safety of the road. Instead, he tipped his head and raised his eyebrows, as though it were some secret sign I should have understood.

'So what of you?' the *jhankri* asked. 'Do you know why you do your deeds, say your words, think your thoughts? If not, are you really so different from a performing monkey or a trained dog, merely reacting with learnt behaviour at the promise of reward and praise, or in fear of punishment and rejection?'

I felt a twinge of indignation rise at his suggestion.

And yet, as I looked into the unfaltering humanity of this man's face, I recognised beneath my affront an uncomfortable admission: that I could claim little, if any, true intention in anything I did, said or thought, beyond the satisfaction of others' expectations and my own interminable self-interest.

By my want of any true self-determination was I really condemned to live a life of repetitive reactions to mundane anxieties of my own making? And was it possible that this little man, with his bone adornments and his clear, bright eyes, could really know a viable alternative?

'Our mountain Tradition offers a different way of being,' the *jhankri* announced with quiet confidence, as though again in response to thoughts I had unwittingly spoken out loud. 'For we are a people whose understanding of ourselves is founded upon the *Moksha Shastra* – the teachings of liberation.'

He drew close enough for me to smell sweet spices on his clothes and breath.

'A solemn title for what are, in truth, simple ways. Ways that afford clarity in every thought, word and act, because all is done with clear intent, with *bhavana* – a word we also use for the place where things grow and flourish, like a fertile field.'

His eyes scanned his vegetables, tapioca and rice paddy, as though to emphasise the point.

'This is the liberating force of our Tradition – for if you choose to change your intent, change your purpose, you change your interaction with the world, and thereby change your life.'

He touched his heart, then placed his hand gently back on mine.

'So again I ask: brother, do you know what you want?'

I looked into his eyes and returned his smile. He had given me my answer.

The learning from Kushal Magar, for which until that moment I had not known I yearned, had already begun.

III

Knowledge is something which you can use.
Belief is something which uses you.
                    Idries Shah

'What do you know of our Thuture Veda,' the *jhankri* asked, 'the Spoken Knowledge of our mountain, Shaiva Tantra Yoga?'

The truth was I knew nothing. I had practised a simple, private, meditative yoga since my teens, when I had first explored techniques learnt from a library book as a way to help ease the emotional and physical anarchy of adolescence. Whilst the term Shaiva remained a mystery, I felt unable to admit that I only associated Tantra with weekend retreats in the West Country involving scented candles and a whimsy of sexual mysticism.

I nudged Samuel, who had shuffled up to sit beside me, and hunched my shoulders.

'Well, the Tradition of our eastern Himalaya is very ancient,' the *jhankri* began. 'Although, of course, age is not a recommendation in itself, except that our ways have been proved and refined by innumerable preceding generations.'

I meant only to glance at Samuel – but in contrast to his earlier anxiety, he had now adopted such an uncharacteristic solemnity that it provoked from me a second, stronger nudge.

'The Tradition of our ancestors is a practical method that guides us to examine our unconsidered beliefs, the assumptions through which we inaccurately see ourselves and others. A method that enables us to press beyond the boundaries of our ordinary perception and thereby recognise the underlying unity of all things. And this that we might learn to live and love more fully, fearlessly – and thereby more effectively, wisely and with greater joy.'

'That's a lot of big promises,' I replied.

'All of which are fulfilled through the gradual deepening of self-knowledge,' he said with a smile, 'by understanding better the choices we make to feel, think, speak and act the way we do, that unmindful, detrimental behaviour might lose its force, that we might render ourselves of ever greater benefit to others.'

This I liked. Not, then, so-called 'esoteric' practices to slow ageing, prolong virility, or win membership of some self-congratulatory, elitist fellowship. Not the 'Raising of Kundalini' or 'Opening of Chakras' for little more than some narcissistic, self-seeking 'personal growth'. Not yet more self-interest masquerading as self-awareness.

This seemed to be different. A practical method, the *jhankri* had insisted, that enabled its practitioners to render themselves of benefit to others.

He had me intrigued.

'So who runs your Tradition?' I asked, assuming there had to be some Brahmin boss or other holding holy court in yet another Western-sponsored ashram.

'There is no organisation of followers,' he replied. 'No priesthood, no dogma, no creed – for our Tradition is not a religion.'

I thought back to the rigour of the religious schools in which I had been raised, with their enforced deference to a staff of Very Reverend men, none of whom had ever seemed more worthy of their venerable titles than the caretakers or dinner-ladies who had dutifully attended to our temporal needs. And then the communal hymns I had been made to sing to a schizophrenic Sunday school god, who beseeched us to be forgiving, meek and mild, whilst having ordered his chosen few to repeated genocidal slaughter without mercy.

Even as a child, I had been aware that I was being trained to worship an apparently sadistic deity who had drowned the world, turned a woman to salt and murdered Egyptian babies. I still recalled my distress when I learnt that this same god had permitted wild bears to kill forty-two boys in a frenzied mauling for no other reason than that the children had called a Hebrew prophet 'Baldie'. I had also soon discovered such accounts could not be dismissed as Old Testament excess, for this had evidently been a psychopathic parent, whose scriptural postscript of Revelation catalogued his intention to starve and poison us, harry us into caves, torment us with a series of imaginative plagues, then burn most of us to cinders.

I had therefore always wondered how this same avenging, jealous god could then command me to love first him and then my neighbour, when he had repeatedly obliged his elect minority to butcher theirs simply because they held a different point of view.

The perplexity on all matters spiritual that this education had instilled had driven the tirelessly curious child I had once been to explore religious traditions beyond the Protestantism in which I had been raised. By the age of ten, Frazer's *Golden Bough* had not only inspired me to earn a Cub Scout badge in Olympian Mythology, but to teach myself the Ionic alphabet of ancient Greece. Bewitched next by *Beowulf* and Tolkien's Baggins, I had studied the Norse gods and, to my parents' dismay, passed an entire summer refusing to write in anything but Elder Futhark Runes.

In my early teens, I had pursued the Abrahamic roots of my own upbringing by first borrowing a Pocket Penguin Koran from the school library. I had then popped into the local synagogue for an introduction to Ashkenazi Hebrew and had explored the possibility of circumcision by keeping my foreskin withdrawn for a singularly vexatious afternoon.

In response to growing academic pressures, I had turned to the unrevised Tridentine Rite both to explore the 'papish' customs of the Roman Catholic Church and to improve my classroom Latin. This in turn had motivated the precocious composition of a liturgy for my own Requiem Mass, which had kept me intensely engaged for the duration of a long and cheerless winter.

At the age of fourteen, I had been approached in the street by an emaciated Brummie and, in spite of her disquieting shaved scalp and persistent finger-cymbals, had agreed to read her complimentary *Bhagavad Gita*. Whilst I had been charmed by the gaudy illustrations of muscle-boys Arjuna and Krishna, its philosophy of devotional passivity, divinely ordained caste, misogyny and deference to an authoritarian priesthood had soon diminished its initial lure.

I had talked to smiling Jehovah's Witnesses, Christadelphians and Scientologists. I had picked up proselytising pamphlets and trawled through tracts. I had invited friendly Methodists and Moonies into the house, to all of whom I had offered barley water and Jaffa Cakes with prudent impartiality.

Yet still I had remained uneasy at what had proven to be their shared tendency to supplant our innate humanity with prescriptive 'moral' law; unsullied human fellowship with new systems of segregation; professed peacemaking with a scriptural language of hypocritical aggression. And, perhaps most disquieting of all, the pervasive inclination to displace common sense with the glorification of a faith so blind that it was degraded to near medieval superstition.

Now to have found myself presented with a way of life that seemed to imply freedom from both overbearing patriarchy and dictatorial doctrine was not only wholly unexpected but undoubtedly worth investigation.

'So if not a religion,' I asked, 'then what *is* the Tradition?'

'A practical approach to life that steadily expands ordinary consciousness,' the *jhankri* replied, 'whose adherents aspire to perceive beyond the limitations they impose on themselves, as well as those imposed by their familial, social or religious culture. And thereby that they might actively contribute to the well-being, the quality of kindness and humanity, of all humankind.'

'Then why the images of deities in your temple?' I challenged, looking towards the scarlet doors beyond his shoulders. Samuel followed my gaze and instinctively raised a hand to touch his heart.

'Our gods and goddesses may seem perplexing to the uninitiated, yet all are simply symbols of the same union of consciousness and energy of which crows, flowers, trees, seasons, stars – and you – are all but one expression.'

I peered into the shadows of his incense-scented sanctuary, to settle on the figure of a goddess draped in crimson cloth. I wondered what, beyond her eight raised arms, benign smile and mount of tooth-bared tiger, I could be missing.

'Perhaps think of them as helpful tools, employed to explore and change the ineffective, self-defeating patterns that we all mindlessly tend to follow.'

My gaze remained held in the temple's shadows.

'For if we change the self-image we believe in and therefore project, we change our destiny.'

'Is that what makes you people so cheerful?' I had to ask, for I had been struck by this very particular quality among the inhabitants of these hills.

'Certainly the Tradition teaches us to seek and embrace joy in life, here and now' – the *jhankri* smiled – 'rather than anticipating it as some promised reward after death for obedience to others' dogmas, their prescribed moralities and priests.'

I recalled the inquisitive, naive adolescent I had been, entrusting clerics with confessions of 'misdeeds' so normal, if not integral to the natural evolution from boy to man, that their threats of certain damnation now seemed pathetic and perverse. Yet at the time, I had allowed them to instil in me a harsh revulsion for my maturing body and a raw alarm for the pleasures it promised. I had even allowed the censure of their scriptures to convince me I was doomed to meet my end as a discarded tare in the divine harvest, to char as stubble in God's furrowed field when humankind faced its Final Judgement.

The contrast between my disquieting memories of ordained men who had insisted that their version of 'salvation' could be earned only by transcending the very qualities that make us human and the *jhankri's* words that now afforded new courage, confidence and perhaps even comfort, could not have been more plain.

'So have no doubt, our Tradition is wholly life-affirming,' he said, beaming. 'For a fundamental principle is that the full enjoyment of human experience and the expansion of consciousness – which some term enlightenment – are in truth one and the same.'

I joined him in his grin.

And, in consideration of the life from which I had so recently stepped, felt like cheering.

IV

Deliverance is not for me in renunciation.
I feel the embrace of freedom in a thousand bonds of delight.
Rabindranath Tagore

Kushal Magar settled a battered metal pot on to his open fire and began to boil water.

'You should know from the start that the Tradition embraces every aspect of life without reservation,' he said with a sweep of his eyes, as though to encompass mountains, trees and sky. 'You see, we prefer to remain fully active and effective in the world, continuing our usual business, attending to our duties and relationships, whilst relishing the innumerable pleasures that afford us health and happiness – and life its meaning.'

Samuel and I had been sitting with the *jhankri* for little more than an hour, and yet he was already turning on its head the very foundation of what I had been taught to believe.

'A spiritual path without austerity and self-denial?' I laughed.

'Brother, any notion of the "spiritual" is entirely of your own making,' he gently corrected, 'for here we do not differentiate between the "spiritual" and "worldly". For us, they are one and the same. Even our Nepali words your people translate as "spiritual" – *atmik* and *chinmaya* – actually refer only to "one's true self" and "purity of intention". And the word commonly translated as "worldly" – *jajaal* – actually refers to "the joyful disorder" of family and children.'

With every statement, the *jhankri* increased my curiosity.

'As for the "austerity and self-denial" you have been

15

expecting, perhaps you would first like to consider your response to the word "pleasure".'

Easy, I thought. Extravagance, debauchery, indulgence. Food, money, sex.

'Perhaps you think pleasure something naughty? Morally corrupt? That a worthwhile, "good" life can only be one of, as you put it, austerity and self-denial?'

I believed myself liberal at heart and wanted to say no.

To my surprise, I now knew my answer would be a lie.

'The Tradition, in contrast, recognises that mindful pleasure is not only the central driving force of human experience, but has a far more profound effect on man's physical and mental well-being than any amount of asceticism.'

'But what do you consider mindful pleasure?' I asked.

'Are you in pain?' he unexpectedly responded.

I had undoubtedly known my share of hurts and aches, for I had grown up with bruised shins, scuffed knees and embedded thorns − all short-lived wounds earned gladly in the company of my siblings as we four built tree-houses in the apple orchard, camps in the forsaken geography of pigsties, straw-bale dens in the rat-runs of abandoned barns.

At that moment, however, my nose may have been cold, my legs a little stiff from sitting too long on an unrelenting floor, but I was certainly not suffering.

'If not in pain, then what?'

I was surprised by my inability to answer such a simple question.

'Then let me teach you some new Nepali words. First, *dukha* − disturbance, obstruction, unease. Discomfort, distress, difficulty. We use it to describe a period of sickness, or our customary year of mourning at the loss of a parent.'

'*Dukha jilo* is a hard and troubled life,' added Samuel,

who was now huddling against my side to keep warm. 'And *dukha bhognu* means "to suffer pain".'

Considering the concern he had expressed upon our arrival at the little temple, my sunny cousin now seemed unaccountably at ease in the company of the 'bogeyman' *jhankri* and his dead men's bones.

'We also use *dukha* to describe a constriction around the heart,' Kushal Magar explained. 'The sort of suffering mankind too often chooses by repeating the same self-defeating habits, the same detrimental thoughts, words, actions.'

It seemed harsh to hear such an observation put in these plain terms. And yet I recognised this trait in friends and family. And in myself.

'Now, the opposite of *dukha*'s suffering is *sukha*,' he continued, a new brightness in his voice for emphasis, 'a word we use to describe ease and balance. Good health. A fertile mind and body. Comfort. All that is prosperous, agreeable, liberating – release of the heart.'

'*Antar sukha* means "to be happy from within",' chipped in Samuel. 'And *sukha purbak* is anything we do with happiness and delight!' he added, playfully running his fingers around my ribs to make me squirm.

'What a gift, then' – Kushal Magar smiled – 'that the Tradition guides us to choose to relinquish our interpretation of life as *dukha*'s suffering, which is merely an imbalance, an aberration, and instead choose *sukha*'s joyful pleasure, which is not only our natural state, but both our birthright and our moral obligation.'

I closed my eyes for a moment to repeat to myself a statement so unfamiliar that it seemed bewildering.

'It is a truth you can know for yourself every day of your life,' he declared, 'by beginning to recognise the pleasure in even the most familiar and seemingly mundane sensations. Whether at your work, at study, or in your bed. In company, or alone.'

I kept my eyes shut to feel my tongue gently pressed behind my teeth, my palms warm upon my knees, the softness of cloth against my skin.

'So why not choose to relish that you have lungs to breathe with? Then inhale every scent, humidity and temperature without judgement as to whether or not it is to your liking. Relish that you have arms to reach out into the world with – then allow your hands to feel earth, bark, stone, leaf, cloth and skin, both yours and others'. Relish that you have legs to stand on – then step with feet bared upon earth, on grass, in water, to delight at every sensation as though it were your first. And why not choose to raise your head against even the harshest wind or rain, to feel its wonder as though you had never before stepped outside?'

I breathed in the cool, sweet savour of mountain air – and vowed to retain this one lesson, since I could already see how its application alone could prove transformative.

'And just as life's most simple pleasures may be a constant, nourishing, uplifting force in our lives if we but choose to acknowledge them, so to be truly happy-hearted requires no reason – other than that we have life, and thereby its gift of illimitable choices.'

I was struck by the almost anarchic force of the *jhankri*'s words.

How starkly different this was from the commonly taught Buddhist principle that all is suffering, which only a detachment from life, and thereby a negation of pain and ultimately the elimination of consciousness, can alleviate.

How unlike the Muslim belief in 'divine destiny',

accepting human suffering without complaint as a manifest test of faith in God's greater righteousness.

How contrary to India's predominant Vedantic philosophy that the entire material universe is mere illusion, worthy only of rejection; a deceit from which 'the pure' alone are able to withdraw into a state of *samadhi* suspended animation, free from the bondage of an endless, suffering-filled cycle of birth and death.

And how very far removed from the Christian idea in which I had been raised: that this is an arduous life, a Vale of Tears, which must be endured until death brings peace and salvation – but only for those who have earned redemption from a divine, judgemental patriarch, whose megalomaniacal ferocity had been catalogued for millennia.

The contrast now offered by the vigorous, joyous humanity that appeared to be both the very heart and purpose of the *jhankri's* priest-free Tradition could not have been more appealing.

V

*Mankind makes great effort to gratify his senses
and thereby fails to experience the lasting joy that resides within.*
Tripura Rahasya

'Does the Tradition really express no contempt for the world or human nature?' I had to ask.

'Brother, our Spoken Knowledge is uncon-ditionally life-affirming,' the *jhankri* declared. 'It requires neither struggle, nor discomfort, nor rigorous self-denial.

Nor does it demand obsessive adherence to somebody else's prescriptive morality or dogmas.'

Again this made me smile.

'Instead, our Shaiva Tantra Yoga recognises that an enlightened perception is most effectively developed without suffering or stricture, as it guides us to live all aspects of this glorious life with greater awareness, understanding and intensity. And thereby with greater pleasure, peace of heart and joy – the reason we employ as the principal symbol of our Tradition the image of Shiva, who we call Sukhin, He who is Happy.'

This, then, was the origin of the term Shaiva that was commonly applied to the Tradition: an adjective referring to the mountain deity Shiva, a name meaning 'benevolence', symbol of the disposition towards order – an essential consciousness, as it is perceived – in the universe.

'It is this recognition of pleasure as not only primary to human nature, but essential to a truly enlightening path, that has been greatly distorted by some who have gained a little knowledge, but no wisdom.'

'Distorted by whom?' I asked.

'By men deficient in integrity, whose hunger for fame and wealth has diminished their truth,' the *jhankri* replied. 'Men who raise themselves up through hierarchical so-called "spiritual" systems that, by their very nature, imply an inadequacy in the individual. Men who appeal to the licentious by claiming our ancient ways authorise indiscriminate, irresponsible sexual abandon.'

It was a pervasive prejudice against anything termed 'tantric' by which I too had formerly been convinced.

'And this when our mountain Tradition teaches that compulsive pleasures, which indulge self-interest and offer immediate though fleeting gratification, will never be enough. Desire becomes insatiable, sprouting ever more desires that demand recognition and satisfaction. We lose our balance. We become unsteady and fickle – until, in time, we surrender the joyful, light-filled limitless self we were born to be to sunless craving, addiction, cynicism and resentment.'

I nodded in recognition. It was a fact that the self-absorbed, acquisitive and often disillusioned society from which I came preferred not to admit.

'In contrast, our Tradition reminds us that there is no benefit to be found in self-indulgence, which only ever leads to self-delusion. Far wiser to move away from mediocre gratification that breeds such unquenchable desire, and instead seek stable, intense pleasures that are beneficial, that improve both physical and mental stability. Pleasures that afford peace of heart and mind. Pleasures that brighten and expand consciousness.'

Kushal Magar let me ponder the possibilities of self-improving pleasures as he poked a new stick into the fire. He threw fingerfuls of leaves into his pot, then added a generous pinch of sweet spices and a juicy crush of ginger root.

'So do you begin to see, brother?' He paused to tip the milk into the tea with a scoop of sugar, then filled three battered metal beakers, which Samuel passed around. 'The Tradition teaches that whilst we cannot resolve all the sorrows of the world, we can always choose to live pleasurably, productively and joyfully, whatever our material circumstances. And then to give as generously as our means and capacity allow.'

I nodded a determined affirmation as I braved a sip of the caramel-coloured liquid – and allowed myself to tingle with a newly heightened awareness of the tea's surprisingly invigorating deliciousness.

VI

Theoretical knowledge makes no one an adept.
Tripura Rahasya

'You're making it all sound very convincing,' I said, imitating Samuel by rotating the beaker to warm my palms.

'Never be persuaded by words,' Kushal Magar insisted. 'Not by anybody's. And certainly not by mine. Another's opinion is not evidence – especially when so many attempt to teach by merely repeating what they have heard from others. Rather live only according to your heart and never according to another's mind. For once you follow someone else, you cease to follow truth.'

'But what *is* truth?' I asked.

'For us, truth is *Sat* – which we represent by the image of Shiva. This is truth that lies beyond faith, ritual and feelings. Truth beyond the self-deception of habitual beliefs, beyond our fearful minds. *Sat* is truth that cannot be imparted by any guru, priest or prophet, nor proven by a book. This is truth that can only be realised through direct experience, through mindful interaction with the world and each other. You see, *Sat* is not a truth of events, but a truth we discover within ourselves – self-knowledge. This truth is a way of being.'

Truth not determined by consensual conviction? Not a creed or catechism, doctrine or dogma? I winced. This was like reading Eliot or Joyce. I might have understood the words and known them to be significant, but I could not pretend to grasp their meaning.

'For this reason, nothing in the Tradition is accepted

22

through blind faith,' he continued. 'After all, knowledge without first-hand experience is not authentic knowledge – for indirect knowledge is no more than a dream.'

In these few sentences he had dismantled the premise upon which my entire education had been founded. And yet in some ways I recognised it to be true. Those long years of calculus, quadratic equations, and learning by heart the gross annual product of the Windward Islands, for example, were all now reduced to an insubstantial, irrelevant memory.

'For this reason, keepers of the Tradition always choose action above theory, seeking out the most direct and efficient route to deepen self-knowledge, and thereby gain wisdom.'

Whilst I found this an easy idea to accept, I was still considering his dismissal of indirect knowledge. Mine was a culture that generally judged unpublished information unworthy of consideration, as though it could be nothing more than unfounded hearsay: if it was not in a book, it was not true. Now to be invited to explore a system that was independent of standard texts or literary exposition was undoubtedly disconcerting.

'But, *jhankri-dajoo*,' I challenged, 'surely the fluency of your English reveals academic learning.'

He smiled with what I judged to be a blush of bashful modesty.

'I am a younger son,' he revealed. 'My brothers inherited our family home and fields, my sisters were married and I was given schooling. I was sent across the hills to an English-medium scholarship in Darjeeling, as my mother was educated and wanted for me the security of work in a government office. But then she died of TB, and my father chose another path for me. He could neither read nor write. And yet such so-called illiterate people, living in what are judged to be poor places, often have practical knowledge and insights far more complex than those taught in schools. My mother may have given me books in English, but my father bestowed the treasure of our ancestral wisdom, for I was the one he chose to inherit the Tradition through initiation with Banthawa Rai, the wisest of our *jhankris* in these hills.'

I found myself yearning to understand this man: his people and his history, his peculiar knowledge and, what I imagined to be, his secrets.

'Of course, the reason the Tradition gives precedence to practical exploration of its teachings is that bookish knowledge is gradually removed by time, dissolved by age – until all that remains exposed at the close of our lives is the true state of our consciousness.'

Never before had I considered that there might be wisdom in regularly reviewing my educational priorities. With what words and images did I daily fill my head? Were they helpful, edifying, enriching and expanding? With what 'state of consciousness', then, was I preparing to be left in my inevitable decline?

'We call this practical exploration of the Tradition's teachings *sadhana*,' he explained, 'meaning the most efficient method to gain true knowledge.'

'But what do you consider true knowledge?' I asked.

'An understanding of ourselves – and thereby of all existence – beyond that afforded by the ordinary limits of the senses. And certainly beyond learning from mere texts or teachers. It is for this reason that a steady expansion of consciousness is primary to the Tradition, for our sense of who and what we are can only ever extend to the present reaches of our perception.'

'Then why do we have "ordinary limits" that need expanding in the first place?' I challenged.

'Our everyday awareness is selective. We perceive and retain only that which is self-serving, only that which we already believe about ourselves, others and our world. The Tradition's *sadhana* therefore guides us to free ourselves from those mindless, reactive habits that lead to detrimental thought, word and action. And this, that we might instead live and love more fully, more effectively, fearlessly, joyfully, wisely and without condition.'

Whilst the practicality he described appealed, I remained unsure how a system that professed simplicity could deliver the impressive range of benefits he listed.

For the time being, however, I decided to remain open to its ideas – some of which had already proved so resonant and reassuring, even whilst others were wholly alien and provocative – because these hill people were delightful, easy with themselves and with each other, revealing a level of contentment and inner peace that was wholly foreign to the culture of self-doubt and conflict to which I was accustomed.

'So how do you "do" this *sadhana*?' I asked.

'By gradually heightening awareness of our ordinary experience, that we might recognise each moment's inherent pleasure, life's inherent joy, and thereby restore balance in and beyond ourselves. For nothing in life has to change for you to find the peace of heart, the sense of purpose and the lasting happiness you seek – except your point of view.'

Although I had never suggested that I was in search of peace, purpose or happiness, now that he had mentioned them, I knew it to be true.

'We each create our own reality, brother,' he declared, 'for the universe will only appear the way we believe it to be.'

I looked back at him with surprise. This last phrase

threatened to overturn the fundamental notion of the wholly physical reality to which I had been raised.

'But for now, just know that our mountain Tradition is a joyful path that embraces everyone and everything,' he said. 'For there is no separation, no division in the universe — except that imposed by man's limited perception.'

His words were gentle and yet I felt each syllable in my craw.

'It is this all-inclusive viewpoint that long ago the people of these hills translated into a practical, experimental system of liberation from self-limitation. This is Shaiva Tantra Yoga. This is our Tradition.'

He looked into my eyes, touched both hands to his heart and smiled.

I returned his smile. And knew that I was ready to begin.

VII

Pure Consciousness is one's own true self . . .
Contemplate on that.
Tripura Rahasya

'*Jhankri-dajoo*, what exactly do you mean when you talk of Tantra?' I asked, taking another sip of his ambrosial tea. 'It's just that where I come from it has very, well, limited associations.'

'Oh, you mean sex' he said. 'Well, of course. Then perhaps you do not know that its particular association with Tantra is a Western fiction, by which foreigners and now Indians alike are most titillated, intrigued — and misled.'

I grimaced in embarrassment, as though I bore personal responsibility for the puerile obsessions of the society in which I had been raised.

'It is a misunderstanding that arose because, unlike patriarchal religions, the Tradition acknowledges and embraces all expressions of energy and consciousness in union, and thereby all human experience.'

This was the principal tenet that had struck me most strongly.

'For this reason, mankind's instinctive sexual drive is recognised in our Spoken Knowledge as but one of many ways to explore our true nature and thereby gain self-knowledge. Yet sex is not, nor has it ever been, the basis, focus or purpose of authentic Shaiva Tantra Yoga. Those who say otherwise are either misguided or mischievous.'

I nodded vigorously as though to prove I was not one of them, even as I winced at the thought of the industry of books, courses and retreats that bandied about the term 'Tantra' as justification for all manner of narcissistic self-indulgence. The full extent of the sexo-mystical mumbo-jumbo thus propagated I felt certain this gentle, smiling hill-man could not even begin to imagine.

'The fact is humankind only truly flourishes when we find sexual maturity and emotional fulfilment in relationships that are mutually respectful, supportive, fearless and joyful. It is for this reason that in these hills we are guided in early adolescence to explore mindfully the sensual potential of our bodies without guilt or shame, to understand better the wondrous forces of the universe we each embody. Practices are then taught to deepen the experience of pleasures that are not merely sensual, but which in time lead to ever greater self-awareness, self-knowledge – and thereby ever greater empathy and compassion.'

I looked at him blankly. Such uninhibited permission could not have been further from my own guilt-ridden blunder into puberty, obsessively monitored as it had been by the likes of the peripatetic vicar who had repeatedly threatened our class of squirming adolescents with the bane of blindness for habits he, perversely, deemed 'unnatural' – or for lingering too long under the school showers with any member of the rugby team.

His condemnation had been supported by Xeroxed handouts of earnest euphemisms, warning us against 'carnal curiosity' in our – or, most heinous of all, another's – God-given 'sacred factory'. And were the Fallen One to stir in us even the slightest urge for 'licentious indulgence', we were either to don our gym kits and run around the cricket field until the Holy Spirit saw fit to 'free us from temptation', or just remove hands from pockets and hum a hymn.

'In contrast, the repression of natural, intimate expression does not lead to wisdom,' the *jhankri* continued. 'Sexual desire instead becomes the cause of hypocritical thinking and behaviour – the primary source of both internal and external conflict, dissolving the heart into depression, the spirit to despair. It explodes as anger, aggression and violence – as much against ourselves as others – leading to acts of inhumanity, cunning, cruelty. Even to the insanity of fanaticism.'

I stayed silent. I was still trying to accommodate the idea of sexual expression without guilt, shame or repression as part of a viable route to 'enlightening' self-knowledge. It was a proposal that seemed almost too far removed from my schizophrenic culture, which so often demonised what it considered sexual 'transgressions', sensationalising other people's perfectly legal libidinal lives on the one hand, whilst sexualising every aspect of ordinary life on the other, whether newspapers, shampoo, cars, soap operas, confectionery or even children's clothing.

In my own growing up, sex had been what frogs did in the biology lab to assist us with our homework; what those oh-so-naughty grown-ups tirelessly attempted in *Carry On* films, yet never seemed to get; and what our tomcat could be guaranteed to do with the neighbour's moggie in the middle of the lawn when uptight relations came to tea. At no point in my upbringing had anyone suggested that human intimacy could be anything more than a frivolous intemperance to which nice people never made reference, and in which nice people certainly never admitted to participating.

In fact, from the very start we had been taught to snigger about all things sexual. We had hidden them from our parents, and boasted about them to our peers. We had been taught to confess them to our priests, and later resolve their 'issues' with our therapists. No wonder, then, that something so entirely natural, pleasurable and essential to our development, our physical and mental well-being, which should have been acclaimed the most positive, nourishing and creative force coursing through our bodies, was too often reduced to a negative and destructive instinct – an uncontrollable energy that, if not 'relieved', made a man depressive, aggressive and promiscuous. Or so he chose to believe.

I listened to the process in my head with some dismay. Never before had I admitted to myself just how disillusioned – perhaps even depressed – I had already grown in matters sexual.

'*Jhankri-dajoo*,' I grumbled, 'the world I come from is so very different. In fact, I don't think you can even begin to imagine how far apart we are.'

Kushal Magar leant forwards to squeeze my knees as though in reassurance.

'You mean people struggling with sexual fulfilment and selfless love? People so removed from each other and themselves that they are struggling to feel the emotions they profess? Lives becoming such a meaningless, unsatisfactory pretence that people turn to material possessions as paltry substitutes? No, brother, people there and people here are not really so very different.'

He had defied my patronising expectations. I had not assumed him to be so worldly-wise. Profound alienation was indeed an integral experience of my modern, mechanised and now hungrily digitising world. Entertainment as the simulation of real life had become so pervasive that a society accustomed to living by proxy through the media now found its own reality too 'stressful'. In turn, as though a production company were in the background to take responsibility, even the most natural of errors and accidents were becoming matters for blame and litigation.

Likewise, our compulsion for ownership of more property and more credit; bigger cars and better holidays; all-pervasive ease, speed, leisure and disposability, had not led to greater social cohesion and personal contentment. Instead, we suffered debilitating anxiety and illnesses in our efforts to fill the emotional void, feverishly acquiring yet more satellite channels to distract us from ourselves, yet more clutter with which to load our cupboards and lumber our lives.

'And then there is the growing obsession with something as irrelevant as external appearance,' he continued, 'which only further diminishes our ability to participate in truly intimate, loving relationships.'

I had never made the connection he suggested, yet was well aware that we were manipulated at every turn. Magazines, hoardings and television adverts all artfully undermining our confidence, feeding us a fear of wrinkles, hair loss and soft bellies —attributes admired in the hills as signs of age-earned wisdom and self-contentment. Big business compelling us to grasp at the promise of the latest youth-restoring creams, virility pills and ever more radical surgical procedures. Yet to keep us spending we were still made to feel inadequate.

Kushal Magar kept his eyes on me as he indicated to Samuel to prepare more tea, whilst I slumped to hug my knees and raged with inexpressible frustration at both myself and the muddled, messy world from which I had stepped.

VIII

Knowledge of the Tradition has two sources —
your teacher and yourself.
Mountain saying

'So if Tantra isn't all about sex, then what is it?' I burst out, with unintentional emotion.

'Brother, the term Tantra may be applied in different ways,' the *jhankri* replied softly. 'It can simply refer to the shuttle of a loom, or the warp of fabric. *Tantra-vaaya*, for example, is an old term for one who weaves. Even for a spider.'

This made no sense.

'Consider that the Tradition compares the entire universe to a piece of cloth in which all things are related and interdependent. Its teachings and practices are therefore often compared to the weaving together of the inner and outer, subject and object – the "you" and "me". A "web" of teachings and practices that guides us towards an expansion of consciousness and thereby wisdom.'

'Tantra can also mean "the chief remedy",' piped up Samuel, as he threw more leaves and ginger root into the pot then stirred the rolling water with a wooden spoon. 'And I believe Keralites in the south associate it with their Malayalam word *thantram*, which means "a very clever idea"!'

'And so it is.' Kushal Magar smiled. 'In our hills, however, the term Tantra is considered an alliance of two words: *tan*, meaning "that which expands, extends or unfolds knowledge", and *tra* meaning "tool". A technique for the expansion of consciousness, heightening it far beyond its normal waking state, in order to deliver us from our potential for inhumanity – which is only ever born of a limited, self-centred viewpoint.'

'Then when you call your Tradition Shaiva Tantra Yoga, what's the yoga part?' I asked. 'Surely not standing on your head and wrecking your knees in the lotus position?'

My limited experience in church halls and gyms had been both uninspiring and discouraging. I had too often sat before self-appointed teachers who indiscriminately assembled, cadged or invented any new practice they wished, to ensure their classes supplied both a satisfying stretch to their students' sinews and a frothy smear of pseudo-spiritual pop psychology. Rarely had I felt the banal gymnastics of such lessons held meaning of any greater profundity than the rhyming couplet of a sentimental greeting card or a gameshow catchphrase.

'Yoga is a term we apply to all the practices of Shaiva Tantra that lead to liberating insight,' he replied. 'It is the active, practical "technology", if you like, that enables us to perceive ourselves and our world more accurately, that we might learn wisdom. The word yoga itself comes from the verb "to yoke", referring to the mindful intention to "engage fully" the ordinarily self-interested and personal with the empathetic and universal.'

'It also has the meaning of "acting with diligence and attention",' Samuel added, 'with "all one's ability".'

I looked at my cousin with surprise. 'You've heard all this before, haven't you?' I asked.

He only cast me a cheeky grin, raised his eyebrows and returned to tending the tea.

'Yoga can also mean "union",' Kushal Magar went on, 'but not in some abstract, esoteric sense. Yoga rather refers to an achievable deepening of the connection with, and understanding of, ourselves and each other.'

I still remained unsure.

'Perhaps it helps to think of yoga as avoiding unproductive thoughts and behaviour. Finding the good, the beneficial in whoever and whatever come our way, then giving as generously as our capacity and means allow. For true yoga could be said to be anything that affords us the freedom of heart and expansion of awareness that enable us to live and love well and wisely.'

As the *jhankri* paused I looked beyond him, towards the blazing orb descending among peaks that marked the west.

I listened to the caw of crows, the cluck of hens, the scuff of breeze-blown bamboo tips against the sky, the sip of Samuel at his tea.

And breathed them in.

IX

Full knowledge of the Tradition is best suited to a calm student who is engaged in meditation and unsullied by malice.
Mountain saying

'Why am I here with you?'

Kushal Magar was gathering bowls of dried herbs, blackened canisters of pungent oil, crimson *sidur* pigment and a length of cotton cloth.

'I wasn't looking for any of this,' I insisted. 'I hadn't even heard of your mountain Tradition until meeting you today.'

Kushal Magar dropped a carefully considered assortment of seeds and leaves into an old stone mortar.

'Then maybe you are here,' he stated quietly, 'because you are ready.'

'Ready for what?' I asked, conscious of the shallow simplicity of my questions.

He tipped dark oil into the mortar and started grinding.

'In these hills, the Tradition's wisdom has long been passed directly from teacher to student – but only as that student shows sufficient maturity to understand each stage of their education. In contrast, I believe your culture holds that all knowledge should be available to everyone at all times.'

I nodded.

'Well, for us, the acquisition of knowledge is given only according to the capacity of the student to assume the responsibilities it brings. The practices and teachings of the Tradition could otherwise be misinterpreted and misused by the unwise and undiscerning. A teacher therefore looks for very particular qualities in every prospective student.'

I nodded to show my eagerness to hear them, in the

hope that I too might one day prove myself suitable to some degree.

'To start with, a healthy body–mind.'

'Body–mind?' I interrupted, assuming there had been a mistranslation.

'What your science differentiates as a "body" separate from a brain-based "mind", we understand as an integral, indivisible whole. In our Nepali, *chaitanya* means "consciousness" and *chola* means "body". Together, *chaitanyachola* means the "dynamic human being", the "living, active consciousness" – the body–mind. Do you see?'

I nodded, eager for him to continue with his list of required qualities.

'Next, a prospective student should demonstrate an honest and sincere disposition, free from pride and with honourable intentions. A sympathetic and open heart that shows invariable compassion to all living things. A capacity for happiness, enjoyment and sensual pleasure, yet with the inclination to master desires and passions.'

I was about to comment, when, to my dismay, I realised he had not yet finished.

'A prospective student should also exhibit disinterest in material wealth and social hierarchies. A willingness to sacrifice self-interest in the discharge of duties to parents, family and teachers. A readiness to explore possibilities beyond the obvious or ordinary. And, ultimately, a genuine desire for liberation from self-limitation, through the fulfilment of the four Aims of Life.'

'The four Aims of Life?' I asked, so daunted by his list of requirements that I recalled only the last.

'These we shall come to. But for now, understand that the knowledge embodied in our Tradition is not given indiscriminately.'

'So can you see even one of those qualities in me?' I laughed nervously.

Kushal Magar looked up from his work. 'You have the potential. And that is all that is required.'

'But how can you be so sure when we only met today?'

'You do not trust me?' he asked, turning to pour a bright gleam of boiling water over the contents of his mortar.

'How can I?' I replied, breathing in a sudden scent of pungent vegetation. 'I don't know you.'

'Do you assume dishonesty and treachery in everyone you meet, until they prove otherwise?' he challenged. 'Are these therefore qualities you recognise in yourself for you to expect them so readily of others?'

I did not know how to respond. Was this a test? Some game of provocation? Or had he seen in me a truth I had never once admitted? Was this then, perhaps, what *jhankris* did?

As I found myself again doubting how well I really knew myself or my motivation, Kushal Magar opened a tarnished metal canister from which he took a pinch of some unseen substance. He mumbled indecipherable words, touched his heart, the earth, then his eyes, and added the mysterious ingredient to his brew. He poked it with a finger and watched it steep.

'Of course, a prospective student would also normally have spent between one and four years living with their teacher prior to initiation, that they might demonstrate their suitability through daily interaction. However, my instincts are keen and your time is short – some man behind a desk has decreed no foreigner may remain longer than fourteen days in our hills – so we must find another way.'

I was grateful for, if somewhat surprised at, the generosity of his concession on my behalf.

'Wise teachers take great care that a student also has the quality of *viveka*,' he added to an already daunting list, 'the ability to distinguish the difference between truth and untruth, reality from self-delusion. In contrast, those who are dissolute or idle at heart, who lack integrity, who are inclined towards the useless and the trivial, or who are obsessively anxious must wait to be accepted by a teacher of the Tradition. For these, the knowledge to be imparted would prove neither useful nor appropriate.'

'But I can be idle!' I confessed. 'I can be as frivolous and neurotic as any other!'

'It is the potential for the qualities of the ideal student – a *shishya*, as we call them – that is sought. After all, if you had no conflicts with yourself, do you think you would have found your way to me?'

But had I? Surely it was he who had, by some means that yet remained wholly inexplicable, found me?

Kushal Magar took up a grass brush and began to sweep the floor on which we sat.

'Of course, in essence, a suitable student must sacrifice his self-interest in order truly to learn,' he stated, through a billow of dust. 'So are you willing to be a *shishya*?'

I considered that I had been raised to regard all learning as a matter of remembering and reconfiguring facts, regurgitating received opinions in order to earn that all-important coloured star or piece of embossed paper. I was also aware that the predominant purpose of all formal learning in my aggressively commercial and materialistic culture was ultimately to increase one's income. However, I was beginning to realise that in these hills this was not considered to be learning at all, but merely the acquisition of socially sanctioned information.

And yet the *jhankri* was not asking me to become

a student in the ordinary sense, but rather an apprentice. He was inviting me to become an initiate into a tradition that seemed to promise a progressive transformation of perception, even of myself and the world through which I moved.

I turned to Samuel, as though he might now intervene to prevent further interaction with this man; as though he might insist this was all mountain madness and hurry me back to the safety of his mother's kitchen, her *sinki* soup and gossip. Instead, he merely tipped his head and smiled, as though in cheerful expectation.

I looked again to the crystalline peak of Kanchenjunga, then back to Kushal Magar – and found myself nodding with unexpected confidence.

'Yes,' I replied and instinctively touched my heart. 'I am willing.'

X

People subject to ignorance wander to this sacred place and that sacred place . . . they do not realise the sacred place that is within the body.
Jñanasankalini Tantra

Samuel and I sat beneath our shawls on the temple steps as Kushal Magar changed his clothes. We watched him pull on his ceremonial *jama pagri* white tunic and a head-dress stitched with peacock feathers and *kauri* shells.

'These shells represent the creative force from which all the complexity of the universe spontaneously emerges,' he explained, as he bound the cloth around his head. 'The force that renders you and me indivisible from stars, sky, forest, seasons, earth.'

'And the peacock feathers?' I was beginning to under-stand that whilst I was accustomed to outward display predominantly being for mere effect or attention, here everything had a deeper meaning and purpose to reveal.

'They represent the inner journey of our ancestors' Tradition,' he answered, 'a journey I repeatedly undertake towards an ever deeper piercing of consciousness.'

I could not imagine what he meant.

Kushal Magar withdrew from a cloth bag long chains of *ghanti* bells, which he draped around his neck and across his chest. He then tied a length of white cotton around his waist.

'Consciousness. Order. Semen. Shiva,' he explained.

He added a length of bright red cotton.

'Energy. Creative action. Menses. Shakti. Together, they remind me that, like all existence, I too am an expression of these same two principal forces in the cosmos.' He paused to look directly into my eyes. 'A fact that *diksha* will now begin to reveal to you.'

'*Diksha*?' My anticipation was growing with his every word.

'Initiation,' he translated, sitting down to face me, his ritual dressing complete. '*Di* is the "giving" of knowledge and clear insight, and *ksha* is the "removal" of ignorance – by which I mean self-defeating thought and behaviour. The root *diksh* also means "to dedicate oneself", for your initiation is an outward commitment to a more mindful, joyful life that will enable you to be of ever greater benefit to both yourself and others.'

These were indeed very big promises to make.

'Of course, initiation is commonly given by a woman in our hills,' he added. 'And no *diksha* is more effective than that performed by one's own mother.'

I thought of mine, thousands of miles away in a bleak north European winter, and wondered what she would make of the adventure I was about to embark upon – although I still retained one niggling concern.

'*Jhankri-dajoo*, I'm confused,' I admitted. 'I've always thought of initiation as a way to secure a place in a tribe or group, to mark a person as different from and better than outsiders. You know, the way Christians baptise and confirm, Jews and Muslims circumcise, and Brahmin priests have their sacred thread bestowed on them. So how does your tantric initiation fit with the Tradition's rejection of hierarchies?'

'You are indeed a suitable student.' Kushal Magar smiled. 'There is wisdom in your questions. Brother, our tantric *diksha* is not performed to imply separation from those who are uninitiated. Rather, it is a rite of passage that sets the initiate on the path to perceive that there is, in fact, no separation. That, like all animate and inanimate life, you too are but one essential, integral phase in an eternal cycle.'

I nodded – even though I did not really understand.

'So there's no problem with me being initiated, despite being a foreigner?' I asked.

'When no division exists between mankind, mountains and weather, do you think any *shaiva tantrika* would discriminate according to nationality, gender or social status? Expansion of consciousness is available to all people, irrespective of culture, religion or biology. For what is consciousness? Not merely the firings of a brain within the confines of a skull, but a primary attribute of all existence.'

Whilst I knew our English word "conscious" came from the Latin for "shared knowledge", I was well aware I had not even begun to fathom his understanding of the term. For the time being, therefore, I settled my curiosity on the rite at hand.

'Then is initiation imperative for all who follow the Tradition?' I asked.

'Not imperative. But it is of greater benefit to some than others.'

He paused and looked me in the eyes.

'It would be of benefit to you,' he stated with calm conviction. 'You would profit from a turning point. And the most effective turning point that I can offer is *diksha*.'

I wondered what his steady, fearless gaze had perceived in me. Could he really see the conflicts I had borne? The raw grief I carried for loved ones lost – that principal inevitability of human experience for which my culture had afforded no meaningful preparation? The crushing self-doubt and confusion that, at times, had spiralled into compulsive self-harm? Could he possibly perceive that near-consuming darkness against which I had battled since my boyhood?

'We undertake initiation into the Tradition on a day determined by the cycle of the moon,' Kushal Magar explained.

'And today is *sombaar*, our day of the moon!' Samuel announced. 'Same as Monday!'

'Which we hill people, by reason of our myths, consider especially favourable for rituals associated with Shiva,' the *jhankri* added. 'Remember him? Our symbol of *Sat*, truth born of self-knowledge. A way of being.'

'And, you know, tonight will also be a new moon!' Samuel added with excitement. 'An *amavasya*!'

This fact seemed remarkably serendipitous. So much so that I wondered whether Samuel had known all along, and that I had been an unwitting participant in some secret arrangement. Recalling what had appeared to be his initial trepidation when we arrived at the little scarlet temple, I dismissed my cynicism and asked, 'But what's the connection between Shiva and the moon?'

'Ah,' the *jhankri* said with a smile, evidently approving of my curiosity. 'One of the forms we attribute to Shiva is the moon god, Soma-shambhu-paddhati, who rides his chariot of glazed water. As such, he represents all trance-visions and dreams – those revelations of the true appetites and ambitions, self-doubts and fears by which we often unknowingly identify ourselves and thereby live out our lives. In this form, Shiva is praised for his beauty and virility, for he embodies *chandramrta*, the nectar of the crescent moon.'

'Nectar?' I asked.

'The sacrificial offering of semen made upon initiation,' he replied.

I looked to Samuel with wide eyes, hoping he might offer some explanation, but he did nothing more than tip his head from side to side as though in reassurance.

'We also call Shiva Chandrashekhara, meaning "moon-crested", for he bears on his head a crescent moon, the symbol of *ojas*, the creative force of semen, which we represent on our *jhankri* altars with lengths of quartz crystal.'

I peered into his sanctuary – and found it to be so.

Kushal Magar touched his heart and closed his eyes, giving me a chance to look back at Samuel expecting to see a flurry of discreet hand signals or enthusiastic mouthings to indicate that we should leave. But he too was sitting silent, his eyes now inexplicably closed.

I turned my gaze to Kanchenjunga, its soaring peak now darkening in descending dusk, and found my mouth dry. I glanced at the swirl of crows around the towering bamboo tops, and was surprised to find my heart pounding.

The *jhankri* stirred. He touched the earth, his heart and mouth, then leant forwards to rest his right hand first on my chest, then my head.

I knew that all talk was now ended. The *jhankri* had placed his blessing on me.

My initiation had begun.

XI

May I ever understand that knowing one is knowing all.
The Vow of Mahamudra

Kushal Magar looked into my eyes and offered a broad smile of reassurance.

He indicated that I was to part my lips, allowing him to place grains of rice on my tongue. He turned to face the *than* altar of his scarlet temple, towards which he released an unintelligible stream of rhythmical syllables.

At his instruction, we made symbolic offerings of raw rice, a mustard oil lamp, three small oranges, cubes of camphor, cones of incense, vermilion paste, areca nuts, betel leaves, cow's urine in a metal pot, handfuls of dried plants thrown into the fire, and a length of gold-trimmed scarlet cloth with which to engulf the multi-limbed image of the principal goddess.

And all the while he muttered an endless stream of *bijas*, anciently configured 'seeds' of sound considered to be of such vibratory influence that they can effect a change in consciousness.

'Brother, it is time for you to remove your clothes,' he instructed.

'My clothes?' I asked, again turning to Samuel for guidance. 'He wants me to take off *all* my clothes?'

A single tip of the head affirmed that I was now expected to set aside my deepest cultural inhibitions, to sit before him bared and unprotected on a chilly Himalayan foothill beneath the snow-topped Kanchenjunga.

And yet, as I inhaled a swell of scented smoke I found myself unhesitating, quickened by a new and unexpected courage finally to face the habitual reticence of my existence. For during these many weeks in India, I had learnt that Westerners so often asked the wrong question.

We asked why?

Here, they asked why not?

So it was that in a moment I sat again before the temple doors on cold, hard stone, almost oblivious to the chill of mountain air against my naked skin.

'The preparatory cleansing often includes the shaving of all body hair, except the eyebrows and eyelashes,' the *jhankri* announced, as he began to wash me with the dark infusion that steeped in gathered bowls.

He smiled as my face expressed my reaction to the thought of the rusty cut-throat blade that hung from a hook by his hut door depilating my every inch.

'However, such exacting rituals have no particular merit beyond their symbolism,' he said, the cloth's wet warmth continuing its course across my chest and down my belly. 'For you, our mountain plants are all we need.'

I sighed in relief at what felt a genuine concession.

Kushal Magar unwrapped the *thurmi* dagger from its cloth binding to dance its length through the smouldering ash of dried *ganja* cannabis, *titepati* mugwort and *hasana* night-jasmine. He raised the blade with both hands above his head, then plunged its iron tip hard into the earth to cut a circle on the ground as he uttered a reverberating chant. He marked the eight directions of his incision with the paper-thin, white *totala* seeds that symbolise the near-mythical *ban jhankri* of the deep forest.

This was now the ritual space, the focus for all the *jhankri's* will and power: the knowledge bequeathed to him by innumerable preceding generations.

Kushal Magar sat cross-legged in the centre of his circle. He sounded the thin, dark pipe of human bone and threw psychotropic *saal* resin on to the glowing embers of the fire. He pricked his navel with the consecrated *dumsi* porcupine quill and offered two drops of his own blood to the new flames as evidence of his self-surrender.

He was now ready to begin.

With a practised sweep of his right hand, Kushal Magar noosed about my neck a *mala* string of brown *vaijanti* seeds. He then covered my head with a long, red cloth, returning to his Nepali to give the instruction, '*Hriday bata suna.*'

I was to listen with my heart.

Kushal Magar partially raised the crimson cotton and drew the *mala* tighter around my throat. He blew hard three times and whispered a mantra into each ear, indicating I was to repeat it back to him until both pronunciation and intonation were correct.

He turned to offer to the rising *saal* smoke his *mura* drum that would take him into trance, enabling him to perceive beyond the ordinary limitations of intellect and self-interest.

Then, as his palms voiced the drum's taut top, its measure mingling with my marrow, I began to feel a rapid change both outside and within, as though a storm approached.

And sure enough, as our eyes drifted close, both he and I began to tremble.

All sense of time was slipping. All sense of self.

Had I been sitting before the scarlet temple for hours, days or months? Had I arrived today or was this the place where I had been born? Was I infant or ancient? Was I man or woman? Tree or crow? Earth or sky?

My awareness of myriad new constellations that had begun to pierce the twilight seemed startlingly heightened as the *jhankri* indicated for Samuel to lay me flat on my back. The drumming did not seem to falter, yet it was Kushal Magar who knelt to pour a viscous liquid into the pit of my throat, chest, belly and the hollows of my groin. It was Kushal Magar who ran vermilion-stained fingertips in long lines across my skin as he pronounced vibratory *bija* syllables.

He dripped a bracing, bitter oil into my nostrils that set my sinuses alight and swelled my tongue; that seemed to cause my face to melt, my head to bloat, my eyes to open wider than the beam of every star.

He doused in new chrism a sudden, inexplicable tumescence.

Kushal Magar withdrew both hands to touch his heart, then plunged into my abdomen with tightened fists and a chant that made my limbs shake without restraint.

My chest began to freeze, as though to mountain ice. My navel to ignite, as though some hidden, residual dock of my infantine umbilicus were now fiercely on fire.

I stretched down to grasp his wrists.

I tried to cry out, to restrain him in his rite.

But my entire body and mind were violently, rhythmically convulsing.

PART TWO

XII

The 'I' that floats along the wave of time,
From a distance I watch him.
Rabindranath Tagore

The sun had yet to rise above the distant snow-topped crests, and yet a molten sky already promised a new day's advent.

I had been woken by crows to find myself curled beneath a pile of woollen blankets and that an entire night had passed. I stirred to rub my chill-nipped nose and uncovered, wrapped around me, the warm, protective water bottle of my cousin.

I began to slip from Samuel's hold, but discovered myself trembling. Nor was this an ordinary shiver, but a tremor centred deep within my bones, as though the fluid membranes of my frame were now vigorously pulsating.

I fought to sit and steady my head, to reconstruct the past twelve hours. And yet however deeply I inhaled a quickening of mountain air, however wide I opened my eyes to the day's fast brightening, my memory remained muffled.

I had no language for what had happened on the *jhankri's* hillside that previous dusk, no words for the unfathomable commotion that had exploded in my every cell and synapse.

With effort, I seemed to recall a confluence of chant and drums, a pungency of smoke and oil. An abstract recollection of a firestorm in my belly, a glacier in the hollows of my chest. A paralysis of relentless spasm.

And then the deep concentric ripples of that ultimate libation.

I clenched my eyes, as though shutting out the rising light might assist my memory. I observed myself and, beyond the unruly quiver of my frame, sensed a change – yet was still unable to define the feeling in my core that was neither fear nor ferment.

It occurred to me to question how I had allowed myself to accept the invitation of this stranger so readily. I was neither particularly courageous nor foolhardy, and yet had willingly handed both mind and body to him with, what in retrospect seemed, outrageous ease.

So what now? Embarrassment at my bold baring? Run away to report this little man? If so, then for what exactly? An unwarranted familiarity in which I had irrationally colluded? A rite that had inexplicably resulted in the offering of my very own nectar of the crescent moon?

A sudden snore distracted the spate of panic in my chest. I turned to tuck blankets tight about Samuel's chin and smiled at the reflexive, closed–eyed grin of gratitude he offered in return – even as I again questioned whether my cheery cousin had been companion or accomplice in my delivery to this isolated temple.

'Brother,' a voice intruded, 'the wisdom of our Tradition is found in the essence of all life, bound into the very structure of soil and leaf, skin and stars.'

I had been so distracted by the oscillation of my atoms

that I had not seen him, the man of whom I yet knew nothing beyond his manifest humanity. Kushal Magar had been tending to a steadily reviving fire, but now approached to press into my trembling hands a beaker of milky ginger tea. This, he indicated with his eyebrows, I should start sipping straight away despite its heat.

'And how do you think our forefathers and mothers first learnt to perceive this knowledge that lay embedded as much in themselves as in the cosmos through which we spin?' he asked, sitting down beside me bearing a steaming beaker of his own.

I blew across the surface of the tea, shook my head in answer to his question and eyed him with new scrutiny as I took a tentative sip.

'From the *gurubuwa*,' he replied. 'The respected parent-teacher who is still here in the forest, in the valleys, on the mountain-tops. And a little in the tea that you are drinking.'

I peered with alarm into the sweet pale liquid, then looked back at the man against whom, despite the inscrutable ritual he had effected upon me the previous night, I could still not rouse suspicion.

'*Gurubuwa* are not people, brother,' he assured me. 'They are our teaching plants – monkshood, henbane and cannabis, cobra lily, saal and datura – each with its own specific purpose and benefit. Even the tree called *jhankri* we use to deepen sleep. All natural means employed by prudent teachers to help the student gain a clearer insight into his true nature – and thereby the nature of the universe.'

I studied the *jhankri*'s bright and steady eyes, around which fans of lines bore witness to his years of carefree smiles. His pale brown cheeks bore the rosy hue afforded by clean mountain air, his mouth the easy calm of honest words. For all I could not understand or yet explain, I knew I liked and trusted this man.

Samuel stirred, drawing himself up to sit in readiness for the hot beaker that was instantly set between his palms.

'You all right, *dajoo*?' he asked

I did not know how to respond. I had just been told I had been drugged.

'Of course, our *gurubuwa* plants are only ever applied with defined purpose by a wise teacher to enable a student to overcome the fears that restrain him,' Kushal Magar impressed again. 'So that the "masculine" mind-set of logic and limitation might be loosened, and thereby perception heightened.'

'Is that what I experienced last night?' I asked hoarsely, still struggling to draw together the elusive memories of my initiation. 'The loosening of logic and limitation?'

'You will soon come to learn that the rites of our Tradition have at their heart the dismantling of conditioning and ordinary references,' he replied, 'in order to reveal the truth within.'

I nodded, as though I understood.

And yet, as I felt again the trembling of my limbs and viscera, I still wondered what I had undergone and to what purpose.

XIII

Unless the four Aims of Life are known,
man performs his actions blindly, and thus keeps
walking in the darkness of his own ignorance.
Tripura Rahasya

I had been asleep again. When I woke, Kushal Magar was washing rice. Samuel was snapping sticks for kindling.

Even though midday had already passed, they both insisted that I rest. On no account was I to undertake a single chore. Not even to help pick grit and beetles from the lentils scattered across a broad woven tray. Instead, I watched them both at their work and sifted through the muddled memories I was still struggling to assemble.

'Aims of Life!' The eddies in my head were only now beginning to disperse.'*Jhankri-dajoo*, in the list of requirements for a suitable student didn't you mention four Aims of Life?'

'The Purushartha, as we call them — literally, "that which is beneficial to humankind",' Kushal Magar replied as he rinsed pale pink grains in cloudy water. 'The practical principles our culture long ago determined to be the most effective means by which to gain self-knowledge, find fulfilment, and establish both personal and social stability. The most effective path to wisdom.'

'But what do *you* mean by wisdom?'

'A suppleness of disposition that enables us to apply whatever knowledge we may have — especially self-knowledge — to the greatest benefit. For us, this means restoring and then maintaining balance in ourselves, our society and thereby the wider world.'

He let me consider his words as he squeezed the rice in

51

his fists, spreading it out to dry in the sunshine. He indicated for Samuel to stoke the fire in readiness for cooking pots, then settled down before me.

'You see, brother, when the four Purushartha are attended to step-by-step over a lifetime, they lead to what we term the "steady sunrise of understanding" – which some prefer to call enlightenment.'

'A lifetime?' I exclaimed with an impatient flush.

Kushal Magar placed his right hand to his heart, then leant forwards to touch mine.

'There is no wisdom to be found in hurry or short cuts. Only broken promises, stomach ache and nose bleeds.'

This was one lesson I wished I might have learnt years ago.

'So, brother, are you ready to begin?' he asked, drawing himself up a little taller.

I looked into his eyes and nodded. Then closed mine to better hear his meaning.

XIV

It is only by attendance to Dharma that both men and Man may flourish.
Mountain saying

'Our first Aim of Life is Dharma,' Kushal Magar began. 'Expansion of consciousness through the fulfilment of moral duty. It is symbolised by the image of Shiva's bull – Nandi, the Happy One – for he embodies the balance of nature, the order of the universe.'

'I'm sorry, but you've already lost me,' I admitted, having to disrupt my focus and open my eyes again. 'What do you mean by moral duty?'

'Well, consider true morality to be an innate sense of what maintains or restores balance in ourselves and the world around us – and what does not,' he replied. 'In essence, it is to choose to think, say and do nothing to the detriment of ourselves or others. And then to become actively engaged by living and loving fully, fearlessly, wisely, that we might all do our part to resolve conflict and ease our own and others' suffering.'

This notion of a morality that was not based on precepts that claimed an absolute unconditional value was deeply appealing. The Tradition, then, had no *Surah Al-Ana'm* to define an irrevocable Koranic moral code. No authoritative Levitical Law to enforce someone else's notion of 'righteous living', with its preponderance of proscriptive *'Thou Shalt Nots'* and the ever-attendant menace of heavenly reckoning.

'Compulsory "morality", in contrast, imposes laws that eliminate personal responsibility,' he asserted. 'Random rules of religion that result in a juvenile sense of "morality" derived from the fear of punishment and the hope of reward. An individual is thereby moulded who follows rules without ever needing to develop personal ethical maturity. An individual who will for ever act "morally" for little more than their own self-interest, in the distorted belief that the love of their particular parental deity is entirely conditional upon their "good" behaviour.'

I winced. He was talking about me.

'The Tradition therefore does not recognise morality to be a code of law that imposes someone else's idea of right and wrong. Not prescriptive man-made "virtues" dependent upon the customs of a particular culture at any one moment in its history.'

'Then if not obedience to a set of rules, of prescriptions and prohibitions,' I pressed, 'what is the "moral duty" of Dharma?'

'You tell me.' Kushal Magar smiled, with an unwavering gaze. 'What do you consider your moral duties to be?'

I looked back at him in silence.

And felt my cheeks begin to flush with the realisation that I could think of nothing honest to offer in reply.

XV

The greatest self-respect of all is to allow yourself true happiness.
Mountain saying

The rice and lentils were simmering in their pots when Samuel settled back down to join us. He had said uncharacteristically little since our arrival on this hillside the previous afternoon, and yet had never once allowed his attention on me to falter.

I now turned to him in the hope that he might say something, anything, to fill the embarrassment of my silence. Instead, he simply rubbed a mark from my cheek with an affectionately wetted thumb and blinked back at me as though in equal expectation of an answer.

I decided the *jhankri*'s questions were just too hard, for they were asked as though I might have actually paused to consider seriously the life I led. As though, being physically fully grown, I might have actually taken the time to examine my motivation, the purpose and impact of my thoughts and actions.

It was only now in sitting here with him that I could begin to see that, in truth, both I and my life were mindlessly, pointlessly adrift. How, then, could he think I was suited for this mountain Tradition? For who was I but yet another Westerner with a backpack, disillusioned – or perhaps just bored – by the self-indulgent life from which I had walked away, and to which I would inevitably return?

'What if I tell you that your first moral duty is to yourself?' the *jhankri* intervened. 'A moral duty to do, say and think nothing to your detriment? To determine your true nature and then to live fully – and happily – in accordance with it?'

I looked towards the mountains, feeling suddenly exposed. Just who was this man, I wondered, who with such apparent ease could catch me at my thoughts and challenge them?

'Brother,' he said, so tenderly that I turned back to look at him, 'self-respect – mindfully attending to the way in which we value ourselves – affords the balance that enables both the individual and the society in which they live to flourish.'

I wanted to believe this could be true, yet was surprised to be confronted by my own, previously unrecognised, pessimism. Was such a Utopian ideal possible beyond the simplicity of the tribal culture in which his people so evidently flourished? Could such a seemingly radical paradigm ever be applied in my own fragmented, materialistic, frivolous society?

'This moral duty to ourselves includes the choice no longer to live life through an endless round of habit. No longer to live through merely learnt reactions to external stimuli – year upon year of the same beliefs about ourselves and the world through which we move. For such a life, brother, is nothing but repetitive self-limitation.'

I considered his statement with rising unease. Had I ever had a single, truly original thought or insight that I could claim to be my own? Was there any idea that I had not inherited from my parents, teachers, Church, books or television? Had I ever had one notion that pressed beyond the mindless norms to which I unquestioningly adhered?

'But isn't this tendency to habit – this "self-limitation", as you call it – a fundamental attribute of humankind?' I contested.

'Habit is a defensive response to what we perceive to be an unpredictable, even potentially dangerous, world. The problem is that we tend passively to accept our particular familial, social and cultural customs as unquestionable truths. We end up living our entire lives through them, without ever stopping to examine their benefit or purpose – even when they diminish us or others.'

Was it really possible that I merely experienced the world and myself through the same endless round of thoughts, beliefs and emotional responses that had been imprinted on me in childhood and adolescence?

'We all do it, brother,' he offered in what seemed like consolation, 'living in a universe of infinite possibilities, yet repeating the same unproductive, even detrimental, choices. Only ever accepting as "true" that which fits our ordinary custom. Becoming so entrenched in habit that we grow stagnant, lonely, disillusioned, depressed or even sick – until we cannot even remember how our true adaptability and joyfulness once felt.'

'But this is me!' I burst out with unintended fervour.

'And so I offer you the Tradition' – he smiled – 'for its principal purpose is to free us from the rigidity of repetitive thought and action by which we limit ourselves. So that we might live according to our true nature which, like the physical universe from which we are inseparable, is in essence rational and harmonious, abundant and joyful.'

I may have been raised to accept mindlessly Judaeo-Christian concepts of talking snakes and giant-killing shepherd boys, a city destroyed by a spirited brass section and corpses rising from the dead – but who had ever talked to me of self-limitation or my true nature?

I turned to look back out across the valley towards the mountains.

And felt myself submerging beneath ideas so unfamiliar they left me breathless.

XVI

All the joy of this world derives from the wish for another's joy.
Bodhicaryavatara

'As our first Aim of Life,' Kushal Magar continued, 'Dharma next teaches that after mindfully attending to our own well-being, we direct our attention to the care of those for whom we are responsible. Such a duty includes neither doing, nor saying, nor thinking anything to their detriment. And to whom do you consider we have our primary responsibility?'

'Those we love?' I answered instinctively. 'Not such a difficult duty to undertake.'

'Why would it be any easier than your primary duty? For if you cannot first nurture yourself, how effective and authentic do you really think your "selfless" attention will be to others?'

I looked back at him – and found that, once again, I had no reply.

'Dharma, then, encourages us to learn to attend to the well-being of our inherited, adopted or chosen families. To honour those who raised us, expressing no arrogance or anger in their presence. To cherish and protect those with whom we share our life. And, of course, never to quarrel.'

Even as he spoke the words, I felt the cold, hard rent of regret.

'Dharma guides us to educate our children – and if we have none, to educate another's. And then to support our friends, those whom we employ and those with whom we work.'

I nodded. I liked this practicality.

'The moral duty of Dharma also includes honouring our teachers, such as our grandparents, mother and father, children, friends. The fields and forest, the weather, crows.'

I raised my eyebrows.

Kushal Magar tipped his head and chuckled. 'Yes, brother, these mountains, their skies and forests, insects and animals are all part of my daily education.'

He paused for me to consider the almost romantic mystery of his words before continuing.

'After our teachers, comes moral duty to our *pitrs* – our ancestors – from whom we inherit our genetic and cultural heritage. It is one reason we place so much importance on our family ties and, of course, nurturing the next generation.'

This honouring of ancestors had been evident throughout my journey across India, both in the garlanding of photographs of deceased relations in homes and shops, and in the annual *pitri-puja* rituals in which some of my own relations devotedly participated. Our relatively recent Western pastime of genealogical research seemed elementary in its fervid acquisition of names and dates when compared with the depth of respect here afforded forebears as a natural part of the daily round. In fact, it might be said that our loss of knowledge of our ancestors had contributed to modern generations not only with a diminished sense of familial responsibility, respect or gratitude, but with little sense of place in the cycle of life, or of the individual simply being but one, fleeting expression of an infinite continuum.

As for nurturing the next generation, I had been struck by the way in which children in these hills were valued and doted upon, both by their families and their community. Children were passed from knee to knee between strangers on public transport, cooed over and dandled with indulgence. Children were massaged by their mothers with vigorous affection, whilst fathers tended them with a natural inclination to nurture. Where my culture could too often treat both the elderly and children as a necessary nuisance, here both were regarded as a cherished blessing.

'This duty to our ancestors is, in effect, another level of responsibility to ourselves,' Kushal Magar revealed. 'For here we consider each of us to be an embodiment – a summary, if you like – of the past seven generations. We inherit their experience, which we have a duty to make conscious and then, where necessary, resolve – thereby ensuring it is not expressed in our own lives as imbalances of unreasonable emotion, obsessive compulsion or disease.'

I was astonished that such an insight should have arisen among a people with no science, as we would judge it, of genetic inheritance. Nor with knowledge of the mechanics of epigenetics, by which the chemical impact of ancestral experience remains attached to our own

DNA, apparently bequeathing us both psychological and behavioural tendencies.

'Dharma next guides us to fulfil our moral duty to those beyond our immediate circle. This we do by show-ing benevolence to one and all, without judgement or condition. You may have noticed that one way we express this generosity of heart is by extending hospitality to any guest, even if a stranger.'

I pressed my shoulder into Samuel in recognition of the remarkable kindness I had been shown since my arrival.

'So do you see?' Kushal Magar asked. 'Dharma is a way of living not just for personal gain, but to restore balance, the natural harmony, where it has been lost, whether in yourself, your family or your society – and, thereby, in the wider world.'

I looked towards the mountains again and smiled.

The late afternoon sun had illuminated their peaks to such brilliance that it seemed I might have pressed my face through the rent of some celestial veil and was now staring into paradise.

XVII

Abundance is found not in what we have, but how we love.
Bindra

S amuel was vigorously scrubbing *karai* pans and metal *thaliya* plates with dry earth when Kushal Magar indi-cated to me that it was time for the second Purushartha. 'Are you ready?'

I pulled my shawl close under my chin, a blanket around my legs, and nodded.

'Our second Aim of Life is Artha,' he began. 'Expansion of consciousness through the fulfilment of social responsibility. In our hills, Artha is represented by Kubera, our symbol of the Earth's abundance and hidden treasure – the greatest of which, of course, is self-knowledge.'

'The fulfilment of social responsibility,' I repeated for my own benefit.

'Artha requires that we prosper in our material endeavours, within the requirements of Dharma,' he explained. 'This means diligently and honourably earning the means by which to support ourselves and provide for those for whom we are responsible. In this way, Artha not only ensures that we function effectively and usefully in the world, but that we maintain a balanced society in which all mankind, even the least able, can flourish according to their own innately rational and harmonious natures.'

I was still puzzled by his insistence that mankind is inherently rational and harmonious by disposition when the sweep of human history was a tireless legacy of cruelty, conflict, greed, violence and self-destruction.

'The word *artha* literally means "to take up one's work", or "to go about one's business",' he continued, unperturbed by my inadvertent scowl, 'yet it derives from the root *ri* – "to gain", "know", "enjoy".'

'We also use *artha* in Nepali to mean "purpose" and "meaning",' added Samuel, who had turned to rinsing plates and pans in a wooden pail of water.

'However, it is important to understand that Artha does not merely refer to monetary reward,' Kushal Magar emphasised. 'You see, Artha also refers to the acquisition of knowledge and friendships, for both are priceless treasures.

We must have – and ensure that others have – all that is needed to be able to fulfil our first Aim of Life.'

'It's hard to grasp how the drudgery of working in an office or a factory to pay the bills bears any relation to an "enlightening" path,' I admitted.

'But only until you realise that there is no sacred *or* profane. No spiritual *or* sensual. No divine *or* mundane. These are simply subjective, culturally dictated notions that do not accurately reflect the reality of existence. Worldly achievements are not separate from any so-called "spiritual" accomplishments.'

'Then I could say that I come from a culture driven by Artha!' I protested. 'Except that in our obsessive pursuit of "material endeavours" as you call them, we are disconnecting from ourselves and each other, whilst systematically destroying the planet!'

'But this is not Artha,' he declared, 'for this Aim of Life is not the pursuit of material wealth for personal gain. Nor is it in conflict with Dharma – the principle of thinking, saying and doing nothing to the detriment of yourself or others. Rather, the purpose of Artha is that all aspects of your life should flourish. That all your life should be abundant. Do you see?'

I nodded cautiously.

'Then engage in Artha as a means by which to express all that you are capable of expressing, in every area of your life,' he directed. 'Through your relationships and education. Your work and recreation. Your loving and passion. And through the dynamic fulfilment of every one of the Purushartha. For it is this that is our true tantric *sadhana*.'

'I'll try, *jhankri-dajoo*,' I replied, when in truth I struggled to believe that such an abundant life could ever possibly be available to me.

XVIII

*An intelligent and perceptive person, attending to Dharma, Artha
and also to Kama, without becoming the slave of his passions, will
obtain success in everything that he may do.*

Kama Sutra

Kushal Magar and I sat in silence.

Another chilly night had passed, yet still we were
wrapped in heavy shawls and blankets. Together
we sipped the day's first brew of tea, and watched for
another dawn to break its beams above summits looming
in silhouette.

Samuel was attending to a call of nature beyond the
jhankri's vegetable patch, behind the maize ears drying
on their bamboo poles, whilst my head was reeling with
questions and conflicts provoked by the previous day's
teaching, none of which I yet felt able to voice.

I raised my face towards a sudden warmth of sunlight
and strained to listen to the tune of an unseen goatherd far
below in the river valley.

'Ready for our third Purushartha?' the *jhankri* asked.

I turned and nodded in reply.

'Then to Kama: expansion of consciousness through
the fulfilment of sensual pleasure. This we represent by
Kama himself, our symbolic god of love and bringer of
joys, embodiment of the profound affections, passions and
pleasures that afford life its meaning.'

Unthinkingly, I raised my eyebrows. This was perhaps
the most surprising of the Aims of Life for one reared in
a culture that, for all its profligate decadence, still deemed
sensual pleasure the antithesis of any 'spiritual' development.

'The Tradition encourages us to embrace, heighten and explore our senses mindfully,' he explained 'for only then are we truly able to engage with ourselves, the world and each other. In this way, the fulfilment of Kama transforms our experience of life, for there is joyful, sensual pleasure to be found in even our most humdrum responsibilities.'

I considered the potential for 'joyful, sensual pleasure' in the mundanities of domestic life back home – of sorting laundry, vacuuming the carpet, choosing supermarket cheese – and felt dismayed.

'Humankind is remarkably adaptable,' he continued. 'An essential quality for our survival, but one that also desensitises us to such a degree that we regard a truly extraordinary world as quite ordinary. It robs us of the wonder to be found in every moment, in every raindrop that falls upon our faces, in every sunrise seen, in every voice heard, in every person met.'

I knew this all too well. Whether shoes, music or holiday destinations, the new always seemed brighter and more exciting – but only until their inevitable absorption into our benumbed 'normal'. Why else did we forever buy new clothes and curtains, change the kitchen cupboards, seek out new lovers and carelessly lose old friends?

And it was undoubtedly the unhappy truth, as others have observed, that if the stars appeared but once in every century, the world would await that rare dusk wide-eyed, ready to celebrate our shared awe. But when those same wondrous, myriad constellations nightly scatter their pin-prick lustre across the sky, we choose instead to stay indoors – and watch the television.

'Consider that if, for example, you are someone who has the privilege of eating an apple every day, yet take a bite without attention, without attendance to Kama, your eyes will no longer thrill at the vibrant subtleties of its colouring. Your lips will no longer feel the polish of its skin. Your tongue will no longer taste the quickening acidity of its sweetness.'

I nodded, for I could recall the time I tasted my first peach. It was a summer's day and I, a four-year-old, was sitting beneath the tree that bombed our garden with its fruits. I could still remember my childish doubt that this soft, warm globe, so delicate in colour and furry to the touch, could possibly be edible. And then the mustered courage of that first bite – the fleecy skin against my palate, the luscious flush of flesh within the mouth. It was exquisite. And yet, in its subsequent familiarity no other bite had stayed in my memory as had the heady fragrance of that first pleasure.

What other abundant daily delights, then, did I no longer notice? How much of my life had already passed me by unseen, unfelt, unknown?

'Kama, then, encourages us to pay attention to all pleasures accessible to our senses,' Kushal Magar stated. 'Through sight, taste, sound, smell and touch. Through art, music, dance and food. Through play, work, *sadhana*, love and breath. Through family and friends. Through attending to the well-being, and thereby the happiness, of others. For when every act in life is undertaken in order to find its inherent pleasure, there is Kama to be fulfilled in every minute of every day.'

As though my eyes were newly opened, I could now see the fundamental ways in which this third Aim of Life was embraced in practice among these mountain people. Kama was fulfilled in their fearless gaze and touch, their unabashed affection and tireless generosity of heart and table. And as the recipient of such repeated benevolence, I had felt myself protected, cared for, nurtured, at ease with them and with myself.

'But, *jhankri-dajoo*,' I said, 'just as Artha could be interpreted as a sanction for excessive, even destructive, materialism, couldn't Kama be taken as licence for intemperate abandon?'

'Except that Kama refers not to selfish desire, but to pleasures that do not diminish the quality of your consciousness. For example, whilst the Tradition does not prohibit intoxicants, such as alcohol, we would not use them to such an extent as to undermine the quality of our consciousness. The same applies to food, our *gurubuwa* teaching plants and sexual play. For Kama is pleasure in accordance with Dharma and Artha, its underlying principle being that only a happy, healthy, gratified body–mind can be effective in achieving the other Aims of Life.'

'May I?' Samuel asked as he returned to sit beside me. 'It's just that in the *Mahabharata*, our great epic, Prince Arjuna and his brothers discuss which of the Purushartha is the most important. Strongman Bhima concludes it is Kama, for without the reward of pleasure a man does not strive to do his moral duty: Dharma. He does not attain earthly profit with integrity: Artha. Nor does he strive to see and live according to the "bigger picture", which I know is Moksha.'

I looked at Samuel with surprise. He had never before revealed himself conversant with the classical texts.

'Bhima's reasoning is that without Kama, a man does not love,' my cousin declared, 'therefore Kama stands above all others!'

'This is wisdom, *bhai*.' Kushal Magar smiled. 'For Kama is indeed the essential, eternal pleasure that brightens both the light within and light without.'

XIX

Liberation is not attained in any other way except by severing the knot of ignorance – and this by the expansion of consciousness.
Tantraloka

amuel had two guavas in his knapsack, carried from his parents' garden. He cut into the fruit with his penknife and presented the pale, solid slices to the *jhankri*.

'*Dajoo*,' Samuel said, offering the fruit to me, 'we must soon begin our journey if we are to reach home by nightfall.'

His sudden talk of home startled me. I had quite forgotten that I had another life to which I was expected to return. I felt no inclination to leave this hillside or these temple steps, this crow-spun sky or the smiling man with eyes as bright as sunlit snow.

'Then, *jhankri-dajoo*,' I appealed with sudden urgency, 'I need to know the last Aim of Life before we leave!'

'An eager student is a gift.' Kushal Magar smiled. 'Mine in return is to share the wisdom of these mountains with one who is both willing and sincere.'

He paused to touch his heart again as though, I suddenly thought, to remind me to keep mine open.

'The Tradition begins with the Purushartha to guide us to embrace every aspect of daily life without reservation, whilst affording it purpose and meaning,' he began. 'So each Aim encourages us to continue in our usual business. Dharma: doing our duty to ourselves and to those for whom we are responsible. Artha: doing our part to sustain a stable society in which all may flourish according to their own nature. And Kama: exploring the pleasure inherent in every moment, in every breath. The Purushartha, therefore, teach us to remain fully active in the world, and yet not to be enslaved by it. It is in this that the fourth Aim of Life plays its part.'

He paused to slip another slice of guava into his mouth and watched my eyes as I struggled with impatience as he slowly chewed.

'And so to Moksha,' he announced with one last swallow, 'the word we use for the end of an eclipse, when darkness lifts and sun or moon are once again restored to their full brilliance. This we symbolise by Shiva himself, our culture's symbol of all that is benevolent and the truth that is a way of being.'

'But what does Moksha mean?' I asked impatiently.

'The expansion of consciousness – self-knowledge, personal order, if you like – by learning to perceive the essential connection that underlies what might initially appear to be difference and separation. This is so that we might develop greater empathy, inspiring in us effective, dynamic compassion, rendering us of greater benefit both to ourselves and to others, in order that we might always think, speak and act out of goodwill, with a generous heart, rather than merely for our own profit.'

Another piece of guava. Again he watched my eyes. Again he slowly chewed.

'But if the Purushartha are so practical, how do I "do" Moksha?' I pressed, wanting a plan of action with boxes to tick and targets to reach before I had to leave.

'Brother, Moksha does not describe a freedom that is to be "done",' he insisted, fingering another slice of fruit, as though to goad my eagerness. 'Each of the Purushartha is interdependent, and Moksha is discovered over a lifetime through the mindful fulfilment of the previous three, as we learn to choose to release our attachment to old, unhelpful patterns. As we learn to free ourselves from the rigid confines of self-interest, and thereby from our self-inflicted suffering. As we come to understand that every aspect of our lives plays its part in the balance of the universe – both our concord and our conflict, our kindness and our cruelty, our compassion and our indifference. All light, all darkness. All beauty, all suffering. All joy, all pain. All life, all death.'

I was bewildered. This was not what I had been brought up to believe. Surely, kindness and beauty: right. Conflict and suffering: wrong. Surely, joy and life: good. Pain and death: bad.

'You see, brother, it is only as we learn to find our own resolution to these apparent contradictions, as much in ourselves as in life, that Moksha arises – the realisation that we already have all we need to be complete, to be all that we can be.'

I returned the intensity of his gaze.

And wondered whether he could even begin to perceive the squall that assailed my heart and mind.

XX

Keepers of the Tradition are not known by 'holy' show or dress, but by unconditional affection, respect, and honest love.
Kushal Magar

Samuel scooped two boiled eggs from the pot and dropped them into a bucket of cold rainwater. Kushal Magar had insisted we take them from his chickens as sustenance on our long journey back towards the town. He had also presented us with a large papaya and a bunch of 'honey bananas' donated to him by a villager in gratitude for restorative ministrations.

'So what do I do now?' I asked, unsettled by the need to leave so soon. I was well aware my permit to remain in the mountain district was about to expire and could not be renewed, yet I was not ready. 'I still have questions – many questions! And I don't even know if I can remember half you've told me!'

'The passage of our lives is directed by our questions – so all is well,' he said, smiling. 'And what more do you think you need? You have an understanding of both *bhavana*'s mindful intention and the Purushartha Aims of Life.'

'But you said they're only the beginning!' I protested.

'Which is the perfect place to start – and very often exactly to where we ultimately return. So consider the purpose of your thoughts, words and actions. Attend to the four Aims of Life. Adopt only what you know you can understand and are capable of maintaining. The rest, for now, is irrelevant.'

Samuel approached with his food parcel wrapped securely in a cloth. He had even boiled drinking water collected from the stream that cut its boisterous course towards the distant river valley. 'I really think it's time, *dajoo*,' he pressed.

I turned to help gather our few provisions, when Samuel whispered that perhaps I should give something to our host to show respect.

'Of course, a true teacher of the Tradition does not impart his knowledge for personal gain,' he assured me. 'Neither for reputation, nor for wealth. However, in our culture it is respectful and polite to give something to support our *jhankri-dajoo* as he earns no wages.'

'But we can't give him back the food he has just presented to us!' I hissed. 'So then what? Money?'

Samuel shrugged.

I dug into my inside pocket and pulled out a single one hundred rupee note.

'That's more than enough,' Samuel said. 'Unless you have a rupee coin.'

I tried my trousers and nodded.

'One hundred is an end,' he explained, 'but one hundred and one is a beginning!'

Every interaction here was an education. I still had much to learn from the sensitivity and respect these people showed one another. I turned towards the temple doors and placed my offering of what amounted to little more than one British pound in a small wooden bowl at the foot of the altar.

I turned towards Kushal Magar, now standing at the base of the dusty path that marked the beginning of our long walk home. I approached him slowly in my reluctance to leave, then bowed, touching my right hand to my heart, to his feet and back to my heart, as a child in these hills would honour a parent.

In return, he placed his hands on my head in *ahashis* blessing, then bent to whisper in each ear a repeated stream of syllables that bestowed upon me the serenity of those vast peaks beyond.

The *jhankri* pressed his head to mine.

'From today, brother, remain wholly engaged in restoring balance in yourself and in the wider world by living with mindful purpose. Learn wisdom from your daily exploration of the four Aims of Life, and always live yours with gratitude. Be free from laziness and apathy – yet addicted neither to work nor leisure. Embrace pleasure – but be moderate in your eating and drinking, your sexual expression and your sleep.'

I smiled that he should have been able to read me with such unnerving accuracy.

'Keep your speech sincere, truthful, encouraging and never to the disparagement of others. Avoid speaking of the good you have done, or of what you have been told in confidence. And think on that which inspires you to live and love well.'

It was undoubtedly Kushal Magar of whom I would be thinking.

'Remain steady in your devotion to your teachers, whoever and wherever they may be,' he said, his smile broadening. 'But most of all, brother, choose always to be happy.'

PART THREE

XXI

Vedic knowledge can always be acquired with money and status, but tantric wisdom lies beyond any wealth or privilege.
Mountain saying

O n my return to the easy domesticity of life in England, I began to question the fleeting contact I had shared with the bright-eyed Himalayan hill-man. Whilst memories of his potent tea and perceptive wisdom retained their lucidity and even infused my dreams, I wondered whether I had even begun to understand his words.

I liked to believe I possessed some skill when it came to retaining new information, but I now began to doubt whether the passage of time and drop in altitude had not distorted my recollection. Although I had been entirely willing to accept the *jhankri*'s assertion that practical knowledge was preferable to mere intellectual enquiry and ultimately longer-lasting, I now allowed my own cultural custom to convince me to pursue a little 'bookish' education, for no other reason than to satisfy my curiosity.

My first foray, however, was unrewarding. The standard high-street bookshop offered nothing with Tantra in its title that bore the least resemblance to Kushal Magar's mountain Tradition. Instead, I immersed myself in the hush of academic libraries, for which I already possessed a lifelong passion. I even braved the studies of university professors, all of whom indulged me with their time, knowledge and lists of otherwise obscure recommended reading.

So it was that I commenced my pursuit of a believable beginning, for in India I had been given to understand that the Shaiva Tantra Tradition was commonly afforded a lineage of some eighteen thousand years, which would have placed its origins at the end of the last Ice Age. It was, therefore, with some delight – as though a vindication of the kindly *jhankri*, and even of my own brief, unsought dealings with him – that I now discovered its roots were 'officially' acknowledged to be firmly founded in the shamanic fertility cults of prehistory.

Nor were its practices and teachings confined to the *jhankri* and his clan, as I had assumed, but remained quietly predominant throughout the entire length of the Himalayan foothills, from Kashmir in the west, to Assam and Kushal Magar's Bengal in the east. Of these, I learnt the latter is generally held to be its original home, a fact that has given the Tradition the alternative name of Bangali Vidya: the Knowledge, or Treasured Truth, of Bengal.

XXII

Whichever river you choose in your quest for self-knowledge,
its bright waters have fallen from the same sky
and flow into the same horizonless ocean.

Kushal Magar

M y subsequent months of study revealed that the Tradition's characteristic rejection of any rigid creed, hierarchy, priesthood or dogma had brought upon its adherents many centuries, if not millennia, of misrepresentation and persecution. And yet in spite of the unorthodoxy that had afforded it a position on the social and geographical periphery of India, the tantric mountain Tradition is technically embraced within the fold of Hinduism.

This term immediately invoked for me the image of Brahmin priests with their caste obsessions, misogyny and stringent rules, none of which I could equate with the gentle wisdom of Kushal Magar. I needed clarification.

The Abrahamic religions of Judaism, Christianity and Islam share deep roots with not only common heroes, myths and ideology, but a resolute belief in the exclusivity of their own celestial sanction. Over time, each of these monotheistic siblings developed their own books of scripture, which they uphold as their particular source of spiritual knowledge and therefore superior to all others. Whilst all three religions promote selflessness and compassion, and across the centuries have inspired thinkers, artists, musicians and poets to heights of breathless beauty, the conviction in an absolute, divinely decreed authority has been invoked as justification for millennia of inhumanity, even 'holy' crusades, inquisitions,

75

genocidal pogroms and atrocious acts of what we now call 'terrorism'.

Hinduism, in contrast, has never been a single monolithic religion with a definitive canonical beginning and a specific creed sustained by one presiding priesthood. The surprising truth is that the term 'Hinduism' is merely a collective noun coined in 1830 by the British East India Company in its attempt to describe in one word on business census ledgers the full compendium of Indian religions that were neither Islamic nor Buddhist. A new 'Hindu' miscellany was thereby created, incorporating under a single heading hundreds of independent *sampradayas*, or traditional lineages, of contrasting viewpoint and practice.

So it is today that 'Hinduism' continues to be applied as an umbrella term to all forms of ritual, mythology or philosophy associated with any of India's indigenous 'spiritual paths'. It does not, therefore, describe a definitive religion, but rather collective experiences and insights into the nature of man, notions of divinity and, notably, of universal consciousness that have arisen among the disparate historic cultures of the subcontinent.

However, the colonial application of 'Hinduism' as a reductive, bureaucratic term did far more than merely extend the Anglo-Indian lexicography. It effectively afforded the priest caste of conservative Brahminism – being just one of these 'spiritual paths' – new status. Following in the consecrated footsteps of the imams of the declining Mughal Empire and the clergy of the ascending *Pax Britannica*, the Brahmana, or Brahmin, priests now too claimed autocratic authority over their 'flock', exerting what they considered to be their religious mandate and the social rights of their high caste upon all Indians who regarded themselves as neither Buddhist nor Muslim.

It was a historically untenable position that was asserted yet further in the nineteenth century with the propagation of the term *Sanatana Dharma*: the unprecedented notion that all Indians belonged to one eternal law; a single religion founded on fundamentalist interpretations, over which the Brahmins alone presided – a lofty station from which they justified shunning their lower caste 'inferiors' in the name of so-called ritual purity and hereditary auspiciousness.

XXIII

Not knowing that the truth lies within one's Self,
the deluded are confused by searching for it in scriptures.
Kularnava Tantra

My studies further revealed that in India all philosophies, styles of worship, texts and practices are classed as being either *Astika*, meaning orthodox 'Vedic', or *Nastika*, meaning heretical 'non-Vedic'. The Tradition of Kushal Magar and his kind was undoubtedly the latter, being condemned as dangerous and 'infidel', denounced by the Brahmin priests as *Vedavahya*: wholly 'outside the Vedas'.

In an effort to understand these terms better, I learnt that just as clerics of the Abrahamic religions claim their authority from the Torah, Bible or Koran, so Brahmin priests take theirs from four books called the Vedas.

Veda is a Sanskrit term meaning 'knowing that which was unknown', whilst the Vedas are the metrical compositions of a nomadic, late Bronze Age, Indo-Iranian people. These texts encompass rules regarding sacrifice, lists of rewards to encourage and punishments to deter, in addition to numerous worship-songs to appease their diverse pantheon.

It is upon the Vedas that Brahmins base both their rites and, by restricting access to these texts, their supremacy. Indeed, their exacting, two-thousand-year-old *Laws of Manu*, or *Manusmrti*, unequivocally state it is by a Brahmin's 'possession' of the Vedas that he is

> by right the lord of this whole creation . . . [for] a Brahmin is a great deity whether or not he is learned . . . Thus Brahmins should be revered in every way, even if they engage in all kinds of undesirable actions . . . [for] by his very birth a Brahmin is a deity even for the gods and the only authority for people in this world, for the Vedas are the foundation in this matter. (IX:317–320; XI:85)

However, the Vedas have always been learnt by rote, one Brahmin reciting to a novice until he could repeat them all by heart. As these works were transmitted through the generations in their original, archaic tongue, in time few, if any, could claim truly to understand their meaning. It was in subsequent centuries, therefore, that the Brahmins attempted to explore and elaborate upon these complex, ancient texts through numerous philosophical treatises.

The result, by the second century BCE, was the development of various systems of philosophy summarised by the term Vedanta: the Conclusion of, or Appendix to, the Vedas. Although differing schools of thought devised numerous speculative notions, the principal tenets to which they inclined – such as the belief that we each earn the social station into which we are born according to the merits of a previous life; or that all physical existence is illusion, human experience a mere mirage worthy only of denial and rejection – were explored and propagated through an extensive canon that came to include the *Upanishads*, *Vaishnava Puranas* and *Bhagavad Gita*.

The conventional society that holds these books sacrosanct continues to disseminate the view that all 'authentic' indigenous Indian religion was born of the Vedas. The non-Vedic is either thereby censured as a corruption of what is imagined to have been a pure and singular source, or conveniently dismissed as wholly foreign in origin. Accordingly, those who hold to this opinion have long regarded the non-Vedic traditions of India as in direct opposition to their own philosophy and practice.

And yet long before Brahmin priests, as self-proclaimed guardians of the Vedic world, rose to prominence with their laws of prohibition, social suppression, suspicions of women and abstemious style of worship, keepers of the Tradition were already embracing life and love in all their diversity as expressions of an all-encompassing, practical and humane truth that surpassed any hierarchy, system or priesthood.

XXIV

The Vedas do not know [Shiva] directly, nor do Vishnu, nor
Brahma, nor the head yogins, nor Indra and the other gods.
Only a devotee knows.

Shiva Purana

The Brahmins' Vedas contain hymns to over fifty gods, including Surya, Lord of the Sun; Varuna, Lord of Sky and Water; and Aditi, the Celestial Virgin. However, with the development of Vedanta's metaphysical speculations, this divine assembly lost their significance in priestly ritual and gradually faded into distant myth.

In their wake, an unlikely candidate came to the fore: a minor deity called Vishnu, who in the Vedas was but a rarely mentioned companion to Indra, Vedic Lord of War and Weather. Over time, Indra's four-armed 'little brother' came to symbolise the domestication of nature, as suited an expanding population troubled by challenging terrain and extremes in climate. He was also soon being appealed to by the orthodox in an effort to secure the people's other principal concern: pregnancy.

So it was that a new cult steadily arose, a devotional sect brought under Brahminical control early in its history, which afforded the priest caste a fresh pre-eminent god: an All-Pervading One to whom – and to whose officiants – devotees were required to offer themselves in complete surrender. It is as such that Vishnu and the most popular and poster-worthy of his ten avatars or 'descents' on to Earth, Krishna and Rama, remain today.

Vishnu's early adoption into Brahminical orthodoxy afforded him an association with social convention and cosmic order, which greatly appealed to the regional rulers of north and central India. As a consequence, Brahmin priests were summoned to royal courts to make a show of offering service to a deity that had come to represent legitimate kingship, and thereby the sovereign's own claims to divine appointment. In so doing, such kings – notably monarchs of non-Indian origin – further sanctioned their position by publicly taking the role of protector and patron of Vedic rites and their elite, Vishnu-venerating celebrants.

It was an entirely natural progression, therefore, that around the fourth century CE, under the aggressive military rule of the Gupta dynasty, Brahminism effectively became the state religion in the urban centres of north and central India.

The priest caste only began to extend its cultural and sacerdotal supremacy into rural districts when subsequent generations offered their services to the courts of provincial rulers, who eagerly employed them as both a status symbol and a means by which to legitimise their power. Paid in royal rights and land grants, Brahmin priests were thus able to settle new regions and, with conscious efforts to convert, spread their ideology, at the same time earning a living for themselves by charging local communities for carrying out their own religious rites.

Given this heritage, it is not surprising that worshippers of Vishnu – called Vaishnavas – uphold a conventional and patriarchal faith. This they express through emotional devotion, or *bhakta*, which by its very nature emphasises the notion of a primary disunion between lowly man and mighty God. The result is a fellowship of devotees who aspire to merit the grace of a separate, unreachable Almighty through reverential ritual and emotive hymns, that they might earn release from what they believe to be the wretched cycles of birth, death and rebirth.

It is perhaps this enthused, devotional aspect of Vaishnavam that has long encouraged its adherents to consider their authoritative scripture- and priest-based religion to be the only valid 'spiritual' path, taking as 'proof' the Brahminical philosophising of Vedanta and the Vedas by which it was inspired. It was principally this conviction that led to a direct attack on the defiantly heterodox Tradition in north India during the great Vaishnava revivals of the fifteenth and eighteenth centuries. As a result, the ancient Tradition of Shaiva Tantra was virtually eradicated in regions where Vaishnava *bhakta* had taken hold, leaving little more than a few distorted echoes of its practices and teachings.

Still today, India's modern conservatism affords dominance to Vaishnavam, with its *smarta* 'conventional religious knowledge' as prescribed by Brahminical law. Accordingly, images of Vishnu depict him bedecked as a high-caste warrior-king who bears around one finger a spinning disc, the *Sudarshan*, to indicate the reliability of his established system, and a heavy mace, the *Kaumodaki*, with which to strike down those who stray from the sanctioned orthodoxy of his priests.

XXV

I am a part of all that I have met.
Alfred Tennyson

One example of the starkly contrasting stances of worshippers of Vishnu, as sustained by the orthodoxy of the Vedic and Vedantic, and that of adherents to the Tradition is embodied in the use and understanding of a single word: *Maya*. Whilst both approaches apply this term to the world, human experience and the material universe, it is generally understood by each in markedly different ways.

Maya is a Sanskrit word that shares its Indo-European root *ma*, 'to give form', with our English 'mother'. Its literal meaning is 'that which can be measured or evaluated', such as physical matter and energy.

Brahminical Vedanta propagates the maxim '*Brahma satya jagat mithya*': 'God alone is real; the universe is a sham, deceit'. The conservative interpretation of *Maya*, therefore, is 'that which veils the truth' – a 'fact', Vedanta insists, that warrants rejection of the 'fiction' that is the world and thereby the 'delusion' that is human experience with all its inherent thoughts, feelings, intentions and actions.

The Tradition, in contrast, considers this orthodox notion of the coexistence of 'real' and 'unreal' an irrational contradiction. Instead, the entire material and non-material universe is perceived to be energy – eternal, amoral, uncontainable and essentially vibrational in nature – the inherent oscillating, reciprocating quality of which brings matter into existence. This in turn leads to omnipresent rhythmical patterns, most easily seen in tides and seasons, moon cycles and magnetic fields, sound and light, birth and death, or even in what we would now recognise as quantum 'wave function'.

The Tradition sees this inherent impulse in the cosmos to organise into illimitable patterns as the expression of an underlying consciousness that brings order to what would otherwise be cosmic chaos, and thereby enables the material universe to exist. Just like the energy that gives it form, this consciousness is recognised as not only eternal and amoral, but also impersonal.

For ease of understanding in a mountain culture that is essentially oral and illiterate, this union of energy and consciousness has long been figuratively expressed as the intimate embrace of the goddess Shakti and the god Shiva.

The Tradition, therefore, embraces the term *Maya* not as a deception worthy only of rejection as Vaishnava orthodoxy teaches, but as an all-pervading consciousness brought into stable, sensual manifestation by energy, to be revealed as light and darkness, matter and non-matter, physical form and self-consciousness.

So it is that for Kushal Magar and keepers of the Tradition, our subjective experience and awareness *is* reality. All people, all life, all 'paths' are worthy of respect. All existence is, by its very being, valid.

XXVI

I love the Beautiful One
with no bond nor fear
no clan no marks
no landmarks
for his beauty.

Mahadeviyakka

The finest spiced tea tasted since the day I had reluctantly walked away from Kushal Magar's blackened pot was served in the London drawing room of an Indian scholar, whose careful attention to his own appearance was made all the more fastidious by the eccentric mayhem in which he invited me to sit. My apprehensive application to Professor Pandey had initially prompted an encouraging response in haphazard script, with the unexpected insertion of a recipe for *ghee*-based Welsh cakes cut from an edition of *Eve's Own*. Evidence, I decided, of a naturally liberal disposition.

Perched on the pile of magazines that cushioned his armchair, my host began by introducing the mountain Tradition of Shaiva Tantra as 'the potent and functional perspective of a resilient and practical people'. One notable expression of this, he asserted, was the Tradition's abundant use of iconographic, geometric and allegorical imagery, which its adherents recognise as the most effective way to engage a human mind that is by nature highly responsive to pictures and patterns.

The fact that the Tradition uses imagery associated with Shiva to express the intrinsic order – the consciousness – that underlies the 'deep structure' of the cosmos, places it under the broad umbrella of Shaivam, an academic term sometimes anglicised to 'Shaivism', applied to all practice and philosophy associated with this boldly heterodox mountain deity.

Shaivam, the professor explained, was once dominant throughout the entire subcontinent, from the snowy peaks and lofty deodars of the Himalaya in the north, to the tropical forests and sandy shores that lie some two thousand miles to the south. However, the Brahmin priests were long opposed to its teachings, for shaivas lay beyond their prescriptive laws and Vedic customs and thereby outside their control. Even so, over the centuries aspects of its teachings and its symbols – notably the imagery of 'male' Shiva (consciousness) and the varied forms of 'female' Shakti (energy) – were not only accommodated but thoroughly absorbed by even the most authoritarian adherents of Brahminical orthodoxy.

This assimilation partly came about when, after the sixth century CE, a great number of Brahmins were drawn to the wandering, ash-smeared, ecstatic Pashupatas, one of the oldest and most prominent sects of Shaiva Tantra. In time, these priestly converts – referred to as *mishra*, meaning 'mixed' – came to dominate the Pashupatas. This not only had an enormous and lasting influence on orthodox doctrine and custom, but these men also steadily changed the Pashupatas' all-embracing ethos to one of hierarchical segregation, with preference inevitably given to members of the priest caste.

And yet despite this interaction, two very distinct traditions became apparent on the subcontinent. On one hand, that of the Vedic Brahmins, which as early as the fifth century BCE had come to represent the institutionalised, patriarchal and priestly aspects of religious practice in north India, with its heartland in what is today western Uttar Pradesh, Haryana and the Punjab. And on the other, the unorthodox Tradition, which stood for self-government, experimentation and free will, its tantric heartland in what is today eastern Bihar, Orissa, Assam – and Kushal Magar's Bengal.

XXVII

Energy . . . is a single entity,
but appears in as many forms as the light of the sun.
Shiva Purana

I n addition to Shiva, other non-Vedic gods – regional deities most commonly associated with animals, trees, geological formations and water sources – were employed in the ritual life and mythologies of ancient India. These nature deities had been especially prominent in India's north-east, heartland of the Tradition, where archaeological evidence has unearthed very little or no sign of early Vedic influence.

As the Brahmin priests had forged eastwards with missionary zeal and royal patronage, they had applied the Sanskrit term *yaksha* to the rural divinities they encountered, assigning them the status of supernatural beings, even ghosts, produced from the 'unclean' feet of Brahma, the priest caste's Lord of Creation. However, such was the popularity of these ancient, non-Vedic deities among the common people that the Brahmins eventually grew to consider the *yaksha* to be benevolent and inoffensive in disposition, as became the lowly station the priest caste now afforded them.

And yet, as the people's gods steadily displaced the Vedic

pantheon, enabling even Shiva to be absorbed into the conventional fold, in time the *yakshas* too were embraced. So it was that Durga, Nandi, Skanda, Tara, Parvati, Lakshmi, Kubera, Krishna, Ganesha, Hanuman, the Nagas and innumerable others were gradually incorporated into the Brahminical orthodoxy. As a consequence, new mythologies had to be invented that might explain, even justify, the assumption of such non-Vedic symbols. This led to the composition, between the third and tenth centuries CE, of the Brahminical mythical 'histories' known as the Puranas.

Many of these so-called *yakshas* were tantric symbols of 'female' Shakti: the energy that is the universe. In an effort to 'tame' the potency and independence they embodied, the priests initially categorised these goddesses as morally ambiguous, even dangerous, frequently consigning them to the roles of controllers of disease or mitigators of misfortune. In time, the Brahmins reassigned them as subservient consorts to their patriarchal gods – Lakshmi being 'married' to Vishnu for example, Saraswati to Brahma. As though to reiterate the misogynistic point, these 'reassigned' goddesses were subsequently depicted by the orthodox as diminutive, almost doll-like figures, perched beside or even dandled on the knee of their presumptive, male masters.

Other *yakshas* were tantric 'fierce' divinities, such as Bhairava, Chinnamasta and Kali – 'fierce' only to those who identify themselves merely through the limits of their own self-interest. In time, these too were embraced by the Brahmins for their potential roles as supernatural 'weapons' that might be offered to royal patrons as an imagined defence against enemies of their states.

Early Buddhism also implemented the same policy of

adopting tantric iconography as a means to draw in the local populations to which they preached with missionary zeal. New myths and texts were therefore created that recounted how the Buddha 'converted' *yakshas* into benign guardian deities, often by killing then resurrecting them in forms better suited to Buddhist thought. In fact, by the eighth to tenth centuries, Buddhism had so widely adopted the 'fierce' male and female so-called *yakshas* that they were commonly employing them at the very centre of their principal meditative tool, the *mandala*.

And yet despite this peculiar history of rejection, reinvention and eventual absorption, today the vast majority of *yakshas* still retain their association with Shiva, the multiple female expressions of the tantric concept of Shakti, and the defiant unorthodoxy of the Tradition.

XXVIII

One who is enlightened . . . requires no ablutions, nor prayer, nor worship, nor fire rituals, nor other disciplines . . . He is not bound by disciplinary codes, nor need he frequent temples for worship.
Devikalottara

I t would seem that the character of my initial questions and the industriousness of my note-taking had endeared me to Professor Pandey. On my second visit to his home, his brew of spiced Darjeeling was accompanied by a biscuit box of 'dunkables' to sustain us both through my new lessons.

He began by explaining that Shaiva Tantra had flourished

after the collapse of the Gupta Empire in the sixth century. A chaotic political period had followed of short-lived regional kingdoms ruled by anxiously militarising monarchs who, in such uncertain times, had grown disillusioned with the old pattern of Brahminical dominance at court. A new source of insight was demanded so that social and state stability might be restored.

It had been to practitioners of the Tradition that these nervous kings had turned, for Shaiva Tantra had long been associated with the mastery of powerful, even 'dangerous', forces. And this principally by the fact of its Vedic exclusion; its purposeful transgression of Brahminical norms; its 'fierce' iconography; and its embracing of the casteless, whose duties included the overseeing of both 'unclean' birth and 'inauspicious' death.

Whilst any reference to 'forces' in the Tradition had only ever been meant as a metaphor for overcoming detrimental habits and limiting self-interest in the individual, over-dramatised hearsay and courtly superstition had afforded the term a new connotation: *shaiva tantrikas* were now accredited with miraculous mantras, 'destructive magic' that might revise nature, ensure both royal virility and longevity – and perhaps even vanquish enemies of the realm.

So it was that, particularly between the eighth and thirteenth centuries, practitioners of the Tradition were for the first time offered protection and benefaction by royal courts. This patronage was notably provided by the Rajputs, who for some six hundred years maintained *tantrikas* in their retinues as counsellors and confidants, whilst these warrior princes extended their kingdoms westwards, as far as Bihar and Nepal.

The fashion for tantric patronage also spread to the royal

courts of Burma, Thailand, Cambodia, Java, Bali, China and Japan, enduring in the kingdoms of Nepal, Bhutan and Java into modern times. The kings of Kashmir even adopted a modified form of Shaiva Tantra, called Trika, as their state religion.

However, such is human nature that the promise of a virtually free hand in royal coffers proved too great a temptation for the unscrupulous. What had always been the entirely personal practice of tantric *sadhana* was now commercialised, reinvented as a public ritual to suit the agenda of paying clients. In these contrived and highly pressurised conditions, an already diminished version of the Tradition was steadily corrupted beyond recognition to suit the politics of state, until even Shiva, tantric symbol of both the consciousness that affords order to the cosmos and all that is benevolent in ourselves and the wider world, was declared a form of the Brahmins' Vedic Indra: a god of war.

XXIX

Every Scripture is but a means. It is not useful to one who has not yet known the Devi [Shakti] and is not useful to one who has already known her.

Kulachundamani Tantra

R oyal patronage may have adapted and distorted the Tradition during India's early medieval period, yet the thriving of an official, urbanised tantric culture had also produced astonishing works of art and sculpture, such as the temple complexes of Konark and Khajuraho.[1]

It had also inspired the writing of literary works, as different forms of tantric thought and practice were set down for the first time in their already long history. The resulting texts were not only egalitarian and universalist in their outlook, but ambitious in their extent, some having as many as five times the number of verses as the Bible. They were principally styled as either *Shakta Tantras*, in which knowledge was expressed through the 'voice' of Shakti, or as *Shiva Agamas*, which employed the 'voice' of Shiva. Together, they contained what was simply termed *Paravidya*, the Ancient Knowledge.

Comprising some two-thirds of all 'Hindu' literature, most surviving *Tantra-Agamas*, as this collected body of texts is known, are written in *sandhyabhasha*, a hidden 'twilight language' of often erotic simile and vocabulary based on early vernacular tongues. The symbolism employed in these texts was purposely misleading, with practices described in such deliberately obscure, even shocking, terms, with essential steps omitted to ensure that teachings inspired by the Tradition could not be easily accessed and thereby misused by the uninitiated. To depend solely on such coded

---

[1] In the fourteenth century, Sufi writers recorded that there was a community of *shaiva tantrikas* living in the precincts of the famous Khajuraho temples. The reason this warranted comment was that these *tantrikas* lived with people afflicted by elephantitis and, most socially ostracising of all, leprosy. The priest caste claimed that the latter disease was a 'karmic' punishment for the two acts of violence they held to be the greatest of all 'sins': the killing of a cow or the murder of a Brahmin; a prejudice that still persists today. Whilst the orthodox perpetuated the horrific notion that the only way to redeem this 'karmic debt' was to bury alive anyone found infected with leprosy, *shaiva tantrikas* took such people into their midst, offering them both physical protection, social inclusion and medical treatment.

and ambiguous written works, therefore, was futile.

Under royal patronage, a vast number of *Tantra-Agamas* were transcribed from their original dialects into a more accessible basic Sanskrit. These patrons included the noble houses of Nepal and Bhutan; the Pala kings of Bihar, Bengal and Orissa; the Pratihara kings of Kanyakubja (now Kannauj District, Uttar Pradesh); and the Candella kings of Bundelkhand, in central India. There was also a vast collection of *Tantra-Agamas* written in the vernacular Malayalam of what is now the subcontinent's most south-westerly state of Kerala, where remnants of its ancient tantric culture may still be found.

As Buddhist monks escaped across the northern mountains to save their libraries and themselves from the hands of fanatical Brahmins, the unified empire of Tibet became a repository of tantric texts from India. Over the years, the heads of Himalayan monastic colleges translated and adapted these written works from their original Bengali, Orya and colloquial Sanskrit, a mutual borrowing and exchange that would continue between Shaiva and Tibetan sources for centuries. These Tibetan renditions, which were a principal influence on the development of Vajrayana Buddhism, are now the earliest surviving versions of any known Indian tantric text.

Whilst many thousands of *Tantra-Agamas* remain extant, the tantric canon has inevitably been tampered with over the centuries. Extreme editing has been applied in some cases, with great passages of 'authorised' works being inserted in order to modify and 'standardise' the knowledge they contain. The result is a confusion of inconsistencies.

The *Mahanirvana Tantra* is a prime example of this process of political adaptation. An eighteenth-century text based on an eighth-century Tibetan original, it is probably the best known *Tantra-Agama* in the West due to its translation by Sir John Woodroffe (1865–1936), a British judge and Orientalist who went by the romantic pseudonym of Arthur Avalon. However, the present version of what he entitled *The Tantra of the Great Liberation* is a gross modification of the original, for it is filled with Vedantic philosophy, even incorporating insertions from the Brahminical *Laws of Manu*, the Vedantic *Bhagavad Gita*, and sermons of the Buddha. These interpolations were made in the early nineteenth century by the joint efforts of a Baptist missionary named William Carey; Rammohun Roy, founder of the Christian-influenced Neo-vedantic Brahmo Samaj; and a Sanskrit scholar named Hariharananda Vidyabagish. The combined purpose of this eccentric coterie was to introduce reforms to the Tradition, which still held sway in Bengal, bringing it more in line with the growing colonial influences of Christian Europe, whilst rendering the text acceptable to the Brahminical elite by passing it off as a devotional text to the One True God. It is, therefore, somewhat significant that its celebrated English translator was himself a devout, if mystically inclined, Roman Catholic.

However, for the numerous tantric texts that have been altered, many thousands more have been lost. Some suffered wilful destruction, either during periods of systematic persecution, or by being burned on funeral pyres. Others, written on such unstable material as palm leaves, have been rotted by monsoons or devoured by insects. Many have simply been decayed by time into illegibility.

And yet, keepers of the Tradition do not consider any of this to be a deprivation, for no words gleaned from a book are considered worthy of use in effective *sadhana*. The oral tradition has always been the preferred and most trusted form of transmission of tantric insight on the subcontinent.

Texts, if used at all, have never been considered any more than an unnecessary, subsidiary support. In fact, in the eastern Himalaya, where the Tradition places all emphasis on practical and dynamic first-hand experience, the written word remains entirely redundant.

XXX

In company a Vaishnava, amongst friends a Shaiva,
in private a tantrika.
Mountain saying

Professor Pandey's introduction to the history of the Tradition in north India had been a revelation. At its conclusion, he had encouraged me to continue my own studies by sending me home with an augmented list of recommended reading and the last Hobnob.

It was therefore back among the weighty tomes of academia, and as proud bearer of a British Library Reader Pass, that over the coming months I discovered the flowering of tantric culture in India had reached its peak at the end of the first millennium of the present era. However, history books disclosed that its keepers continued to suffer at times fanatical persecution: repression for the symbolism they employed in practice, vilification for the veiled language of tantrically inspired texts, and violence for what was judged the 'amoral' unorthodoxy of their teachings.

As a result, over the centuries shrines raised to the symbols of Shiva and Shakti had been violently destroyed throughout the country, replaced by temples dedicated to

Vishnu and his avatars under the administration of Brahmin priests. The tantric way of life had also been put under pressure by authoritarian Jain and Buddhist teachings, which perpetuated new patriarchal 'spiritual' hierarchies whilst advocating physical renunciation and unquestioning conformity to their particular notion of prescribed 'morality'.

This persecution had only been furthered by invading Afghan, Persian and Turkish Muslims, European Christian missionaries, and then by the conservative political and yogic cultures of the modern day. Even in the historic tantric heartland of Bengal, to the north of which lie Kushal Magar's mountains, the long-ruling Communist Party of India has made concerted efforts to belittle, discredit and suppress the teachings of the Tradition and its practitioners with fantastical allegations of intemperance, sexual aberration and even cannibalism. Such charges continue to be propagated through the politically motivated Anti Superstition Clubs, which have been set up in many Bengali schools and communities. The result has been a marked increase in incidents of *tantrikas* being sought out and brutalised by politically sanctioned thugs.

Only regions south of the Central Highlands of the Vindhya Mountains (notably the Western Ghats), and the northern kingdoms of Assam, Nepal, Sikkim, Bhutan, Kashmir and Tibet have offered refuge to the Spoken Knowledge. Elsewhere, almost all the ancient tantric pedigrees have simply been wiped away, whilst those who have attempted to preserve the teachings and practices have been widely denigrated as figures of either fear or fun.

The thought that generations of 'Kushal Magars' could ever have been so aggressively abused, maligned and even murdered left me in dismay.

XXXI

The Tantra is for all men, of whatever caste, and for all women.
Gautamiya Tantra

A principal reason for these centuries of tireless harrying is the Tradition's nonconformity and anti-elitism, which has always proved hugely challenging to a priest caste that condemns tantric egalitarianism as a threat to all social norms. In addition, there have long been specific Brahminical practices and social principles, which Shaiva Tantra has not only always openly rejected but courageously defied.

Keepers of the Tradition have, for example, never tired in their active condemnation of such practices as *sati daha* (often simply anglicised to 'suttee'), which not only forbids a widow to remarry, but requires she prove fidelity to her husband by throwing herself on to his funeral pyre. It was a practice that the orthodox fiercely enforced for centuries, as their scriptures brutally and repeatedly instruct:

> It is the highest duty of the woman to immolate herself after her husband. (*Brahma Purana* LXXX:75)
> On her husband's death, the widow should . . . ascend the funeral pyre after him. (*Vishnu Dharmasutra* XXV:14)

The mind-set that established *sati daha* as an acceptable practice in conservative society is impossible to conceive – until the abhorrent misogyny that has been propagated for millennia by the 'sacred' texts of the priest caste are exposed in such texts as the following:

The mind of woman cannot be disciplined; she has very little intelligence. (*Rigveda* 8 – XXXIII:17)

Women are light-minded. They are the root of all troubles. Attachment towards them should not be pursued by wakeful persons who desire liberation. [For] there is none more sinning and more sinful than women. Women are the root of all sins . . . fickle-minded, of evil deeds and emotionally incomprehensible even to an intelligent man. (*Uma Samhita* XXIV:3, 16)

One should approach [a] woman and invite her to have sex. Should she refuse to consent, [a man] should bribe her. If she still refuses, he should beat her with a stick or with his fists and overpower her, saying: 'I take away the splendour from you with my virility and splendour'. (*Brhadarankyaka Upanishad* VI.IV:9, 21)

The *Rudra Samhita* (book III – chapter LIV) bears the further Brahminical decree that a 'chaste' woman is never to defend herself against a husband who scolds or rebukes her, for 'even when beaten by him she shall remain glad and say, "I may even be killed, O lord".' She is never to show the least maturity or initiative, except, of course, 'at the time of sexual intercourse', whereupon she is to 'like whatever her husband is interested in . . . [for] to a wife the husband is god, preceptor, virtue, holy centre and sacred rite. She should cast off everything and adore him alone.' Therefore, if she has the audacity even to consume sweets without sharing them with him, she is to be reborn as 'a wild goat eating its own dung', whilst if she dare retort to her husband's unkindness, she is automatically damned to 'be born as a bitch in a village'.

Such misogynistic scripture has afforded unthinking followers of Brahminical orthodoxy full justification for the subjection of their women, who, being deemed both inferior and dangerous, were not only traditionally denied an education, but forbidden even to touch a book. Indeed, the threatened 'divine' punishment for such precociousness was premature widowhood, with its terrifying consequential burning; after all, it was customary for every Vaishnava woman to be held responsible for her husband's death, whatever its actual cause.

It is a mentality that remains alarmingly evident in India's conservative society today, as revealed by the rising rates of selective female abortion, sexual violence against women, bride torture and burnings, dowry killings (nearly one an hour recorded in 2012), or even the persistence of the public intimidation termed 'Eve-teasing'.

Of course, all this is anathema to *shaiva tantrikas*. Indeed, the cruel censure of priestly scripture could not be in greater contrast to the millennia-old *Niruttara Tantra*, for instance, which details a wholly liberal attitude towards female independence to ensure that men and women enjoy complete equality. The *Kali Tantra* extols female qualities, whilst the voluminous *Yogini Tantra* defiantly states that the 'moral' codes of the dominant Vedantic, Vaishnava culture should be actively broken, all women being encouraged to speak and act with the same social, familial and sexual liberties as their menfolk.

Still today in the eastern Himalaya, where the Tradition maintains its benevolent influence upon the people, a man who raises his voice in disrespect of any woman is required to undertake a day-long fast in reparation, and the house in which a woman resides is considered worthy of the same honour as any temple. In the unequivocal words of the *Kaulavalinirnaya Tantra*:

> Respect and consideration for women mark the very foundations [of the Tradition]. All women are to be looked upon as manifestations of the Great Mother [Shakti]. An offending woman should not be beaten even with flowers. A woman of any age, even a girl, or even an uncouth woman, should be bidden a respectful farewell after salutation. (chapter X)

XXXII

Numerous here on earth are those who are intent on social class, who follow the rules of caste. . . But he who is devoid of all such concerns . . . is difficult to find.

Kularnava Tantra

Another orthodox principle wholly rejected by the Tradition is the tenet of exclusion. In India and Nepal, this is most obviously expressed by the 'spiritual' and social hierarchy of caste.

Called *varna* – meaning 'colour of the face' or 'outward appearance' – caste is a Brahminic imposition on a society of which they regard themselves to be at the preordained apex; in their own words, they are 'the best of all men'. Below the priestly Brahmins, in descending order, lie Kshatriyas, the aristocratic warrior caste; Vaishyas, the merchant and artisan caste; and finally Shudras, the servile class, whose duty is to 'meekly' labour for the benefit of their superiors, 'in order to make himself liked by them'. As numerous Brahminical texts unequivocally declare:

> The Vedas enjoin rituals for the first three castes. The Shudras are excluded since their only activity is service. (*Kailsa Samhita* XII:22)
>
> A Brahmin who takes a Shudra wife to bed will sink into hell . . . Let a Brahmin not give a Shudra advice, or the remnants of his meal . . . Having defamed a Brahmin . . . a Shudra shall suffer corporal punishment . . . A Shudra who insults a twice-born man [one initiated into Vedic study] . . . shall have his tongue cut out. (*Manusmrti* III:17; IV:80–81; VIII:267, 270)

To justify such cruel prejudice, numerous Brahminical texts, beginning with the Vedas, declare Brahmins to have been born from the head or mouth of God; Kshatriyas from his arms or shoulders; the Vaishyas from his belly or thighs; and the Shudras from what is regarded in India as the most polluted part of the body: his feet. The orthodox authors of the later mythologised Brahminical 'histories', or Puranas, even went so far as to state that the 'divine' Brahmins were born from the Vedic Creator's sweet breath, whilst the *asura* 'antigod' Shudras were produced from his foul flatulence.

The *Bhagavad Gita*, which maintains such popularity in the West despite its discriminatory philosophising, further entrenched the birth-determined caste system to the benefit of the Brahmins by conveniently proclaiming it to be a divine, Vishnu-originated construct. In this way, priestly law was able to justify denying their forcibly assigned servile caste access to the 'sacred' knowledge of the Vedas.

Indeed, a 'low-caste' Shudra was not only forbidden to learn Sanskrit, but were he to overhear the recitation of any part of the Brahmins' sacred books he was to have molten lead poured into his ears (*Manusmrti* XII:4). Even then, if a Shudra were ever to admit that he remembered a single word of what he had accidentally overheard, his body was to be torn to pieces (*Apastambha Dharma Sutra* III:10–26). And still further:

> If a man of one birth [low-caste] hurls cruel words at one of the twice-born [those initiated into Vedic study], his tongue should be cut out, for he was born from the anus.
>
> If he mentions their name or caste maliciously, a red-hot iron nail ten-fingers long should be thrust into his mouth. If he is so proud as to instruct priests about their duty, the king should have hot oil poured into his mouth and ears . . .
>
> If a man of inferior caste tries to sit down on the same seat as a man of superior caste, he should be branded on the hip and banished, or have his buttocks cut off.
>
> (*Manusmrti* VIII: 270–72, 281; see also *Vishnusmrti* V:19–25)

And yet, even these reviled Shudras are not at the nadir of social order, for whilst they may be the lowest of the four priest-promoted castes, below them lie the casteless Antyaja – the so-called Untouchables – whose only permissible occupations have traditionally been those of 'beggar' musicians, collectors of excrement and carriers of the dead.

Today these 'illegitimate' Untouchables number about

170 million of India's vast population. Calling themselves Dalits, meaning 'the oppressed', these men, women and children continue to suffer religiously sanctioned bigotry and abuse, such as exclusion from orthodox temples and communal water sources, inequity in the education system, and alarming levels of physical and sexual violence. And this despite official anti-discrimination policies that were first introduced in India as long ago as 1935.

XXXIII

An outcast . . . is equal to a leading Brahmin, a sage, a glorious ascetic and a learned scholar. A master of the four Vedas is not dearer to [Shiva] than an untouchable . . . He shall be shown the same respect as [Shiva].
Shiva Purana

In contrast to the divisive exclusivity of Brahminical orthodoxy, one of the defining qualities of the Tradition has always been its defiant inclusivity. For Kushal Magar and his kind, all existence is an expression of the same consciousness and energy in union. All life is worthy of respect. They therefore reject any purported 'spiritual path' founded upon any form of hierarchy, or that entertains discrimination between man and woman, maharaja and beggar, Brahmin priest and Dalit 'Untouchable'.

It is this all-encompassing approach of the Tradition that has proved particularly challenging to those who prefer to estimate their worth by the subjugation of others. Even Shiva, as 'male' symbol of the tantric path, is fiercely denounced in

Vaishnava scripture for his open contempt of the Brahminic social prohibitions:

> The Brahmins will not sacrifice to you [Shiva] along with the other gods, for Shiva has defiled the path followed by good men; he is impure, an abolisher of rites and demolisher of barriers [by giving] the words of the Vedas to a Shudra . . .
>
> Let Shiva, the lowest of the gods, obtain then no share with Indra and Vishnu at the sacrifice; let all the followers of Shiva be heretics, opponents of the true scriptures, following [Shiva's] heresy. (*Bhagavata Purana* IV – II:10–32; *Brahma Purana* II – XIII:70–73; *Garuda Purana* VI:19)

Keepers of the Tradition continue to reject self-esteem through social or 'spiritual' status. They even deem the mindful effort to disregard all such hierarchies – whether those of kings, priesthoods, politicians, 'holy' men and women, or celebrities – a defining mark of a *shaiva tantrika*. As Kushal Magar once asserted, it is always fruitful to consider which hierarchies we mindlessly accept, whether they be to our aggrandisement or diminution.

It was with this memory of his teaching that I knew my many months of scouring card indexes and currying favour from tired librarians and an indulgent Professor Pandey had come to their end for the time being. My research through obscure publications may have appealed to my intellectual curiosity, but in reality I knew that the knowledge for which I truly yearned would never be found in books.

The time had come for my return to distant mountains, a river valley and a crow-topped scarlet temple.

PART FOUR

XXXIV

Seekers of Liberation should begin to practise Shaiva Yoga . . . to enlighten their understanding.
Yoga Shikha

A pewter sky bore down upon our heads as Samuel and I paused at the top of the powdery path. Kanchenjunga lay concealed within an ashen veil that threatened precipitation, whilst, far below, the river valley was already beginning to vanish beneath a listless mizzle.

A year had passed since last we had stood together on this hillside. A long, slow year since I had unwittingly stepped into the *jhankri*'s world and found myself confronted by the mindless, self-involved drift I had unquestioningly accepted as my life.

In addition to my studies, for the past twelve months I had begun to reconsider choices made without awareness, beliefs assumed without enquiry, company kept with no consideration of its influence. I had sought ways to fulfil the first three Aims of Life in every interaction: the personal responsibilities of Dharma, the social duties of Artha, and Kama's sensual pleasure. In so doing, I had found myself challenged, even provoked and perplexed. And yet at every new confrontation with myself, I had known my life enriched.

I now placed a hand on my cousin's shoulder, indicating that he should lead our descent back towards a little hut and temple that had been too long consigned to dreams.

All was as we had left it.

Geraniums and marigolds bloomed from neat rows of thumb-pinched pots that lined our path. Carefully tended soil bore lush lines of mustard leaf and radish. A scrawny cockerel minced his realm on yellow shanks, as biddies pecked and puttered through tidy ranks of cauliflower and carrot.

Only two things were amiss. There were no crows to herald our approach. There was no *jhankri* to surprise in eager greeting.

I paused before the temple steps where I had first learnt of the Tradition, and recalled the tea-stained smile that had assured my welcome. I looked at the scarlet temple doors, now tightly shut, before which ordinary notions of my self had been contested. I turned to the adjoining, shuttered sanctuary in which I had circumambulated the *linga* – the ithyphallic upright stone that represents Shiva and all his meanings – and had first reflected upon the perception of an essential unanimity.

A ruffled cluck of chickens caused me to look round to meet the eyes of a hardy adolescent girl, her arms heaped high with maize cobs. She stopped quite still as my foreign features met her stare.

'*Namaskar bhaini*,' Samuel intervened. '*Jhankri-dajoo gharma cha?*'

'Yes, the *jhankri* is home,' she replied in perfect English, her broad cheeks flushing as she tipped her head. 'But not today,' she added, exhibiting the quaint custom of these hills of never answering a question with a negative. 'You must be the brothers he's expecting.'

'We're certainly cousin-brothers,' Samuel affirmed, casting a grin in my direction. 'But we'd sent no word that we were coming from Kalimpong this morning.'

Her bright eyes widened. 'So far? Then you must have started before dawn! Please sit.'

The girl set down her load and quickly lit a fire. She merged with the darkness of the *jhankri*'s hut to retrieve the same blackened pot from which I had been served seemingly endless mugs of suspiciously spiced tea the previous winter. I watched her at her work with such candour that she caught my curiosity and quickly announced, 'I am Jai Kumari, brothers – the *jhankri*'s daughter.'

I turned to Samuel. Kushal Magar, an unmarried *jhankri*, had a child? Samuel responded with a shrug so indiscreet that Jai Kumari noticed.

'I was an orphan from beyond the village,' she explained without the least unease, 'until the *jhankri* took me in and raised me as his own.' She dropped ginger root, cinnamon bark and cardamom pods into the wooden *musli* mortar. 'He's a good and kindly father,' she continued, gently bruising the spices with a well-worn *okhli* pestle. 'And now, like him, I study at college in Darjeeling.' She tipped the contents of her mortar into the rolling water, added sugar, then prepared to heat a little milk.

I leant forwards, eager to inhale the scent of *masala chiya* that I had so often found myself craving throughout the intervening year. My own efforts to replicate this perfect mix had never borne such exhilarating fragrance.

'You must be the foreigner who came before,' Jai Kumari said, glancing towards me in an effort to satisfy her own curiosity whilst maintaining customary Nepalese propriety.

I nodded. 'Of course,' she replied. 'My father spoke of you.'

'We thought we'd surprise him by turning up today,' I admitted, satisfied at the fulfilment of many months' hard work and prudent economising that had returned me to these temple steps.

'Here,' she said, offering a metal beaker of steaming, scented tea with her right hand supported by her left to show respect, 'drink it hot before your climb.'

'Our climb?' I laughed.

'Yes, brothers,' she answered, 'to the rock temples.'

'But why would we want to climb to the rock temples?' Samuel asked.

'My father's waiting there,' Jai Kumari replied. 'He's been expecting you since sunrise.'

XXXV

Shiva expounds for the benefit of His devotees the Discipline of Yoga, so that they may . . . gain beneficial knowledge and an undistracted mind.

Shiva Samhita

Samuel and I rang the heavy bell that hung above our heads. Its vibrant toll resounded through the cloud that clung to trees and veiled the steep, stone-cut steps ahead.

'Why do we do that?' I asked as we began our climb.

'To wake the deity within,' Samuel replied, his shorter legs doubling their pace to keep alongside mine.

I slowed. My initial visit to Kushal Magar, the year before, had revealed that my cousin had known far more of the teachings of the Tradition than he had at first let on. In fact, he had told me on our long walk back to Kalimpong that he had undertaken initiation with a female *jhankrini* four years earlier. Samuel's apparent trepidation as we had approached the *jhankri* on that first introduction had merely been to test my nerve. If I had been put off by mountain myth and dead men's bones, he had admitted with a laugh, then I would never have been able to accept the teachings that were to come.

And yet when I had pressed him to confess some conspiracy to trick me into tramping across the hills to an allegedly unfamiliar scarlet temple, he had insisted that he had never visited the place before. He vowed that, until that day, Kushal Magar had been unknown to him – which I wholeheartedly accepted to be true.

However, Samuel's sudden talk of deities now perplexed me.

'I thought the Tradition didn't teach the concept of external gods.'

'Yes,' he confirmed with short-winded concision.

'Well then, accepting that there is no divine Father Christmas either bestowing blessings or punishments from beyond the clouds, who exactly are we waking up?'

Samuel paused to catch his breath. The air was cooler and much wetter here. The sweetness of damp leaf and moss permeated our nostrils. The savour of moist humus and bark suffused our tongues.

'*Dajoo*, we don't sound the bell to rouse a holy something up there in the temple, but to awaken our true selves,' he began. 'A reminder to enter this place without our habitual presumptions, expectations or desires.'

I smiled. Samuel sounded like the *jhankri*.

'Of course, no temple is any more sacred than our houses or cowsheds,' he continued. 'It's just that these are places dedicated to reflection, meditation and teaching. So in preparation we remind, or "awaken", ourselves to put aside the ordinary limits of our self-interest.'

'You never cease to amaze me,' I admitted with a beam of fraternal pride.

'It's just my culture.' He shrugged. 'And I'm honoured you wish to share it.'

Samuel held firmly to my arm as we resumed our arduous route towards another archway from which hung the flared rim and pendulous clapper of a larger bell.

'This is where we remove our shoes,' he instructed, indicating that we should sit on a wooden bench to expose our socks. One of mine also exposed a single toe.

We touched our hearts, sounded the second bell and stepped into the temple courtyard. A natural granite floor, scuffed smooth by centuries of unshod soles, led to a craggy rock-face pierced by decorated hollows, crevices and caves. We stood and listened for any hint of life beyond the misty trees, but all was silent. No squirrels, birds or monkeys. No pilgrims, *sadhus* or . . .

Samuel and I started as a scant shadow seemed to material-ise out of the looming darkness of the cliff beside us. It pressed forwards into corporeal solidity with every soundless step – until I could brave a tentative, '*Jhankri-dajoo*, is that you?'

Kushal Magar appeared from the fog and bowed in *pranam*. Samuel and I in turn bent to touch his feet as he touched our heads in *ahashis* blessing, like a father to his sons.

'Welcome,' he offered in warm and smiling greeting. 'I have been expecting you.'

XXXVI

Yoga functions through knowledge.
Through yoga, self-liberation is effected.
Linga Purana

The cave was warm.

A low fire licked its tower of twigs on a floor of flattened earth, illuminating a rocky, sooty ceiling that pressed so low I could not stand.

Kushal Magar pointed to a tatty roll of matting and indicated that I was to sit in front of the narrow niche in which a *linga* stood, a single upright stone marked with crimson *sidur* and scattered flowers. I shuffled to make room for Samuel to join me, but he shook his head.

'No, *dajoo*, I'm back off to the village,' he announced. 'You'll be ravenous in no time, so I'll return with the best hot *daal-bhat* our good *jhankri*'s daughter and I can prepare!'

I was surprised to be left alone so soon, but before I could say a word in protest Samuel had raised his eyebrows, grinned his broadest and disappeared back into the honeyed mountain mist.

I wrapped a shawl around my shoulders and looked at my companion in anticipation. In my excitement to be sitting with the *jhankri* after so many months, I instinctively touched my heart and for a second time leant forwards to touch his feet.

'I do not require such reverence,' he said, again placing his hands on my head. 'I am not your master, but your *dajoo*, your elder brother.'

I smiled and instinctively bowed again. I liked this gentle man. He deserved my deference.

My mouth was full of questions, none of which now seemed more than trivial inquisitiveness. I kept them to myself as his gaze looked far beyond my eyes and countenance. With sympathetic non-judgement, Kushal Magar was scrutinising me.

'I've spent this past year reading up on your history,' I announced. 'And I've done as you told me by trying my best to apply the Aims of Life.'

'So, you have fulfilled your promise and have returned safely across the Seven Rivers,' he observed, ignoring my keenness to earn his esteem.

This prompted me to acknowledge that in craving his approval I was only diminishing myself. Instead, I simply nodded in silent and respectful affirmation.

'Then today I introduce you to our yoga,' he revealed, 'that you might live and love more effectively, productively, justly and joyfully. So here begins the mastery of your body–mind.'

XXXVII

Yoga is not [attained] through the lotus posture and not by gazing at the tip of the nose. Yoga, say the great yogins, is the identity of the individual self with the Supreme Self.
Kularnava Tantra

I skimmed my eyes around the shallow, smoky hollow in which we sat.

'*Jhankri-dajoo*, how exactly do we do yoga in such a little space?'

'*Do* yoga?' he asked. 'You think you are here to stand on your head? Brother, we do not begin with postures – otherwise what would we do but energise distortion and invigorate imbalance? Instead, the Tradition offers us Eleven Vows before even a single *asana*, or yogic posture, is taught, that we might begin to learn to resolve the conflicts between our conscience, thoughts, words and actions.'

I felt embarrassed to admit that I had never considered yoga to be much more than an exercise routine best suited to easing backaches and lengthening hamstrings. His talk of vows and conflicts was very far removed from any of my expectations.

'The first six of these vows are called *yamas*,' he stated. 'The Restraints in Personal Conduct.'

Kushal Magar paused again. He had seen my eyes tighten at the mention of restraints, a term that had evoked too many memories of enthusiastic wielding of cane and brogue as schoolmasters had resorted to brutality in their efforts to curb the natural, impulsive behaviour of my boisterous, hormone-maddened peers. The *jhankri's* use of the word seemed unsuited to what I had understood to be a remarkably non-prescriptive path.

'Be assured, brother, the *yamas* do not require that we hold ourselves back or suppress our feelings,' he insisted, seeming to read the flutter of my thoughts. '*Yama* is a word for a charioteer, whose mastery enables him to drive a team of otherwise wild horses at full force and with single focus towards his chosen objective.'

The one horse I had ever been closely acquainted with had been a dozy mare in the field beyond my grandmother's rows of runner-beans. She had only been saved from the knackers' yard by a peculiar compulsion to tap her front hooves in a rhythm reminiscent of the opening lines of

'Camptown Races'. I had once climbed on to her bare back in an effort to perfect the circus trick I had been practising on the ironing-board. Although hardly 'wild' in temperament, Doodah, as we called her, had found no pleasure in my clumsy efforts on her spine and had simply slipped me off her neck, face first into the hawthorn hedge. Driving her with 'full force' or 'single focus', even towards a proffered apple, would have been an impossibility. Perhaps, then, it was time for me to admit that much of my own mind was quite as obstinate and unyielding.

'Perhaps think of a *yama* as a valuable skill,' Kushal Magar continued. 'A means by which to learn self-mastery and forbearance. To concentrate the mind and focus the will. To live more fully and effectively. With purpose.'

It was this very possibility that had brought me back so soon to this simple, smiling man and his compelling teaching.

'If we lengthen the first "a" – *yaama* – we have the word for a path, or progress,' he added. 'For each *yama* is applied to your relationship with the world, guiding you to develop respect for yourself and all those with whom you come in contact. Remember, the fulfilment of your own Dharma must never impose on others, nor prevent the most vulnerable members of society from thriving fully.'

I found these lexicographical additions hugely helpful – yet still felt a growing trepidation, which sent me rummaging in my backpack for a pen and notepad.

'But no need to worry about the detail,' he advised. 'Just know that the combined purpose of all our vows is to encourage us to recognise our outdated, detrimental habits and then release them. So are you ready?'

I nodded impatiently.

'Then let us begin.'

XXXVIII

There are but two 'sins':
doing harm to yourself, and doing harm to others.
Bindra

'So to the first of the *yamas*, our Restraints in Personal Conduct,' Kushal Magar announced. '*Ahimsa* – the wisdom gained in learning to avoid causing harm to ourselves or others, by either thought, or word or action.'

I scribbled down an approximation of his words, wincing at the thought of just how far from this one preliminary concept alone I stood, even though he had already touched on it a year ago with his introduction to Dharma.

'Even personal gain at the detriment of another, by whatever means – including at the price of your own self-respect and integrity – is considered a form of violence.'

'But you've just described my world!' I muttered miserably. 'I don't think you can imagine the ways that the pursuit of our own self-interest to the detriment of ourselves, each other and even the planet, has become so ordinary that it could be said to be acceptable.'

'The very reason that *Ahimsa* is the foundation for all that follows,' he asserted. 'For any society is only the collective expression of the individuals who comprise it. A society that is mistrustful and destructive, for example, is only the communal expression of personal conflict. We must therefore take responsibility for our own thoughts, our words and actions, since they contribute to either the accord or discord of our community. It is this that both the Purushartha – our Aims of Life – and this first *yama* teach us.'

Although this fact now seemed obvious, I had never before acknowledged the true impact of personal responsibility for the greater good. I had never considered that the social ills over which I often fretted and complained could be the magnification of individual inner conflict. Expressed in this way, before we sought to attribute blame beyond ourselves, we needed first to confront the prejudice and cowardice, conceit and apathy, anger and avarice through which we personally responded to the world.

Perhaps for the first time in my life, I was pondering how my behaviour, both towards myself and all those with whom I interacted, contributed to the self-destructive state of the society in which I had assumed I played a wholly insignificant part.

'To help along your way, consider that *Ahimsa* has three secondary *yamas*,' Kushal Magar continued. 'First, *Akrodha*, the wisdom found in freedom from anger. Second, *Kshamaa*, the wisdom of forgiveness, both of others and ourselves, to encourage us to move beyond merely identifying ourselves through the past and our emotional reaction to its memory. And third, *Dayaa*, the wisdom found in mercy and compassion – again, as much for ourselves as for others.'

I jotted each word on to my notepad.

'And all these, that we might learn no longer to demean and discourage ourselves. No longer to judge our worth by our appearance, our possessions or our social status. No longer to diminish our body–minds by the food we eat, the books we read, the words we use, the company we keep.'

I listened hard and tried to learn.

'However, *Ahimsa* does not imply a passive state. It is the mindful consideration of all living beings, to whose well-being we actively dedicate our energies and means.'

'But meat is eaten in these hills,' I challenged, having seen for myself the daily slaughter undertaken to supply the wealthy Buddhist monasteries with their insatiable demand for flesh – a wholly hypocritical taste, it seemed to me, for to avoid their notion of 'karmic debts' they simply hired non-monastic neighbours to commit the killing. 'So how does that fit with the concept of *Ahimsa*?'

'The Brahminical philosophy of vegetarianism in India was inspired by the asceticism of the Jain religion,' Kushal Magar explained. 'In our hills, only worshippers of Vishnu profess to adhere to such strictures, whilst we *shaiva tantrikas* have never considered ourselves under the command of such priestly prohibitions. Even so, if keepers of the Tradition do choose to eat meat, it will normally only be once a year, during the autumn festival of Dashain, straight after monsoon, when Durga's mythical defeat of the buffalo-demon is celebrated – a reminder for us all always to overcome our self-defeating thoughts and behaviour with ever deeper self-knowledge. But even then only a male animal whose life has been ritually and respectfully taken is eaten – and never a monkey, bull or carnivorous beast.'

'So *Ahimsa* does not require vegetarianism?' I pressed for clarification, even though I had not eaten meat since the day I had first made the alarming connection between the chicken casserole on my plate and the much petted broody hens that pecked my grandmother's kitchen scraps and nested in her outside loo.

'Only according to your nature,' Kushal Magar replied. 'If you are inclined to consume meat, then acknowledge that the taking of any life is a sacred act, and only eat an animal in whose killing you have taken a respectful part.'

'As unlikely as that will ever be, I still don't see how I can possibly go through life without causing harm,' I protested.

'I mean, can I really tiptoe through the world to avoid stepping on an ant or swatting a mosquito?'

'But *Ahimsa* is not a simplistic concept of non-killing,' he insisted. 'Ours is not the pacifism of the Jain *shravak* or the Theravada Buddhist. Dissolution is essential to the balance of existence, whether in plucking fruit, scything grain, or taking milk from a cow. Instead, think of the principle of *Ahimsa* as a way to learn that, whilst the path of wisdom will never be found in the wanton destruction of any form of life, we may develop a true understanding of the value of all life only by eradicating every feeling of hostility in ourselves.'

'And all this is just *yama* number one?' I winced.

'You think it already enough?' he asked with a smile. 'Well, in many ways it is, for as you learn to apply the principle of *Ahmisa* first to yourself, to your significant relationships, then to the wider world, you will undoubtedly discover that the experiences you call your life will be transformed.'

XXXIX

What is the value of eyes in which there is no kindness?
Thirukkural

'Our second *yama* is *Alobha*, the wisdom gained by learning to live without selfish ambition.'

Kushal Magar paused to let me consider the implications of such a notion as I penned this new word and its meaning on my pad.

'But does that mean no aspiration to better yourself?' I

asked, troubled by the potential passivity that this *yama* might suggest, for since childhood I had worked enthusiastically at self-improvement. There had been the practising of scales and sight-reading to assure good marks in my music exams; the learning of languages in preparation for the foreign climes my young heart had been set upon; and then the fitness regime over which I had perspired throughout my teens in the narrow space between bed and chest of drawers, in the vain hope of growing up to look like the Hellenic heroes I most esteemed.

'*Alobha* is the absence of *selfish* ambition,' Kushal Magar reiterated. 'And this, to free us from the inner violence of greed, pride and jealousy.'

The notion of 'inner violence' was revolutionary to me.

'However, aspiration in every aspect of life is essential,' he impressed, 'for the very vitality of our interactions with the world is determined by our willingness to adapt, grow and change. It is rather the purpose of our objectives that *Alobha* asks us to examine.'

'But I've been raised in a world driven by greedy, egocentric ambition,' I complained. 'Even at the expense of personal integrity or social harmony!'

'And yet it is you, not your culture, who is master of your life,' he insisted. 'It is you who mindfully applies the intention, the *bhavana*, to your exchanges with the world. It is *your* knowing of *your* purpose that determines both the outcome of your actions and thereby the quality of your daily life.'

I knew his words were true. I also knew that there was much I had yet to address in the innumerable unthinking choices by which I clumsily lived.

'So learn to apply the wisdom gained through the exploration of *Alobha*,' he concluded, 'and you will discover for yourself that it is not in taking from others, but by giving of ourselves without thought of personal profit that we truly gain the most.'

XL

Whatever is done with truth bears fruit.
Mountain saying

'Our third *yama* is *Asteya*,' Kushal Magar stated, 'the wisdom gained by learning not to steal – neither by body, nor intellect nor word.'

I immediately recalled a boy who had been relentlessly unkind to me at school. The son of the local policeman, he had behaved towards his fellow pupils as though his father's profession had afforded him impunity. It had been his repeated determination to make me spill my mid-morning mini bottle of milk over my new blue blazer that had finally sharpened my resolve. When the lunchtime bell had rung and backs had turned, I had slipped my hand beneath his desk-lid to remove a little red box in which his father had once received a presentation watch. Back in my bedroom at the end of the day, I had hidden the plunder in my 'Secrets' drawer. And there it had remained, among treasured mouse bones, a goat's tooth and desiccated baby bats, for I had never been able to put the cardboard carton to even the most frivolous of uses. The thought of the little red box, and the dishonest act by which I had acquired it, had always left me so queasy that I had never been tempted to pilfer anything again.

As to how I might have stolen by either 'intellect or word', however, I was less certain.

'This *yama* does not merely guide us to avoid taking that which is not freely given,' Kushal Magar continued, 'but that there is wisdom in extinguishing the very desire to possess something that belongs to another. Nor does this simply apply to another's material wealth, but their social rank, talents, employment, reputation and appearance. The heart of this *yama*, therefore, is to accept that so long as we are able to maintain our physical, emotional and mental health, and those for whom we are responsible, we already have enough.'

I grimaced. For one who had been raised in a world driven by feverish consumption and acquisition, even when it was so evidently to our own injury, this was undeniably a great challenge to comprehend, let alone live. I had always envied others their popularity and friends, their prowess on the sports field and in the swimming pool, their natural confidence and wit. I had victimised myself with the greatest of deceptions that if I had just had that, or had looked liked this, then my life would have been better, more satisfactory and fulfilling.

'There are, of course, additional *yamas* to assist us to this end,' the *jhankri* said, as he observed my struggle. 'Consider *Satya*, truth without distortion – honesty, sincerity, the fulfilling of your word. And *Arjava*, the renunciation of deception – straightforwardness, impartiality, living your life in accordance with your conscience.'

'Honourable in theory,' I agreed. 'But aren't there times in life when truth without distortion and straightforwardness could cause all sorts of trouble? Couldn't such total honesty prove damaging to relationships?'

'Not when in accordance with *Ahimsa*, thinking, saying

and doing nothing to the detriment of ourselves or others,' he replied. 'For as we teach our children here, say what is true and pleasant, but not what is unpleasantly true.'

I smiled. In the simplicity of a single sentence he had dissipated my concerns.

'So do you see? *Asteya* inspires us to master greed, that we might free ourselves from self-defeating selfish desire in all its forms,' he summarised. 'The Tradition therefore attaches one more additional *yama* to *Asteya*: the principle of *Aharalaghava* – the wisdom of moderation in eating, applied both to those who overindulge and those who subject themselves to levels of self-denial that cause them harm.'

I widened my eyes at the thought of my native culture of extremes that I still did not believe he could even begin to imagine.

XLI

Sin is not a mere action, but it is an attitude of life which takes for granted . . . that we are not all essentially one but exist each for his own separate individual existence.
Rabindranath Tagore

'Our fourth *yama* is *Brahmacharya* – literally, knowing the absolute. The wisdom learnt in seeking to live according to your true nature.'

I had met the term before, but was puzzled by his definition.

'Don't the orthodox usually interpret *Brahmacharya* as celibacy?' I asked.

'A common misunderstanding,' he replied. 'And this because *Brahmacharya* was used as a term for students under the age of twenty-five, who were unmarried and lived with their teacher. Perhaps today it is forgotten that their learning traditionally included the *kamashastra*, the erotic sciences, which were considered imperative to their education, with sexual experimentation, even ritual intimacy, employed by such students as an essential source of wisdom and self-knowledge.'

This astonished me, when the narrow, conservative interpretation of the term was now so widely propagated that it had become blindly accepted as fact.

'The word for sexual chastity is actually *Upasthanigraha* – literally "restraint of one's genitals" – although even this does not mean celibacy,' he continued. 'Rather, it refers to sexual mastery, when a man is no longer at the mercy of his desires – as expressed in Shiva's unfailing *linga*. After all, our myths are keen to emphasise that he certainly does not symbolise an abstention from intimacy.'

I looked to the ithyphallic image in its niche with renewed fascination.

'But for keepers of the Tradition, *Brahmacharya* is a primary step towards resolving the deep conflict we suffer as a result of the disparity between our true nature and the familial, social, religious expectations, the mindless habits and beliefs, to which we ordinarily conform. You see, *Brahmacharya* is yet another level of *Ahimisa*. And to assist, we have the additional *yamas* of *Dhriti*, stability and resolve; and *Java*, alertness, meaning living and loving with mindful awareness.'

I looked back at him so blankly at his talk of my 'true nature' that he smiled and turned to rummage in the tatty cloth bag that bulged beside him. He withdrew a pale, oval acorn, which he held up towards the firelight before passing it to me.

'Have you ever wondered how such a small object could contain the entire history of our mighty Himalayan oaks?' he asked. 'All the millennia of knowledge, the wisdom required for its species to survive? And had you never seen a mountain oak, would you believe that such a towering tree was contained within that tiny kernel lying on your palm?'

I stared at the smooth shell and shook my head.

'And what is an acorn anyway? Not a separate object in its own right, but an expression of innumerable generations of oaks, which have soared from the soil and then returned to the earth from whence they came. That acorn in your hand is simply one aspect of a perpetual process.'

This at least was a familiar concept I could comprehend.

'So, now look at yourself. What do you see?'

'Just a chilly me?' I suggested sheepishly, staring my shawl-draped knees.

'And yet you are not in fact a separate "me" at all,' he replied. 'You are an expression of the same union of consciousness and energy that constitutes the entire universe. For you – like all that was and is and will ever be – appear and then return back into the underlying, energetic matrix from whence you came. Do you see? Each season, star, mountain, tree, animal, human and beam of light is like that acorn. All but one essential event in a perpetual, universal process.'

I looked back to my hand, not to reconsider the acorn, but my own pink palm upon which it lay.

'And understanding this is *Brahmacharya*?' I asked.

He tipped his head. 'So that in time you might begin to see all life as an expression of yourself' – he smiled – 'and yourself as an expression of all life.'

XLII

Whatever we treasure for ourselves separates us from others; our possessions are our limitations.
Rabindranath Tagore

'Our fifth *yama* is *Tyaga*, the wisdom gained by learning to release attachment to material possessions. Its purpose, to encourage us to accept the stewardship of all that life affords with integrity, modesty and gratitude.'

'But the world I come from is wholly founded on the attachment to material possessions!' I complained. 'In fact, we've given everything – even time – a monetary price. And in the process, seem to have abandoned all sense of the true value of anything!'

'This is happening here also, even in our hills,' he said. 'Look at the aerials appearing on every other house and hut. And then the giant pictures raised above our heads to tell us we need new phones and cars to make us truly happy, shampoos and perfumes to ensure that we are truly loved.'

'Then where's the balance? Obsessive accumulation as in the West – which is clearly spreading here – or *Tyaga*'s abandonment of material possessions?'

'But brother, *Tyaga* does not propose a state of poverty,' he insisted. 'That would be unrealistic, irresponsible and miserable for most of us. We would be left unable to realise the second Aim of Life: *Artha*, the fulfilment of social responsibility. *Tyaga* rather encourages us not to identify ourselves by or seek happiness in the things we own. Instead, it guides us to recognise that the desire to possess is a tireless cycle that can never be fulfilled. And then to value only that which is necessary to live healthily and freely.'

This was an idea that I had seen exemplified by the indigenous Lepcha people of the eastern Himalaya, in whose Rongring language all possessions, property and people are only ever 'ours', and never 'mine'.

'*Tyaga* might even be explored through a period of wandering in our lives, abandoning all we own to take to the dusty roads of the Plains and the forest footpaths of these hills, never resting in one place for more than three days. And this to understand better the truth, the wisdom and the peace that lie within, which identifying ourselves through material goods and social status so often veils.'

I nodded, for in my youth I had spent months 'roughing it' on several occasions. I had wandered across Africa for a season with little more than a tent and a toothbrush. I had rambled through Scandinavian forests to swim in lakes as the setting summer sun merely skimmed the surface before rising to another dawn. I had, of course, roamed alone across India from the distant western seaboard, through village and temple, palace and slum, before first finding my way to these eastern jungle-clad hills. All had been equally difficult and invigorating times in my life, each one revealing to me a state of freedom and challenge to which, in subsequent years, I had often desired to return.

'No doubt you have met *sadhus* on your journeys,' he added, 'men and women who have chosen to renounce material comfort for a month, a year, or even longer, and have taken to the road as a period of self-discovery. A re-evaluation of all values.'

This reminded me of a young, naked computer programmer from Bangalore I had once encountered on the Plains. We had spent two days talking and sleeping together beneath a peepal tree as he had told me of the busy business life and impending marriage he had chosen to postpone, abandoning all the social and material trappings by which he had judged his own worth, in order to reconsider the principles by which he lived.

Following his example, I too had begun to assess my own largely unconsidered purpose, for that young *sadhu* beneath his tree had opened my eyes further to the fragile brevity of life, which demanded an inner freedom for which I yearned, but knew I had not yet truly known.

'However, remember that *Tyaga*'s releasing of attachment to worldly possessions demands no extremes,' Kushal Magar insisted. 'For every *yama* is moderated by the principle of *Ahimsa* – thinking, saying and doing nothing to the detriment of yourself or others.'

I nodded in appreciation of his simple words and his practical teachings.

And yet, the way of being he described still seemed so far removed from the person I was or believed I could ever be, that at that moment the very notion seemed as inaccessible to me as any hermetic mystery.

XLIII

The greatest gift you can give another is the purity of your attention.
Rabindranath Tagore

'So to our sixth and final *yama*,' Kushal Magar stated. '*Shaucha*, the wisdom gained by learning to maintain internal and external cleanliness.'

At every town and city where I had stopped in my journeys across north India, I had been astounded by the general air of decay. Roads had been piled with rubble and rotting refuse, gutters with litter and sewage. Public buildings had been left to moulder, facades to fall, their staircases sprayed with urine and betel-reddened sputum. In all my travels around the world, I had never seen a country like it. To speak of *Shaucha* in such a land as this initially seemed laughable.

Once again, Kushal Magar seemed to predict the pattern of my thoughts, a talent of discernment to which I was now becoming accustomed.

'Perhaps you would judge cleanliness by appearance?' he challenged. 'On a lick of paint or a well-washed shirt? And yet whilst part of our Dharma duty to ourselves is certainly to tend to our physical well-being, this is not true *Shaucha*. Instead, our last *yama* guides us towards the wisdom inherent in purity of thought, speech, action and intention – which brings us back to *bhavana*.'

I nodded. And felt shallow.

'For whatever another's nature or appearance, isn't the way in which we approach the world the only quality that truly matters? Whether we are able to know ourselves and thereby fully engage with kin, friends and strangers alike, devoid of prejudice, enmity or resistance?'

'I like the theory,' I admitted. 'But how do I start?'

'You have already begun with the Purushartha and *Ahimsa*. However, *Shaucha* also guides us to add to them by caring for the mind through the study and contemplation of beneficial subjects.'

'Such as?'

'That which is enriching and uplifting. That which enables you to know yourself better and thereby refine your intention, that you might apply the principle of Ahmisa more fully to yourself and others. For the benefits of this last *yama* are many, including a heightening clarity of thought, mastery of the senses and a cheerful disposition.'

Then just like Kushal Magar, I thought.

'And all this, that we might be moved to do our part in restoring balance in ourselves and the world, through purposeful, selfless action,' he concluded. 'For in this, brother, lies both wisdom and freedom.'

PART FIVE

XLIV

For the benefit of those weakened by lack of purpose, fatigued by
self-made conflict, the Tradition is given.
Mountain saying

The buoyant whistling of a jaunty tune heralded Samuel's return. He was carrying newspaper-wrapped canisters in his arms, fresh faggots for the fire tied across his back.

'Wood's a bit damp, but it'll do,' he announced cheerily. 'Might make your eyes smart – but then who needs to see their food to eat, or their teacher's face to learn?'

He laid down his load, then sat close to share my shawl and warm himself.

'So, finished all your *yamas*?' he asked, poking my ribs.

'How do you know what I've been learning?' I responded with surprise.

He said nothing, but reached out to unwrap parcels and prise off lids, scenting our smoky grotto with the steam of *chana daal*, cumin rice, *aloo dum* and a steaming curry of gingered egg. Another package revealed three small *tapari* leaf-plates, whilst tight twists of paper provided portions of pink salt and dry *mulako achar* radish pickle.

'It's a feast!' I declared.

'And I'm famished!' added Samuel.

We three shuffled forwards to serve each other, until our plates of stitched *saal* leaves were flattened with the weight of food.

'Did you know that in these hills we consider every mindful mouthful to be a *puja*?' asked Kushal Magar as we plunged the fingers of our right hands into the spread. 'For every act of self-sustenance can be a meditative undertaking.'

I reflected on his words in hungry silence as I bound fluffy rice with runny *daal* between fingertips to form a manageable ball, and considered the potential extent of 'self-sustenance' beyond simple nutrition.

'You see, the Tradition talks of different ways by which to comprehend our true limitless natures,' he continued between mouthfuls. 'One of these is consciously to settle awareness on moments of intense pleasure – such as the savouring of good food, a reunion after extended separation, the touch of water on the skin.'

'Or, traditionally, the memory of licking a beloved!' added Samuel, protruding the pale tip of his tongue and wiggling it at me in threat, until I prodded him away with an elbow.

I offered the last of the *chana daal* to Kushal Magar, which he declined.

'So *dajoo*,' Samuel said, scooping up red *aloo dum* and white *achar* pickle, 'are you counting?'

'Counting what?'

'Your mouthfuls!' he replied. 'Didn't you learn about moderation in eating this morning, as part of the *yama* of non-stealing?'

I raised another generous scoop of rice and *daal* and shook my head quizzically.

'Well, traditionally we say moderation is thirty-two

mouthfuls per meal for a householder, sixteen for a forest recluse and only eight for an ecstatic – and if you ask me, jolly hungry – sage!'

'So are you counting yours, *bhai*?' I challenged, as he served himself yet more *aloo dum* potato.

'But of course!' he retorted with a spicy grin, sweeping fingers around his leaf-plate to gather more rice. 'It's just a good job that nobody says how big those thirty-two mouthfuls ought to be!'

XLV

My body, once restless as the waves, he in calmness fixed.
Thirumandiram

Pots had been gathered. Hands and mouths washed and wiped.

Samuel bowed in respect to the *jhankri* as he left our sooty huddle, then offered me a leave-taking grin.

'Good luck with part two, *dajoo*!' he called through the deepening mist, as he commenced his muddy descent along the forest path a second time. 'But watch out for *Tapa*! It might give you blisters!' he concluded enigmatically.

'So to our five Observances of Personal Conduct,' Kushal Magar announced, indicating that I should settle comfortably and restore my focus. 'The *niyamas*, a word that means "precept" or "determination". But lengthen the first "a" – *niyaama* – and you have a boatman, able to maintain his chosen course even against the fiercest mountain rivers in full spate.'

I nodded, even as I resisted a creeping, post-prandial compulsion to nap beside the fire.

'In combination, they are a personal code applied to your relationship with yourself, guiding you to reduce the conflict between your internal perspective – your thoughts and conscience – and your external action. In this way, over time and with mindful effort on your part, the body–mind is rendered increasingly calm and trouble-free.'

This, I could not imagine. In addition to the daylight struggles with myself – the anxious obsessions, at times crippling self-doubt and a tendency to near asphyxiating depression – I had not known a peaceful night in years. Since childhood my sleep had been so regularly tormented by unhappy dreams that my restless sleepwalking about the house had become a natural part of my long-suffering family's domestic round. In deep, dark slumber I had sought lost loved ones in the garden; scrawled visionary poetry on tabletops; piled furniture into towers; and laid out cutlery, pins and buttons in complex labyrinths, without the need for light to guide my way.

My parents had done their best. They had endeavoured to douse my young cheeks with water to interrupt my troubled sleep, but I had cowered at all attempts to touch me. They had sat me on the loo and read aloud *Black Beauty*, but in my somnambulist sobbing I had repeatedly fallen in the bowl. I had been poked by doctors and grilled by therapists, had had my soul blessed by a bishop and my skin pierced by an acupuncturist. Yet nothing had delivered me from the impenetrable and distressed sleep I had so long endured.

'Then are you ready for our *niyamas*?' Kushal Magar asked.

I nodded eagerly and raised my pen and notepad – for I trusted that if anyone were able to guide me towards the lasting changes in myself that would prove imperative if in the coming years I was to survive my own internal chaos, it would be this smiling man.

XLVI

If you wish to avoid thorns, don't cover the earth with leather – put on sandals.
Mountain saying

'Our first *niyama* is *Santosha*,' Kushal Magar began. 'The wisdom learnt in choosing to be content with the necessities of a healthy, fulfilling life.'

'All right,' I responded, 'but how do I determine what my necessities might be?'

'Well, what more do you really need than sufficient food and physical security; mental stimulation and purposeful, rewarding work; human intimacy and meaningful friendships?'

He was right, of course. The necessities of life were not the alternating annual holidays of sunny Med or snowy Alps. They were not the New Season's colours and cuts, the relentless tedium of celebrity, or the altering of perfectly healthy bodies by diet, syringe or knife to emulate someone else's fickle notions of beauty. Nor were they the fortunes and time spent on securing some promised, otherwise inaccessible 'spiritual enlightenment'.

'In practice, *Santosha* could simply be to reduce your needs,' he suggested. 'Therefore, attached to *Santosha* is the *niyama* of *Hri* – modesty in all things.'

135

'But,' I interjected, even as I wondered whether my persistent challenges were a source of quiet irritation to him, 'doesn't the contentment encouraged by *Santosha* suggest an impotent, passive condition? A submissive attitude to life, in which hardships, poverty or perhaps even abuse are meekly, hopelessly tolerated?'

'What you describe is complacency and compliance, not the active, mindful contentment of the Tradition,' he asserted. '*Santosha* does not suggest that nothing requires change or challenge. Do not forget, the moderating heart of each of our vows is *Ahimsa*, in which nothing is thought, said or done that is of detriment to the well-being of yourself or others. Perhaps, then, think of *Santosha* as contentment with the necessities of life that you have attained through your own sufficient and suitable efforts.'

I nodded, knowing that I had barely begun truly to understand the premise of these Eleven Vows.

'And yet wherever it may be applied, *Santosha* teaches us to embrace the pleasure of the moment, whilst mastering desire,' he concluded. 'For a primary principle of the Tradition is that it is not pleasure but selfish desire that limits the boundaries of man's consciousness.'

Again I nodded – but now with new determination to acknowledge the innumerable yet too often unnoticed delights my daily life afforded. And this, that I might one day know the wholly unfamiliar contentment, the ease of heart and mind, and the lasting self-acceptance, this first *niyama* alone seemed to promise.

XLVII

Learn to receive in order to give.
This is the order of Nature, the balance in the universe.
This is Wisdom.

Bindra

'The second *niyama* of our Tradition is *Dana* – the wisdom gained by learning to give of oneself without thought of reward.'

He slowed to allow me to catch up with my note-taking.

'However, *Dana* is not merely the handing out of alms or charitable acts, but a liberality of spirit in every interaction. A warmth and openness of heart to all life, without condition.'

'Where I come from, people have a strong inclination to donate time, money and cast-offs to good causes,' I assured him. 'But in ordinary dealings I sometimes think we have been led so to mistrust our fellow man that we have forgotten the rewards of being open-hearted.'

'Which is a reason why here, with our preference for the practical, we remind ourselves of this *niyama* in our daily domestic rites, our *puja*,' he explained. 'For *Dana* is represented by one of the eight flowers we place at the feet of whatever symbol we have chosen to represent our true, limitless nature.'

I looked at the fresh petals clustered at the base of the flame-lit *linga* that nestled in the niche before us. I had never considered they might embody far more than a simple, customary symbolic 'offering'.

'You see, these flowers represent the eight qualities we are encouraged to strive for in our lives,' he continued, following my gaze. 'Tolerance, self-discipline and patience.

Knowledge, dedication and contemplation. Honesty and generosity of spirit – *Dana*. In fact, these qualities are of such importance to both individual and, thereby, social well-being that we represent them in the eight lotus petals of Kali, in the eight arms of Durga, and by the eight teeth of Kubera, our Himalayan symbol of life's unfailing abundance.'

I sat in silence, my eyes fixed on the delicate blooms scattered about the *linga* in an effort to retain his every word.

'To assist in the exploration of *Dana*, we have an additional *niyama*,' he added. '*Huta*, self-sacrifice – but only ever in keeping with *Ahimsa*. Their combined benefits in the path to freedom from all our mindlessly adopted limitations are immeasurable.'

Kushal Magar paused to feed the fire, as I considered the potential benefits of giving without thought of reward and of self-sacrifice without harm to myself. I reflected on those times when I had shown a false generosity, begrudgingly and with ulterior motives, and remembered too well how I had resentfully complained that life was friendless, mean, affording me nothing. In contrast, when I had deigned to approach the world with a liberality of character, unprompted altruism and benevolence of spirit, I had found life unfailingly abundant.

'For of course, brother,' he offered in conclusion, as I leant in to help him with his kindling, 'none of us really sees the world as it is, but only ever as *we* are.'

XLVIII

Freedom from ignorance is the goal.
Vidyeshvara Samhita

'Our third *niyama* is *Tapa* – a word that literally means to "glow", or to be "consumed by heat", for it signifies the wisdom learnt through demanding dedicated practice.'

I wrote the word with ease, yet could not imagine what he meant. A fiery *sadhana*? The source, perhaps, of Samuel's parting joke about blisters?

'Think of *Tapa* as any mindful practice that assists us to develop self-discipline and willpower, or physical, emotional and mental endurance – qualities without which life cannot be fully and fearlessly lived.'

He waited until I had finished taking notes before continuing with careful emphasis.

'There are some, of course, who take this notion of endurance to debilitating extremes, with little purpose beyond competitive self-interest. Or to earn some imagined celebrity – even "sainthood" – among the gullible.'

I knew exactly what he meant, for I had once had a disquieting encounter with a *sadhu* on my journey across the Plains. He had been sitting beneath a palm umbrella on a river *ghat* at Varanasi, his right arm raised and withered to near fossilisation, a feat of such alarming self-abuse that it assured attention and even monetary veneration from the passing hordes.

Nor were such traits to be found in India alone, for a plethora of Christian saints had similarly earned their hagiographies through well-publicised 'salvific' masochism.

I recalled from school divinity the fervid flagellations of Francis, Catherine and Thomas More; Ignatius with his iron chains and knee-ties, accoutrements I had always envisaged as a pair of unyielding Boy Scout garters; and Sister Mary Lucy of Jesus, who had blithely given away her packed lunches and flogged herself with stinging nettles.

'In the Tradition, of course, *Tapa* is only ever undertaken in accordance with *Ahimsa*,' Kushal Magar emphasised. '*Tapa* is therefore never a punishment, nor cruel. Never disrespectful of the body–mind. Never to our own or others' detriment. The self-inflicted torture or neglect found among orthodox and exhibitionist fanatics alike are not *Tapa*, for they produce little more than disordered psychological imaginings.'

'Then if not standing on one leg or lying on a bed of nails for years, what exactly is it?'

'True *Tapa* is any restraining practice by which we may learn to remain steadfast, in balance, unaffected by external circumstance. A demanding yogic posture, for example, may be maintained whilst the body–mind is focused on the antithesis of what the practitioner wishes to overcome. Heat to defeat cold, joy to defeat sadness, pleasure to defeat pain. Compassion and forgiveness to defeat the desire for revenge. In this way, *Tapa* may be applied to help us overcome a self-defeating habit.'

He peered into my eyes to ensure I was still following.

'*Tapa* can also be the withholding of our ordinary impulses through intense, single-minded concentration – in darkness or silence, or by the simple repetition of monotonous sounds – as a means to afford ourselves a tranquillity of heart and mind. And this that we might steadily learn to remain unaltered by gain or loss, praise or insult, victory or defeat.'

I thought of the drumming and chanting that had played a central a role in my own initiation, the impact of which I still could not properly explain.

'*Tapa* can also be selfless action,' he continued. 'Even hospitality is regarded here as one of its expressions.'

I wondered whether this last might, in part, explain the extraordinary generosity I had been privileged to know among these mountain people. The helpful hands to ease and guide my passage through their jungled hills. The proffered cups of tea and feasts of food from people who were in far greater need than me. The smiles that cheered my heart and brightened every day of my course across the subcontinent's vast breadth.

'And yet whatever form they take – whether over-loading or withholding impulse, or simply acting selflessly for the benefit of others – all *Tapa* focus our will and energy to free ourselves from the limitations of detrimental self-interest,' he concluded. 'And this – as with all teachings and practices of the Tradition – that we might learn how to live and love fully, fearlessly, joyfully, wisely and without condition, in a world with which we are more meaningfully connected.'

XLVIX

Liberation is not attained in any other way but by severing the knot of ignorance and that . . . is brought about by the expansion of consciousness.

Tantraloka

'Our fourth *niyama* is *Svadhyaya* – literally "one's own study". The wisdom found in remaining open to new learning, expanding our ordinary ways of thinking through personal enquiry, contemplation and mindful *sadhana*.'

I scribbled down my notes in the hope that I might understand them later.

'So how open are you?' he challenged. 'How willing to sacrifice your own self-interest in order truly to learn?'

'Oh, very much so!' I exclaimed, exposing pride in what I believed to be my irrepressibly enquiring character, for I had been compelled from childhood to seek out insight deeper than the superficial recitation required by school curricula, or the restrictions of religious rhetoric.

'And yet, from our earliest years we decide the way the world is through the filter of our familial and social cultures. We become so attached to habitual thought and action that many of us rarely accept new learning. Instead, we only accept that which supports the beliefs we have already chosen or have been trained to make our own. And whatever does not fit that narrow spectrum, we simply reject as untrue.'

I recognised such behaviour in religious fundamentalists of all creeds whose tightly blinkered eyes refused to see rational evidence before them when it did not support the irrationality of their faith. And yet, I found myself struggling to admit that I too could be limiting my intimacy with life by comparable narcissistic filters.

'The purpose of this fourth *niyama* is therefore, first, to develop a greater understanding of our true nature, in contrast to our impermanent personality – that microscope through which man tends to view life in obsessively insignificant detail.'

I had never before considered that the 'personality' – upon which my culture placed such excessive attention – might be a restrictive lens that merely maintained its focus on the trivial and self-serving.

'Second, it is to develop in the student a greater under-standing of the teachings given, and thereby their practical application in the wider world. For the primary purpose of *Svadhyaya* is never merely personal reward, but always for the benefit of others.'

Again the tenet of social betterment that had first convinced me to pursue the *jhankri*'s teaching.

'The Tradition adds to *Svadhyaya* the supporting *niyama* of *Sravana*,' he revealed. 'Attentive listening – not only to music or words that inspire the mind, or to the insights of another's experience and wisdom, but to your true heart through honest self-reflection.'

As I noted this new Sanskrit word, I pondered how a life moderated by the principle of avoiding causing harm in thought, word or action might be when lived according to one's 'true heart'.

I imagined a life in which even the domestic and banal might gain new significance, every interaction meaning. A life of fearless, passionate engagement with everyone and every moment.

It was undoubtedly the only life for which I yearned.

L

Whoever wishes to, may sit in meditation
With eyes closed to know if the world be true or false.
I, meanwhile, shall sit with hungry eyes,
To see the world while the light lasts.

Rabindranath Tagore

'Our fifth and final *niyama* is *Pranidhana* – the wisdom learnt through applied endeavour and focused attention. And this not only in everyday life, but specifically to the three-part tantric practice of self-mastery we call *ulto sadhana*.'

He paused as though to test my interest.

'Which is?'

'The supreme *Tapa* of "reversed" or "contrary discipline" – so called because it goes against the current of ordinary processes.'

I could not imagine what he meant. And yet the notion of self-mastery appealed, for I was too well aware that my thoughts and feelings were undisciplined and all too often detrimental to myself. I was impatient with my failings, resentful of my weaknesses, for they affected my relationships and the colour of the world through which I moved, whilst filling my nights with disruptive dreams as evidence of perpetual and profound disquiet.

'So where does this *ulto sadhana* begin?'

'With the Eleven Vows I have described to you today, that you might learn to release habits of unhelpful behaviour at every level. Next, the physical practices of Hatha Yoga to afford mental and physical stability. Only then may we explore the first step of tantric *ulto sadhana*: mastery of the

144

breath, learnt through the progressive practice of *pranayama*, for nothing restores balance to the body–mind so effectively as mindful breathing.'

I knew of *pranayama* through my elementary yogic explorations. Even its most simple techniques of *bhramari* 'gallant bee', *ujjayi* 'victorious' and *anuloma viloma* 'alternate nostril' had already proved their benefits to me.

'Second, mastery of sexual response. This is explored through practices we call *bindusiddhi*, for when we pause at the pinnacle of pleasure, a tremendous, positive force is made available that might be directed to any meaningful purpose.'

This was an idea so new to me, so far beyond the least hint of possibility afforded by my upbringing, that I struggled to accept it could be so.

There! I thought. I had caught myself rejecting another's experience for no other reason than that it did not fit with my culturally dictated perception of reality.

'Third comes mastery of the mind, truly achievable only once breath and sexual response are mastered. This we call *pratyahara*, an attentive withdrawal of the senses that promotes a spontaneous state of meditation. For only when the mind is brought to stillness can we know the inner truth of ourselves – the "enlightening" piercing of consciousness, as we call it – through which we are able to resolve the conflict between our internal perspective and our external actions.'

I struggled to see this potential in myself. My 'internal perspective' seemed one of only faults and failings, selfishness and muddle.

And yet I sensed that I now sat before a man who had resolved his conflicts, restored his balance, 'reversed' the ordinary in himself and 'pierced' the reaches of his consciousness. And if he were to be believed, as I thought he was, then the qualities I perceived in him were also already mine. And to reveal them to myself was all I truly wanted.

'Attached to this *niyama* is *Gurusushruta*, respect for one's teacher,' he explained, 'through whose careful guidance the process of *Pranidhana* can be most effectively achieved. And all this, that you might learn to be happy in yourself – with clarity of mind, peace of heart, free from the limitations of selfish desire – and thereby, of course, of ever greater benefit to others.'

I nodded, my heart swelling with gratitude for this opportunity, wholly unexpected and unsought, to sit before a man so unsullied by self-interest and so willing to share with me something of his learning.

And in that moment I knew with more than mere intellect that I no longer wished to live an 'edited' life, filtered through the cultural norms in which I had been raised. No longer for me the life of easy, empty comforts buoyed on the single hope that the years of unthinking self-absorption might draw to their close with a medic at hand to ensure a pain-free death. Instead, I now chose to challenge and dismantle my every limitation, that I might plunge in with open hands and hungry eyes, living, feeling, knowing every exquisite, precious moment.

And even as I felt this new determination in my heart, heard this new vow resound within my mind, Kushal Magar touched his chest and leant forwards to place both palms on my head in blessing.

LI

Here, we prefer to choose a bright, open, fearless consciousness, free
of everyday concerns. So why don't you?
Kushal Magar

I had been asleep.

On completion of the *niyamas*, Kushal Magar advised me not to ask more questions. He suggested instead that I put aside my frenzied note-taking and simply let the long day's teachings find their proper place. I would remember what I needed.

In reflective silence, I watched him boost the fire to boil another brew of ginger tea. We sipped together at our beakers, captivated by the energetic dance of flames across each other's faces. And once the dregs of root and leaf were reached, I laid my head to rest on a bundled blanket at his encouragement, my body wrapped in two warm shawls.

'Just a little nap,' he said. 'We'll be on our way once you're awake.'

And then a soothing chant of undetermined end. A lilting, languid lullaby.

It was the scuff of feet that woke me to new light. I had slept untroubled until Samuel returned with breakfast eggs and *puri aloo dum* still hot inside their tiffin tins.

'Good dreams, *dajoo*?' He grinned, sitting down beside me to brush dust and ash from my face and hair.

'None at all,' I grunted, still surprised that I had slept so long.

Samuel warmed water for me to wash in, for only once I had shown my body the required respect could we together undertake our morning Ganesha *puja*. We first lit mustard oil lamps, then unfurled twisted strips of paper that we might each place a pinch of rice, *sidur* and jaggery – emblems of life's irrepressible creative energy and intrinsic pleasures – on the elephant-headed image in its niche.

'Ever noticed what the figures we employ for *puja* are usually sitting on?' Kushal Magar asked.

I re-examined the carving we had just smeared with vermilion. 'A bed of petals?'

'A lotus, symbolic reminder of the unlimited possibility and inherent joy in life found through our daily fulfilment of the four Purushartha and by applying the "mindful intent" of *bhavana*. And this that we might learn truly to know and value ourselves, living with honest and constructive purpose, whilst overcoming fear, anger, conceit and envy; duplicity, regret, hypocrisy and resentment. Only then may we learn really to live and love without attachment to our own past – without condition.'

I looked back at the cheerful Ganesha in wonder that there was always new learning to be found here, even in the most unlikely places.

Next, Kushal Magar led Samuel and me in *japa* – tantric chant employed to quieten the body–mind's ordinary obsessions – that we might affirm our intention to be receptive to the new wisdom our day would inevitably bring.

We finally voiced our gratitude to sky, earth, cow, chicken and loving hands that had produced the food before us, then tucked in with relish, until all was hungrily consumed.

'So how am I to "do" all that you've taught me here, *jhankri-dajoo*?' I asked as fingers were rinsed and fire doused. The truth was that I felt almost overwhelmingly daunted at the thought of the Eleven Vows.

'You have the *yamas* and *niyamas* in theory, so now explore their practice, one by one from the beginning,' he replied. 'Simple!'

'Simple' was not the word I would have used – but still I asked, 'So starting with *Ahimsa*?'

'Exactly,' he replied, preparing to tie blankets across his back. 'All else is based on this one principle. So first discover the wisdom in avoiding harm in thought, word and action to yourself and others. And then see what your life becomes.'

LII

A man who has a sceptical nature and is without conviction can never receive the desired fruits of his actions.
Tripura Rahasya

Samuel had doused the remaining embers with the dregs of tea, and was already gathering up the charcoaled canister and tins.

'You off somewhere?' I asked.

'Jai Kumari-*bhaini* is expecting to give us *chiya* down at Lapu,' he replied. 'And then we need to be getting on our way back home. The weather's changing.'

'Already?' I exclaimed. 'But why so short? I have a week left on my permit – and still so much to learn!'

I turned to Kushal Magar, who was binding his head and shoulders with a shawl.

'Dedication to your learning and practice is one of the *Tin Gunharu*,' he responded, reading the plea in my eyes for him to intervene. 'One of the three qualities that all who choose the Tradition are wise to cultivate. For it is only by following the path that we discover it.'

With an insatiable hunger for his teaching, and desperate that it might not finish so abruptly for yet another year, I stopped Samuel in his preparations and asked Kushal Magar to explain.

'Well, dedication is that essential longing in the heart for new insight, learning and wisdom,' he replied. 'The desire to liberate ourselves from detrimental behaviour, expressed by a fearlessness of change. Without it, all study, contemplation and *sadhana* are fruitless.'

I stood still to assimilate his words, but noticed Samuel slowly edging back towards the cave's narrow entrance, his arms filled with tiffin tins.

'In a hurry?' I challenged him.

'Just chilly now the fire's out. And desperate for hot *chiya*!'

Puzzled by his impatience, I picked up the last blankets.

Only once I bent low to follow his passage through the cave's tight entrance and stepped out into the chill of mountain mist did I feel the full frustration of what seemed a hasty, if not enforced, dismissal.

LIII

The Tradition: Self-discipline without rigour,
positive-living without sham or excess.
Brajamadhava Bhattacharya

Kushal Magar was evidently impervious to the mountain chill. He strode ahead on bare feet to mark the path for our descent, leaving Samuel to beckon me to follow in his footsteps.

'*Jhankri-dajoo!*' I called out towards the dark smudge already forging fast into the mist. 'You said there are three qualities. So what's the—'

I hit the cold, wet stone with such speed and force that I had neither opportunity nor breath to express my consternation. With arms still clutching the blankets, I had no hands to ease my fall and felt anew the bony parts of elbows, knees and chin.

It was Samuel who cried out on my behalf as he ran to rescue me from my foolish inattention. Thick winter wear had saved my joints from all but bruising, but my unshaved jaw was cut, against which my cousin now pressed a cotton hanky from his pocket.

Samuel's alarm had summoned Kushal Magar. He hurried back, insisting he check for himself that my head and limbs were unharmed.

'So now to answer what might have been your last question.' He smiled with relief. 'The second quality we choose to develop is concentration – being aware of every moment of our lives . . .'

He paused.

And we three burst into laughter.

'Concentrating on what we think and speak and do demands that passivity in life is dispelled,' he continued, helping me back to newly conscientious feet. 'Remember the importance of *bhavana*? The setting of your intention, free of everyday concerns, that life might be lived with honest, constructive purpose?'

I did. This one aspect of his teaching had proved remarkably challenging to me, and yet had afforded a new intensity to the past twelve months. I had noticed how the trivial and unconsidered had begun to lose their lure, even my words to bear more meaning, my actions to be more thoughtful – and thereby more fruitful.

In just one year, my life had gained a greater value to myself and, I liked to believe, was therefore already gradually beginning to prove of greater benefit to others.

LIV

Those who have seen never tell;
Those who tell have never seen.
Pampatti-Chittar

Our descent through forest fog had been so fast, the smarting of my chin and jaw of such distraction, that we reached the road before I had time to think about the grazes on my knees.

We hurried on towards the village far below, its corrugated roofs and weather-stained walls reflecting sunlight as we escaped the woodland clouds. And then the little temple in its bamboo grove, the drying cobs, the smiling daughter with her chickens, and the crows that now alighted as though in welcome.

I noticed the eagerness with which Samuel offered Jai Kumari the cheerful benefit of his assistance, even though the fire was already lit, the *chiya* prepared and, as I had hoped, fresh *daal-bhat* rice and lentils bubbling for our pleasure. We gathered close to warm our hands in celebration of our return from what had seemed quite another country, and thrilled at steaming cups of tea spiced with black pepper and cardamom that promptly passed among us.

'So, brother.' Kushal Magar smiled. 'The third and final quality that those who choose the Tradition are wise to focus on is discretion.'

This was not the concluding attribute I had imagined. Fortitude, perhaps, prudence or temperance – all evidence of my own upbringing. But discretion?

'All that you learn is for *your* benefit. There is no profit in drawing the attention of others, for pride is an easy downfall for any student of our – or any other – Tradition.'

I flinched. Had I not already known the tempting glint of smugness that I was privy to some mystic mountain knowledge?

'Consider that the open discussion of one's initiations, for example, or glib conversation about one's practice, dissipates the force of their experience. There is no benefit to be gained in attempting to share such details with others. Authentic inner experience cannot be expressed in language. For that which can be told is not the truth.'

I was astonished by this assertion.

'A true *shaiva tantrika* makes no show of his knowledge. It is wise to be wary, therefore, of those who do.'

'Then I shall tell no one – unless you give me permission,'

I vowed. 'I'll keep it to myself and just work hard to make myself a better person!'

'Brother, permit me to suggest that you do not allow an obsession with what you imagine to be "self-development" to become its own hindrance,' he advised. 'Attend instead to the application of the teachings you receive purely for the benefit of others, rather than yourself – and their profit will be greater.'

'Of course.' I nodded earnestly. 'Always for the benefit of others.'

'Always,' he repeated. 'For as we like to say, in those whose intention is unselfish – who are tranquil, yet passionately engaged in life, who apply the practice of the Tradition as given by their teacher without drawing attention to themselves – shines wisdom.'

I bowed my head in gratitude. I had no more to ask.

Kushal Magar responded by touching his heart, then placing his hands on my head.

His blessing of farewell had been bestowed.

His teaching was finished for another year.

PART SIX

LV

*According to the profound path of the Tantras, besides the outer
there is the inner and secret meaning, given only from the
lips of a master teacher.*
Kagyü Gurtso

'*J hankri-dajoo*, are you my guru?'

Another year had passed since I had last trudged
through mountain mist to the confines of the cave
temple. As the warmth of summer rain dissipated into a
cool, grey autumn, I knew the time had come to return to
Kushal Magar.

For the past months, his practical guidance in the Eleven
Vows had motivated me to maintain the simple daily yogic
sadhana I had been given, after which I would set my *bhavana*,
my mindful intention, towards the Aim of Life I had chosen
to direct my day.

I had explored Dharma, finding better ways to fulfil
my 'moral duty' to myself, to those I loved and beyond. I
had tried to embrace Artha more effectively, fulfilling my
responsibility to social stability, whilst embracing life's full
abundance through friendships, work and learning. I had
more frequently remembered to acknowledge Kama,
allowing myself to welcome every pleasure accessible to my

senses, even – and perhaps most especially – when engaged in the monotony of domestic chores.

In addition, I had chosen to dedicate each day of the intervening seasons to the principle of *Ahimsa*, the *yama* Kushal Magar had emphasised was the basis of all vows. The others, I decided, would have to wait their turn, for this alone required of me an untried attention to every thought, word and deed, that I might be the cause of neither careless nor intentioned harm to myself or others.

It had not proved easy, for these daily efforts had exposed the mindless regularity with which I passed judgement on both myself and my fellow man, only to be buffeted by my own feelings of self-doubt and resentment, guilt and envy. And ever the fear of criticism and rejection, habitually emphasised by the insatiable need for approval and praise.

Yet through it all, I had begun to perceive that the means Kushal Magar had given me to temper my response to life's natural and necessary tides had initiated a previously unknown moderation in my dealings, both with myself and others. A new enrichment of the ordinary. An evident yet intangible 'enlightening' in the mundanity of my daily round, affecting for the good my every exchange, the outcome of my actions – and thereby my sense of my own value and my life's worth.

Even the nightmares, which had harassed my sleep since childhood, as evidence of hidden fears and conflicts, had begun to ease away. And as I had persevered, I had known moments of unfamiliar stillness in my mind. An untried peace of heart. The beginnings of a new contentment.

But now I sat again below Kanchenjunga, its supreme peak ablaze in morning sun, a beacon bright enough to steer me from my native soil. My companions and I were pressed around a meagre fire when Samuel's laugh at my question as to whether Kushal Magar was my guru billowed into vapour then dissipated back to clear, bright air.

I glanced at him in puzzlement.

'Sorry, *dajoo,*' he said. 'In Nepali, it's just a funny thing to ask. You see, *guru's* slang for bus-driver. And if you were to say it twice – 'Are you my *guru-guru*?' – you'd be asking our *jhankri*-brother if he's responsible for the rumbles in your stomach!'

'However, in the way you meant it, brother,' Kushal Magar interjected, turning to look directly at me, 'guru literally means "a dispeller of darkness". One who routs ignorance.'

This I did not know.

'You may remember that the teachings of the Tradition are termed *Thuture Veda* in these hills – the Spoken Knowledge – for they are taught intimately and directly, that the recipient might gain greater self-awareness, better understanding of his true nature, his own natural order. And this that he might be of greater benefit to himself and others – and thereby learn wisdom. So it is that such teachers are commonly addressed here as *Gurudeva* – Bright Being – by their students.'

I struggled to relate these terms to the robe-wrapped men who stared from billboards and television screens in innumerable Indian shops and homes. Men who drew followings of international reach, ensuring they were not only venerated as incarnations of an otherwise inaccessible Divine, but became the figureheads of multimillion-dollar 'spiritual' empires. I had seen for myself the fanatical *bhakta* devotion they inspired, notably among young Westerners who crammed into ashrams for what were all too often distorted philosophies and fraudulent esotericism. Such personality cults promoted a co-dependence that gave birth to the same phenomenon of 'group mind' as any proscriptive religion, with both overt and subtle rules defining how adherents were to dress, speak, behave and think.

'I'd always thought guru meant something like "master",' I confessed. 'You know, a man or woman who sets themselves up – or is set up – as the big chief of their own little tribe of believers.'

'And yet, for us, a true guru is not a leader of any sort and would certainly not build an institution around themselves, nor procure a lifetime of devotion and dependence from their followers,' Kushal Magar insisted. 'For true knowledge affords self-reliance, developing in the student courageous independence not only from limiting social and religious structures, but also ultimately from their teachers.'

Nor, would I imagine, did true gurus have Swiss bank accounts, palaces on the Ganges, or multi-*crore* mansions in the Himalayan foothills, like certain of their breed I had already encountered in both the fashionable superfluity of yoga literature and in person. It seemed equally unlikely that a true guru would wish to broadcast their 'spiritual gifts' to prove how 'enlightened' they are, taking out adverts in newspapers, presenting their own television shows, registering trademarks or publicising Hollywood patronage. Nor would they go by such titles as Her Holiness, count a personal hairdresser in their entourage, fly first class to meet their international devotees, or spend donations on plastic surgery to maintain their 'miraculous' eternal youth.

'A true guru is one who offers guidance and comfort gained from their personal experience,' Kushal Magar confirmed. 'And certainly with no thought of personal reward or notice. Of course, there are students who seek a sense of personal worth in the fantasy that their teacher is *their* god incarnate. Equally, there are some self-professed gurus who, for reasons of their own self-interest, actively encourage such misplaced expectations. It is therefore always wise to question anyone who chooses to adopt a role in any system founded on "spiritual" hierarchy.'

Since my first introduction to India, I had explored shrines, temples and 'holy places' of every age and religion. I had walked with *sadhus*, monks and naked Jains. I had sat with sweet-scented mullahs, turbaned Granthis and Brahmin priests. I had been served tea and biscuits by dour, young *repas* before the embalmed body of their Bhutanese bodhisattva. I had been bitten by a Rajasthani saint that had supposedly been reincarnated as a rat, and had been robbed by Bihari pilgrims whilst I stripped and dipped in 'hallowed' waters. I had even joined a crowd of hundreds that had gathered in a big top to honour a rotund man who sat on cushions between shaven-headed bodyguards and babbled 'divine' nonsense with a demented grin.

I had listened to earnest foreigners compete in tales of their particular guru's sleight-of-hand 'miracles' of materialising plastic beads and scented ash. I had watched them surrender to sleep- and food-deprived hysteria, mistaking their heightened imaginations for the mystical. I had heard gratuitous self-absorption proclaimed 'spiritual enlightenment'. And whilst their 'holy' men and women enjoyed chauffeur-driven cars and holidays in Barbados, beyond the confines of their ashrams incalculable numbers of the native population suffered curable diseases, sewage-soiled water and no access to basic education.

It was exactly these cults of 'spiritual' celebrity that had rendered me sceptical of any hint of guru-dom, for in the self-perpetuating hierarchies I had encountered at India's most revered sites, I had found no 'dispelling of darkness'. I had seen no 'brightness'.

'In these hills, a guru is simply a conduit of the Tradition,'

Kushal Magar said. 'A single, selfless current in a continuous stream of knowledge, whose purpose is to guide the initiate to perceive their true nature, enabling them to live and love more honestly, more effectively and joyfully.'

I nodded and offered silent thanks to an inherently unpredictable universe that had brought order out of chaos – and into my life my own Bright Being.

LVI

There is no being that is not enlightened,
if it but knows its own true nature.
Hevajra Tantra

'*Jhankri-dajoo*, you described the Tradition as knowledge that enlightens. But what exactly is enlightenment?'

I glanced at Samuel in case he was going to tease me again for my question, but he now seemed so absorbed by the smoulder of embers glowing at our toes that he did not say a word.

Samuel had laughed and talked with characteristic mischief the entire morning's trek. He had mentioned in passing that political tension had been brewing in the hills since my last visit, with a resurgence of increasingly aggressive calls for the establishment of a hill state independent of the Communist government of West Bengal. Just last week, there had been outbreaks of public disorder in Darjeeling, which explained the noisy convoys of army jeeps and lorries on the roads that had convinced us to take the slower and more arduous cross-country route on foot.

However, Samuel's principal concern had been to disclose the details of family gossip that his mother had prudently omitted the night before around the kitchen table. Together we had sniggered at Aunt Dilly's attempts to threaten a bank clerk with accusations of corruption, sending anonymous letters on which, in her fastidiousness, she had mistakenly penned her return address. Together we had chortled at the tales of Aunt Kanti's kleptomania, compulsive thefts forgiven only by the ready distribution of her spoils among street urchins and beggar widows, but which had earned her a life ban from Shri Ram's Bengali Sweetshop cum British Bakery and Guesthouse.

As we approached Lapu-*basti*, Samuel's natural ebullience had heightened and he had quickened his pace, revealing, it had appeared to me, an eagerness to return to *jhankri*, crows and scarlet temple. However, once I had begun my clumsy questions to Kushal Magar, I noticed Samuel's attention drift. Indeed, he had not said another word beyond his *guru-guru* pun. He had not yet finished his beaker of tea, when normally he was eyeing the pot for another before I had barely managed half of mine. And instead of his usual banter, his eyes had begun to linger on the hill path as though in anxious expectation.

'You all right, *bhai*?' I asked, pressing into him with my shoulder.

'Oh yes, *dajoo*, most muchly so!' he mumbled, confirming my suspicions.

I sensed it best to pursue his unfamiliar demeanour later, so squeezed my cousin's arm and turned back to Kushal Magar, who was ready with his answer.

'Brother, long ago the quest for "enlightenment" seeped from our mythologies to consume the most capable and courageous men with self-doubt. It is an ambition that has driven generations to grasp their version of an imagined heaven, whilst rendering them beholden both to priestly canon and the superstitions of fraudster "chicken-*gurus*". And all this for an illusory reward that they conclude they are not worthy of, for they are still engaged in its pursuit.'

I too had been raised in the promise of a Christian paradise, ironically little different from the Islamic Jannah, Buddhist Trayastrimsha, Jewish Olam Haba, or even the Lokas of Brahminism. Each offered the assurance of perpetual peace and painlessness. Each was either bestowed upon divine whim, or proffered as a barely reachable reward for compliance to an unbending dogma that had been determined by another man or men from some other distant time and place. It had always struck me that in every case the promise of perfection was defined by the extent of its exclusions – a fantastical host of heavens only identified as such according to those to whom a welcome would never be extended.

'For whatever name or qualities given to the so-called "blissful goal" of enlightenment,' he continued, 'its pursuit invariably implies the divinity or sacred state that man believes he seeks are not here but elsewhere. That they must be earned by submission to authorised books, rituals or hierarchies of ordained men – to all of which personal power and moral responsibility are unquestioningly given.'

He paused to reach for dried cornhusks and more wood. I joined in feeding the fire, as I considered that all I really knew – or thought I knew – of enlightenment was that it had been found by Prince Siddhartha Gautama beneath a fig tree near the Indian town of Gaya. Or so they said. Whatever he had discerned had earned him the title of Buddha, the Awakened One – and at the same time inadvertently afforded almost every New Age book, workshop and yoga class a mystical, and thereby conveniently inaccessible, holy Golden Fleece.

I now had to admit that I too had bought into the fantasy, long imagining that this insinuated Supreme Condition was available only to emaciated, celibate *yogins* hidden away in Himalayan caves; to aged *lamas* privy to arcane knowledge and occult rites in mountain monasteries; offered only in austere ashrams where refraining from all human intimacy, appetising food or sufficient sleep were integral to that ultimate discovery.

'Then tell me,' I pleaded, reaching out to touch his knee, 'what does "to be enlightened" mean?'

'Depends who you ask,' he replied, as though with purposeful ambiguity. 'Buddhists and Jains talk of *bodhi*, "perfect knowledge", or *nirvana*, literally "a land that has no trees", for their interpretation of enlightenment is the complete extinction of individual desire and passion.'

I screwed up my nose. I much preferred Tagore's poetic 'hungry eyes' – 'to see the world while the light lasts' – rather than the abstemious notion of some 'enlightened' state that afforded no feast of forests, ardour or delight.

'Brahmin priests, on the other hand, apply the term *kaivalya*,' he continued, 'meaning "total unity with the Brahman" – their notion of a timeless, passive absolute. For them, "enlightenment" demands a detachment of what they perceive as the eternal "soul" from all human experience or material existence. A "supreme state" in which all further learning, and therefore growth, ceases.'

This priestly interpretation simply sounded far too much like death to me.

'And you?' I pressed.

'Well, here we prefer the term *byunjhanu*, meaning "to be fully awakened", for it implies a practical, active shift from night-time sleep to sunlit life. From ignorance to self-knowledge.'

Again he poked the fire, as though to give me time to think.

'But in these hills you will also hear the word *divyachara*, going by daylight,' he continued. 'Perception beyond mere mental conditioning. Beyond the ordinary, all-consuming preoccupation with our physical, emotional and sexual responses to external stimuli. For *divyachara* describes the personal experience of engaging with every moment of your life through an expanded consciousness – an enlightened mind.'

And with this, I raised my head as though to pierce the sweep of lucent blue in its eternal, shining span above us.

And tried and tried to grasp how to be fully awakened might truly be.

LVII

The real magic of discovery lies not in seeking new landscapes,
but in having new eyes.
Marcel Proust

Kushal Magar bent low to blow fresh life into tongues of flame, which we watched curl and char his cornhusks.

'Of course, the term "enlightenment" does not describe a permanent condition,' he said. 'Rather, it expresses an on-going heightening of awareness that gradually expands consciousness beyond its normal waking state. A steady sunrise of understanding.'

Not then, as I had imagined, the atomic blast that blows the head into some other, previously inaccessible, celestial dimension.

'So how do I begin?'

'You think you have yet to start?' he replied. 'An awakening mind first requires a heightening of your awareness of the present by fully experiencing what you already have, fully embracing who you already are. By relishing every moment for its own sake, rather than anticipating some imagined reward promised at a later date. By perceiving all tastes, sounds, sensations and feelings as blissful. Do you recognise this?'

'Of course!' I laughed. 'It's in everything you've taught me from the start! *Bhavana*. *Sukha* and *dukha*. The four Purushartha. The eleven *yamas* and *niyamas*.'

'Each step of the Tradition is practical and with purpose' – he nodded – 'for enlightenment is found in a steady dismantling of learnt barriers. This, in turn, leads to an understanding free from prejudice and fear, free from social conditioning and our need to control. An understanding free from the distortions of our own self-interest.'

'And really all that is required is a change of outlook?' I asked, trying to rest my eyes anew on *jhankri*, gliding crows and resplendent mountain ranges far beyond.

'Enlightenment is not something to attain by arduous effort and training. It is an awakening to the reality that the finite and infinite, the mortal and divine, are not separate but the same. That the truth, joy, peace and knowledge we seek are neither conditions of circumstance, nor qualities we must anticipate as some "divine" reward. They are already here, now, if only we would accept, recognise and embrace them in ourselves and each other.'

My head was spinning with the implications of this assertion.

'You see, brother, you already have all you need to be all that you truly are,' he declared, leaning forwards to touch my heart. 'And the only thing you need to do is choose to put aside old, unproductive habits – your detrimental thoughts, words, actions – and step into the daylight.'

LVIII

Imperfection is not a negation of perfectness; finitude is not contradictory to infinity: they are but completeness manifested in parts, infinity revealed within bounds.
Rabindranath Tagore

Samuel was too quiet for my comfort.

Twice I caught him looking at his new birthday watch, only to stare again along the path that cut its course back through dense bamboo and leafy scrub.

As Kushal Magar seemed wholly unperturbed by Samuel's distraction, I returned to the subject that continued to perplex me.

'You've told me what enlightenment is and what it's not, but can you explain how "awakening" might actually feel?'

'Imagine a moment when awareness is heightened and yet individual consciousness is free of all thoughts. Like when a lover embraces his beloved, every sense so sharply brightened by his passion that he no longer has any sense of himself as separate. This is an awareness comparable to "going into daylight".'

At these words Samuel burst back to life, almost throwing his neglected beaker of tea to the ground as he leapt to his feet. He listened keenly to what seemed to me like silence, stared at his watch as though in expectation of some long-awaited wizardry, only then to slump down again.

'What's got into you?' I asked, wrapping a fraternal arm around him.

'Sorry, *dajoos*,' he mumbled.

I raised my eyebrows to Kushal Magar, who merely tipped his head from side to side, as though this was entirely reasonable behaviour on my cousin's part. He then turned to pour water from a metal milk-can into his pot. His answer, it seemed, was to boil more tea.

'Sorry, *jhankri-dajoo*,' I persisted, tousling my cousin's hair, 'but I still don't really understand how this "going into daylight" is ultimately achieved.'

'The only "achieving" that you need attend to is applying with composure and integrity the practices of the Tradition that are most useful and relevant to your present life. This is what will lead you to perceive your limitless nature, your true self. And the "daylight" that you seek.'

He paused to drop cinnamon sticks, cardamom and cloves into the rolling water.

'So value your life as you live it today. Honour who you are *now*. And love the best and most honest way you know – for nothing is more healing, nurturing or enlightening than to give and receive selfless love.'

Again I closed my eyes and held my breath to feel more deeply the tender, winter sunlight stream contentment through my skin. To smell more intensely the spices suspended in my nostrils, to feel the inestimable comfort of toes in socks and shoes. To discern for myself more clearly the invaluable knowledge that out in this vast and restless world lived loving family, devoted friends and yet new companionships waiting to be forged.

At that moment, Samuel looked back at his watch and bounded to his feet. His reanimation was so sudden that he nearly knocked me sideways as he ran towards the hill path up which he quickly disappeared.

Kushal Magar made no remark, but simply turned to add milk to the brew that bubbled in the flames.

'Is he sick?' I asked, standing tall to peer for some last glimpse of Samuel in his maniacal flight, unsure whether I should not have already hurried off in pursuit.

'In a way.' Kushal Magar chuckled, binding the pot's handle in a cloth in readiness to pour new tea. 'Don't you see? Your carefree cousin-brother is quite obviously in love!'

LVIX

What you are you do not see.
What you see is your shadow.
Rabindranath Tagore

I might have considered myself alone, but for the chickens scuffing round the flowerpots, the clamorous crows, and a single hefty hornet whose curiosity required repeated dissuasion.

Kushal Magar had excused himself to visit the bamboo outhouse that teetered on the hillside's slope.

Samuel had yet to return from his impulsive sortie in the direction of the village road. The *jhankri* had showed such little anxiety at my cousin's sudden madness that I could only trust that Samuel would soon return, his normal self.

I sat relishing air in my lungs sweetened by warming vegetation. I gazed out towards distant peaks that, through the rising haze, seemed more intangible than their myths.

In this place where skies and mountains merged, the *jhankri*'s talk of limitlessness was more accessible than in my ordinary landscape of tidy terraced houses. Here where weather, forest, beast and man combined in the essential practicality of every day, his talk of universal union seemed more lucid than at home where individuality is deemed so sacrosanct that we let it lead to loneliness and fear.

And yet as I sat on the temple steps and prodded ash in search of hidden embers, I set my mind to a single question for which I still did not have an answer.

'What is the true self?' I asked the chickens pecking at my feet.

'What is the true self?' I asked the shining summits soaring high above.

'Who do *you* think you are?' Kushal Magar intervened, laying a soap-scented hand on my shoulder as he settled back before me. He touched first his heart and then mine, his sign that I was now to receive new teaching.

'Perhaps you are the clothes you wear,' he began, reaching out to tug the hems of my travel trousers. 'Perhaps the society you entertain, the car you drive, the house that binds you to its wood and brick. Perhaps you are your education, your sense of humour, your passion for sport, your sexual prowess. But then who are you when naked, silent, or alone? Who are you when homeless, penniless, or impotent?'

I blinked back at him, bewildered.

'Perhaps you are your mind,' he suggested. 'Then who are you when unconscious, unbalanced or asleep? Or are you your body? But then who are you when sick, in pain – or dead?'

He paused to let me consider the options his questions might have left me with, then looked into my eyes to ensure my full attention.

'My primary purpose as a teacher of the Tradition is to reveal to you that you are not who you think you are,' he stated. 'That you are not what you believe yourself to be. So again I ask, who do you think you are?'

I looked back to bamboo, crow and mountain.

And found I had not one inkling of an answer.

LX

Break barriers all your life long.
Trust your heart and break barriers.
Marie-Paule Mourik

'So you tell me, *jhankri-dajoo* – who am I?' I asked, hoping that a direct question would prompt a comparable reply.

'Brother, it is not for me to give you answers,' he replied. 'There is no dogma here. No rigid rules. No rights and wrongs by which you might be judged for praise or punishment. The wisdom of the Tradition is not found in an objective doctrine and creed, but in the heightening awareness of a sunlit mind.'

Coming from a culture largely founded on objective

'truths', the idea that personal insight might in some way be of greater value or veracity was still not easy to accept.

'Your steady "sunrise of understanding" again,' I said with a momentary twitch of frustration.

'Then let's begin with two new terms – *Nama* and *Rupa*. The first literally means "pasture ground", but we also use it to describe the inner nature of an object or being. The very essence of who and what you are is your *Nama*.'

He tipped his head. I tipped mine back. He had my interest.

'*Rupa*, on the other hand, means "material form" or "colour", for it describes the external manifestation of *Nama*. So what of yours?'

I looked down at my pink knuckles, unsure of what he was asking.

'Well,' he tried again, 'to begin with, what is your *Rupa* made from?'

'Oh, basically air and water, coal and chalk,' I replied, relieved to be able to answer this unexpected test, and newly grateful for the attention I had afforded school-lab Bunsen burners and the Periodic Table. 'With a pinch of iron, zinc, phosphorus and sulphur, of course, to make us fizz.'

Even as I said the words, I looked up to Kanchenjunga and grasped a momentary insight. Had Kushal Magar not impressed that he and I, the earth on which we sat, the tea we drank, the megalithic peaks above were all, in essence, indivisible? With my material *Rupa* form of moistened rock and metal, gas and crystal, was I not then just another form of mountain, crow and ocean, cabbage, hen and weather? Was I not but one expression of the same elements, atoms and vibrations? The self-same truths?

Even in the vagueness of my own academic learning, I had already acknowledged a fundamental natural law that I could so easily accept in the far-flung reaches of the universe. Why, then, did I still struggle to recognise it in myself?

'So upon which do you base your self-image, brother?' he persisted. 'Your *Nama*, or your *Rupa*? Your inner nature, or your outer appearance?'

The honest answer to this question was not comfortable to admit.

The truth was that my self-image and thereby self-confidence were entirely capricious, chiefly founded on my response to the reflection of the cluster of basic elements that made my flesh and bones in the bathroom mirror in the morning. If on that day I deemed myself passable to the fickle cultural standards by which I had allowed myself to be indoctrinated, I could face the world with buoyant poise. However, if I judged myself 'sub-standard', as was my usual response to skinny legs, nondescript features and thinning hair, then I would skulk internally, unable to muster the least self-belief or look a stranger in the eyes.

'Of course, *Rupa* is applied to much more than just the limits of your skin,' he continued, not needing to wait for my reply, 'for *Rupa* also refers to your outer life. But if this outer life is not a true reflection of your *Nama* – your "inner nature" – then you will find yourself in perpetual conflict. You will feel dissatisfied, restless, unhappy. You will feel profoundly, and yet often indefinably, ill at ease.'

Kushal Magar had exposed me.

Dissatisfied. Restless. Unhappy. Ill at ease.

In those few words he had described with unsettling precision the filter through which I had so often experienced my life. Perhaps, then, it was by reason of this uncomfortable catalogue that I had found my way to his hillside hut in the first place.

'In contrast,' he continued, 'when your *Nama* and *Rupa*

172

are in harmony there is a remarkable, intensely pleasurable sense of wholeness, of being complete – which you may have already known in your life, even if fleetingly. A moment, perhaps, when you tasted your limitless capacity by exposing vast reserves of strength or stamina, mental clarity or insight. A moment when even all sense of time and space is lost. Such as in the throes of loving passion. Or during periods of intense creativity.'

In some small way I had. I had grown up in a household of music teachers and choristers, with a grandmother who should have been a concert pianist had her father permitted the opportunities her talent deserved. Accordingly, I had first sat on her knee when less than two years old to explore the keys at her instruction. Thereafter, the piano had become my passion and my friend. In future years, as technique and confidence had improved, it had afforded me opportunities to know for myself those moments of union between the inner and the outer, when staves and fingers, polished bone and ebony, time and self seemed to merge into nothing but the music.

'You may also have met people who live with their *Nama* and *Rupa* in harmony,' he added. 'People who stand out because they are fully engaged in a life that is lived with clear and mindful purpose. People who possess a remarkable capacity to influence others positively, even to change for the better the world through which they move.'

I nodded in fondest memory of a tutor engaged to teach me music, but who had extended our curriculum from counterpoint and symphonic form to languages, literature, philosophy and Belgian cooking. She would challenge me to compose variations for cello and piano on a given theme, then reward me with an afternoon perfecting a recipe for *mousse au chocolat* and *Galettes de Tilff*. She would walk me through a gallery to sit before a single painting, a library to read one poem, to a concert hall for a specific movement. And then, when our separate households were fast asleep, she would throw pine cones against my bedroom window so that I might join her amble beneath a midnight moon and pursue discussions inspired by Gide or Gibran, Caravaggio, Mahler or Krishnamurti.

But far above her many matchless talents as a teacher, this gifted, industrious, sharp-witted friend had encouraged me by both her example and tuition to learn to trust my heart beyond others' expectations. To believe in myself beyond others' praise or denigration. For she had been one of those uncommon few who live in full accord with their internal world, their ardent outer life as their lucid inner truth – their *Rupa* with their *Nama* – by which she had wrought a beneficial change on all with whom she had engaged. But especially on me.

'Such a capacity is also yours,' Kushal Magar announced.

'But how?' I asked, struggling to believe that the confusion in myself, reflected in an enduring frustration with what I still perceived to be a fragmented and dissatisfactory life, could ever be resolved.

'Apply the wisdom of our Tradition to your daily life, and you will steadily learn to create that balance between the inner and the outer. And this that you might live and love to your full capacity, through a passionate, abundant, honest life, brother, that is entirely your own.'

LXI

If the mind, when filled with some desire, should seek a goal,
it only hides the Light.

Song of Mahamudra

'I can accept that the real me is more *Nama* "inner nature" than *Rupa* "outward appearance",' I conceded. 'But *jhankri-dajoo*, I still don't understand – who or what is my true self?'

'Let us unravel a little further who you think you might be,' Kushal Magar replied, as though intentionally to tease me, when all I really wanted from him was the revelation of some insightful truth.

'Well, I know I'm a bit of loner,' I began, 'but on the whole good-natured, I think. Curious about the world. Largely liberal in attitudes and politics. Something of a dilettante if I'm honest—'

'But is this who *you* are?' he asked, interrupting what threatened to be a lengthy and indulgent list. 'Or are these just qualities of the external personality – a role you have been taught to play by the culture that has "civilised" you to see, think, act and even feel according to its preference?'

I felt myself draw back, as though such a proposal were a personal affront.

'But surely we all need roles for society to function,' I insisted.

'We certainly have a responsibility to maintain social stability through the fulfilment of Artha, the second Aim of Life. However, we diminish, even harm ourselves and others by identifying solely with roles that we adopt in mindless compliance.'

He paused to offer a kindly smile, as though to ease the force of his next assertion.

'The truth is, brother, you have played your assigned roles for so much of your life that you can no longer differentiate who you really are from the person – or people – everybody else expects you to be.'

My mind was in ferment, for if this were true then it was time finally to admit that the inherited burden of familial, social and religious expectation had indeed borne down heavily on my perception of myself and thereby my experience of life. That the requirement to conform to a tyranny of approved norms so contrary to my nature had, in truth, delivered me to a lifetime of disquiet and depression.

'So what are the roles that you have learnt to play?' he pressed. 'The Victim or the Hero? The Bully or the Clown? Is yours the biddable Good Boy or the delinquent Bad?'

I had no notion of how to respond beyond the discomfort his enquiry provoked.

'Important questions. And invaluable answers. For the roles by which you identify yourself have a far greater impact on the choices that determine your experience of life than you might ever wish to imagine. The words you say to yourself have power – whether or not you know you hear them.'

I thought of my parents' female friends who had identified themselves solely as nurturers and devoted mothers for so long that when their children had grown up and moved away they had found themselves depressive and adrift. I thought of my parents' male friends who had identified themselves as the man-behind-a-desk-with-nameplate-on-the-door for so many years that on retirement they had lost all sense of self or purpose, quickly faded, ailed and even died.

'So learn to free yourself from such a compromised version of your sense of who you are, and you will still live in a world you have always known, but no longer be limited by it,' Kushal Magar declared. 'You will find yourself able to live life intuitively, creatively, joyfully – even playfully – as you once did in childhood. Then just imagine how different your experience of life might be!'

I stayed silent. And tried to envision what seemed at that moment to be a wholly revolutionary proposal.

LXII

In darkness the One appears as uniform;
in the light the One appears as manifold.
Rabindranath Tagore

'So again I ask,' Kushal Magar persisted, 'through which roles do you identify yourself and thereby experience your life?'

I was unsure even where to start to answer such a question. I tried skimming back across the convoluted route of years to search for echoes of the child I had once been, a child unsullied by the roles dictated by family, Church, school and wider culture.

My quest returned me to a loving and supportive home of Goons and Danny Kaye, dressing-up and windfall pears, tuna tarts and Surrey curry. A home of parlour games and treasure hunts, comb-kazoos and patter songs, limericks and Granny's Supper. High teas of mustard pies and finnan haddie, Cheddar cheese on ginger biscuits, and home-churned butter on home-made bread. And always to mark the year-long round – whether Advent, Passion, Patronal Feast or Sea Sunday – the reassuring sugared trail of my mother's indefatigably inventive cakes.

Amid the memories of those easy, early days, I could still recall the free spirit I had been born to be: that joyful boy whose companions had been squirrels, tadpoles, bees and hedgehogs, barleybirds and shufflewings. Whose internal landscape had been post-prandial sun on flint-flecked fields and downland chalk. Whose dream had been to be a doctor on a bicycle, stethoscope round neck, pockets plump with vaccinating sugar lumps. That little lad whose secret longing had been only for a ploughboy with weather in his hair and eyes, in whose straw-stacked stables and loyal embrace his life would be for ever spent.

This brought to mind my childhood struggle to keep on my clothes when my impulse had always been to welcome summer sun with naked skips through stands of beech. And then to run, to leap, to laugh through cowpat-spattered meadows towards the skinny-dip in Pigwood Pond with minnows, sticklebacks and newts.

I could almost remember back before that fearless boy was moulded by well-meaning to sit through Sunday school without a fidget, close his eyes and bow his head for prayers, and know the words to every verse of every hymn. To keep his blazer meticulously clean and never once mislay its matching cap or Grandma-knitted mittens. To coax with spit and comb his cow-lick to a parting. Until that bold, blithe boy learnt deference to those he did not like or trust. To disguise dishonesty with politeness. To doubt himself. To seek esteem. To be for ever Good.

Nor was this the only role I had adopted, for throughout my early efforts at grown-up-commended conduct, I had found other children a conundrum – particularly when faced by their unseemly nasal habits or inexplicable compulsion to play ball games. My preference had therefore soon become for hours alone of secret dens and ciphers, invisible ink and experimental alchemy; the construction of shoebox homes for field mice, the tireless study of anatomy books and the sleuthing skills of Nancy Drew.

Only now had this new reflection made it clear to me that by identifying with the roles of both Good Boy and Outsider so early I had inadvertently drawn unwanted attention to myself. When I had stepped into the sanctuary of our garden, for example, the neighbours' boys had bombarded me with wasp-cored apples to drive the bone-collecting misfit back indoors. And when my mother had sat me on the lawn in an upturned-table-and-sheet-topped covered wagon for a Pioneer Lunch, these same fruit-flingers had hit me with spit and stones, issuing such threats that I had found myself too frightened to face my Sloppy Joes, Skedaddle Spuds or Buckaroo Baked Beans.

In turn, my earliest memories of school had been of interminable brutality – violence no doubt exacerbated by an instinctive sensibility that had been most obviously exposed by my fascination with naked ancient Greeks. Of course my talk of an imaginary friend named Henry, who hovered in the corner with an untrimmed beard and elongated red tan shoes, could not have helped my cause. Nor the admission that in my bedroom I bred albino gerbils, stick insects, butterflies and frogs. Or that my grandmother could forecast storms, claimed to commune with dead relations and start fires without matches.

The daily kicks and thumps, the cruelty of scornful names, the repeated spoiling of my homework, the stampings on my feet that had eventually broken bones, had left me with feelings of such intensity that they had often proved too great to bear.

In response, that boy, so soon in conflict with the world into which he was expected to advance, had learnt the role of Victim. To quell his curiosity, still his voice, erase his smile and drop his eyes. To creep through corridors, skulk behind the toilet block or keep cover in the long grass beyond the cricket pitch at playtime. And once back home, to hide in the bedroom wardrobe and press his sobs into the muffling drape of clothes, in secret hope that he might one day escape his life by tumbling into Narnia to live with Mr Tumnus in the daytime and Prince Caspian at night.

So there it was. The truth of the *jhankri*'s words and the trio of related roles I had unwittingly adopted were now quite clear: the Good Boy, the Outsider and the Victim. Three labels to which I had unthinkingly adhered for over twenty years, even as they had deadened my senses, fed my fears and rendered me compliant. Three roles by which I had constructed an artificial self that had left me so discontented with who I seemed to be, my body and my choices, that I had too often been engulfed by dangerous self-loathing.

'Now do you see?' Kushal Magar's voice gently interrupted, as though my thoughts had played before him in full cinematic clarity. 'Be attentive to the roles by which you live, brother, and choose them well. For ultimately, you will become whatever you identify yourself to be.'

LXIII

Space is everywhere; it is the foundation of all.
Tripura Rahasya

'So if the real me is not the roles I have adopted,' I asked, determined not to leave this subject until I had secured a concise reply, 'then who – or what – am I?'

Kushal Magar's response was yet another smile. Perhaps it was too plain to see that for all the years of academic study and my pretensions of an open mind, my heart had been conditioned to seek a creditable creed – an easy list of truths and falsehoods, rights and wrongs, dos and don'ts.

'Consider *ka*, the Sanskrit word for not only "splendour", "light", "joy" and "pleasure", but also the name given to the space between earth and sky, planets, mountains, trees and people,' he offered in baffling reply.

Despite the apparent tangent we were now pursuing, Kushal Magar had my attention, for one of the very few details I had retained from compulsory double physics was the startling fact that at an atomic level, less than one billionth of our physical form is measurable material. In fact, the closer science looked at our fundamental building blocks, the less was found. Matter was insubstantial. Atoms were just electron clouds around a nucleus. Particles were just energy interactions – waves, charges, vibrations. The rest was only the space that lay between.

In terms of the *jhankri*'s teaching, I could therefore confidently state that he and I, and the ground on which we sat, were indeed more *ka* than anything else. More like a thought than any solid object.

'*Ka* also describes the gap between stimulus and reaction,' he continued, 'a gap the Tradition teaches us to widen, that we might free ourselves from destructive, self-limiting behaviour.'

Another new paradigm of unimagined possibility.

'So are you saying that the real me is nothing more than the "space between"?' I pressed. 'That the real me is merely *ka*?'

'Would that change the way you see yourself and your version of the world?' he asked. 'Would that enable you to live and love more fully, freely or fearlessly? Without detriment to yourself or others?'

He tipped his head.

'Because after all,' he added with a smile, 'what else really matters?'

LXIV

That 'I' is not my real self.
Rabindranath Tagore

'But,' I persisted, 'if the real me is neither my external appearance, nor my impermanent personality, nor the roles I've adopted – and if all that's really left is the space between – then what am I? A waft of ether? A puff of smoke? Or just a breath of fresh air?'

'The *you* you seek is not something or someone found if sought with sufficient diligence,' Kushal Magar replied, unresponsive to my effort at a joke. 'For your true self is but one expression of universal consciousness made active through energy.'

'Like bees and trees and stars.' I nodded at a concept that I still resisted, despite it evidently being at the very heart of Kushal Magar's understanding of himself, the world and his place in it.

'All the same consciousness, all the same energy,' he replied, 'their union expressed through illimitable forms.'

He paused to watch my eyes intently, as he so often did, as though reading my every thought.

The fact was my culture had raised me to conceive of energy as a single, universal force that could be neither created nor destroyed; a force that could be neither claimed as 'mine' or 'his' or anybody else's, nor designated 'good' or 'bad' for it possessed no innate moral quality of its own. Yet still I struggled with the notion of consciousness as an equivalent, essential and all-pervading reality.

'Perhaps it helps to think of a flock of birds at dusk,' he ventured unexpectedly, 'switching this way and that in complex patterns and yet seeming to move as though with one intellect, even able to navigate the vastness of the skies as if a single, self-sustaining whole.'

I nodded, remembering seaside starlings reeling about piers where I had passed numerous sunlit rock-pool, windy-picnic holidays.

'Well, humankind functions in much the same way, for like those birds we too affect each other's personal, and thereby our collective, behaviour. We also move in complex patterns, in sympathetic response to our environment and one another. It is a fact that leads humankind through repeating waves of self-induced chaos, order and again chaos; development, decline and again development, throughout the recurring tides of history.'

I recognised in his description of sympathetic response the way in which biological systems develop features: morphogenesis. The way cells are alike at the outset, then adapt their behaviour and structure to one another, until increasingly intricate organisms arise. Evolution through interaction. Order from disorder. Dynamic, disparate life from inanimate dust. Heart cells co-ordinating to stabilise the organ's essential beat. Pigment cells responding to create the configuration of a tiger's stripe.

Likewise, fractal geometry: identical shapes replicating at ever smaller scales into infinity to form the structure of trees and lungs, blood vessels and broccoli. Cloud and wave, lightning and snowflake. The geography of canyon and peak, shoreline and sand dune. All the wonders of the cosmos in their boundless complexity and diversity – including us – all derived from the very simplest of rules.

And of course, even the atoms we are made of are not our own. They came into being millions of years ago in the nebula – that vast cloud of cosmic dust and gas which collapsed to form our solar system. Every one of our atoms has, therefore, already been something or someone else: many other men, women, sparrows, elephants, trees, the rain, the stars.

Nor are they ours for our lifetime, for atoms are in a constant state of flux. In fact, at an atomic level some 98 per cent of our bodies is not what 'we' were even one year ago. We are constantly merging, mixing with the world we think stays on the outside; mingling, interacting with the universe we mistakenly believe lies beyond our skin.

At every moment, we are breathing in each other, rubbing off – until with each time we say farewell and go our separate ways, we are all less who we thought we were and more each other.

LXV

With one meaning, they are the same thing,
the Absolute, the cosmos, all that moves and all
that does not move.

Jñanasankalini Tantra

With a tilt of his head to indicate that I should follow him, Kushal Magar and I stepped between chickens, marigolds and spinach, to stand together at the very edge of his garden.

The valley's breadth before us was immense, its hazy depths delineated only by the gilded furrow of a distant river. Its borders a chaotic collage of step-cut fields and empty paddy. The darkness of unscathed jungle. A scattering of tidy cottages. And high above, the blue sky soared from the forest-darkened hills on which we stood to the summits of snow-bleached Himalaya beyond.

'You might prefer to imagine boundaries – limits between you and me and "them" and "that" and all of this – but in truth, there are none,' he declared, placing his left hand on the centre of my back. 'Do you see, brother? The *you* you seek is this.'

I closed my eyes and put aside my usual slurry of assumptions that I might hear his words more clearly.

'All that I have taught and all that I will teach is but to guide you to fearlessly embrace yourself and your life in all its fullness. And this by recognising that you are not your external appearance or personality. You are not your social or familial roles. You are not your thoughts, your emotional responses or your mind.'

I nodded. This I could understand.

'Your true nature lies beyond all such differentiations, for all matter is energy and consciousness. And all energy and consciousness are but forms of light,' he said, placing his right hand against my heart, as though in a gesture of support. 'Your true self and my true self, the mountains and the sunshine are not separate. The universe and the individual are one and the same. It is only the limitations of man's self-interest that afford the illusion of separation.'

I breathed in deeply, almost as though to inhale the place where we stood so that I might better perceive what he professed to be our essential union.

I then mindfully exhaled all my reserve, all ordinary perception of my boundaries – of flesh and skin, of inner and outer, self and other.

'*Aung aham-idam-idam-aham*,' Kushal Magar intoned beside me. 'I am all this – all this is me.'

'*Aung aham-idam-idam-aham*,' I repeated into an infinite, horizonless expanse of which, in that bright moment, I could suddenly conceive that all that is and was and will be were but an indivisible expression.

'The self for whom you seek, brother, is this,' I seemed to hear him whisper. 'For you and me – and everything – are but limitless sky.'

LXVI

The power of knowing all is not externally attained,
but resides within.
Paratrimshika

I heard Samuel's laughter long before I saw him.

I had been so enraptured, standing on both the garden's brink and what seemed the very limits of an entirely other sense of being, that I had not noticed Kushal Magar withdraw to rekindle his fire. With eyes still shut, I focused on the sound of ginger root and peppercorns pulping on his grindstone. And then the rush of water as he filled the old charred pot.

I resisted peering back into the day's last light a little longer, relishing the loss of any sense of time or place or person that I had been unexpectedly afforded. For in that moment I had known in myself a new reality. A different truth. The radical discovery that man, nature and who or what we might wish to name 'god' are indistinguishable. Perhaps even that the resolution of all our conflicts and imagined mysteries may ultimately be found in the awareness of this unity.

And there, an insight more than mere cerebral analysis or wishful fantasy: that beyond corporeal elements, beyond the mind, that which I am is boundless. A self in which the universe is reflected.

But even more than this, I had found within me a certain joy – instinctive, without rational or external cause – that brought with it a sense of freedom that I had never known. As though this bliss were, just as Kushal Magar had once said, inherent.

Samuel's laughter provoked a caw of crows, prompting

me finally to open my eyes and gaze again at the sky and river valley that had, in some inscrutable way, enabled me to know myself beyond the limits of my limbs.

I turned to find, still far off, a miniature version of my cousin dawdling down the rough rock steps that rendered the hillside traversable. I focused on his figure as he paused to offer hand, arm, then shoulder to a nimble companion I could not identify.

'Come, brother,' Kushal Magar called, indicating that I should press through radish leaf and potato top, to join him at his tea.

I breathed the valley air again, then wandered back to the promise of sweet, milky spices. Yet even as I took my usual place before the fire and felt the familiar heat of the beaker between my palms, even as I looked into the face of a man I had in some ways grown to love, everything had changed.

It was more than the lightness in my step, or the brightness of the colours. I felt different in myself. About myself. No longer did sky and air terminate at my clothing. No longer did I finish at my skin.

'The knowledge you have gained today is sunlight with which to illuminate your darkness,' Kushal Magar said, as he sat down beside me. 'Knowledge that can, if you so choose, liberate you from the disservice of self-interest. For in glimpsing life's essential unity, you might know empathy in its fullness, and thereby a new, practical compassion, both for yourself and others.'

'But how do I keep this feeling?' I asked, my analytical mind already interjecting.

'Feelings are a reality only for the moments that they linger in our chemistry. It is the way we choose to respond to their ephemeral impulse that enables them to leave their mark on us and on our world – whether for betterment or for harm.'

Samuel and his companion had momentarily vanished into trees on their descent. Yet still I could hear his laughter.

'A man with self-knowledge beyond his bones, beyond his learnt reactions to life's essential unpredictability, no longer identifies himself by transitory feelings. A man with such self-knowledge can feel more acutely and more honestly, for he is free.'

'Then I asked the wrong question,' I conceded. 'I should have asked what am I now to do with this new insight?'

'Live your life with less self-interest and greater self-respect. In this way you will learn to love more freely, fully, wisely and without condition. Speaking of which . . .'

I followed the fading intonation of his voice to the sight of Samuel's advance along the final span of path. My cousin seemed in no great rush to join us, yet waved, whilst beaming through his cheeks' bright flush.

The movement of a limb behind him revealed a glimpse of the companion he had kept so well hidden in his wake. Not until they reached the tidy lines of marigold-filled pots did a smiling face appear to offer a respectful, '*Namaskar buwa!*' to Kushal Magar and a 'Hello, *dajoo!*' to me.

The college term was over.

The *jhankri*'s daughter had come home.

PART SEVEN

LXVII

That which removes sorrow should be considered the highest good.
Tripura Rahasya

Samuel was as radiant as the new day's sunlight.

After our evening meal the night before, we three men had made our usual beds beneath the stars, whilst Jai Kumari had spent the night inside the wooden hut.

For the first time, I had been the earliest to wake, my head brightly alight in marvel at the previous day's lessons. Whilst my companions and the chickens had remained asleep, I had watched the planet's spin turn night to dawn, pondering the remarkable fact that my own modest frame, mind and senses were expressions of the same boundless universe into the very heart of which I seemed to stare.

A busy morning had followed, the four of us together sharing chores. But now midday had passed. Samuel was picking grit from rice with listless inattention as Jai Kumari ground roasted sesame and coriander seeds with lemon peel and chillies. She talked of heightening tensions in Darjeeling as she worked – spreading strikes and angry threats, violent protests and rumours of gun-running – which I only partially understood.

I tended to the fire, bundling cornhusks and breaking

twigs, pretending not to notice that Jai Kumari's quiet confidence and easy wit left Samuel flushed and breathless. I smiled as they laughed together through what could easily have been the tireless, natural banter of devoted siblings. These two were undoubtedly well suited.

I turned to scrubbing soil from miniature potatoes, and scolded myself that I had been so involved in my insatiable hunger to pursue new learning that I had not noticed Samuel's discovery of a new emotional landscape of his own.

I had also not noticed that Kushal Magar had left us whilst we prepared an evening meal's *daal bhat*, *tarkari* and *aloo achar*. When eventually I asked, Jai Kumari told me that he had climbed the long, steep path to the cave temples. However, I had not seen him leave and puzzled that he would slip away in silence, with neither word of farewell nor explanation.

Once food was cooked and scarlet temple, hut and breath suffused with seasoning, Jai Kumari invited me to carry a well-packed set of tiffin tins to her father in the hillside sanctuary. There would be more than enough, she assured me, for both of us to share.

'But go quickly, brother,' Samuel called, as I began my climb, 'before the jackals wake up hungry and have to choose between our *bhaini* sister's cooking and your sweet white shins!'

We all three laughed – but still I felt a new unease that sped my step until I broke the tree-line and reached the Lapu road.

LXVIII

There are some things one can only achieve
by a deliberate leap in the opposite direction.
Franz Kafka

The village was curiously quiet as I passed along its empty, dusty thoroughfare.

I wondered whether it was the talk of growing troubles that had driven every family to settle so soon behind bamboo wattle and cow-pat daub. Only itchy dogs and chickens in their final dusk-lit fossick revealed the cosy domesticity that lay behind each cottage wall.

Despite the sudden chill, my brow moistened as I forged up the final incline to the temples' threshold. In the forest, the last light slipped from between the trees as I sought for any signs of dangerous dogs returning to nocturnal life. But nothing moved. Squirrels, tragopans and babblers were already settled in their nests. Even the grumpy rhesus monkeys had gathered their fuzz-faced babies into the protection of a sleepy communal embrace and had fallen silent.

I removed my shoes and socks, sounded the bell and winced at the chill of courtyard stone. I scanned the looming rock-face for signs of firelight, but found nothing more than shadow. I sniffed the air for wood smoke, but found nothing beyond the sweet mould of forest humus and the distinctive fusty damp of trees.

'*Jhankri-dajoo?*' I hissed, for fear my voice would disrespect that peculiar enchantment found only in a woodland dusk. 'Jai Kumari's sent your food!'

I padded forwards to seek lamplight in any of the crags

and caves that breached the granite thrust that rose beside me. But all was dark.

I was almost ready to assume that I had missed him and commence a hurried descent, when a throaty grunt close by my feet caused me to flinch.

'*Dajoo!*' I exclaimed in relief that I had stumbled upon a *jhankri* and not a jackal. I bent to place the tiffin on the ground to find that Kushal Magar was not seated, as I had assumed, but slumped. He smelled of urine.

'Are you hurt?' I gasped. 'Are you sick?'

I moved to feel his forehead, but he pulled away with a growl of protest and wildly thrashing limbs.

'*Bando ko chaak!*' he bellowed, suddenly lunging at me as though to grasp the manhood in my trousers.

I recoiled and stumbled back against the cold, wet stone. His words were not only vicious and offensive, pronouncing me the least attractive aspect of simian anatomy, but slurred and strongly scented.

'*Bando ko chaak!*' he spat again, menacing me with staring, reddened eyes, before again lunging at my crotch.

I pushed him off and pulled away, but could not speak.

I could not think.

Kushal Magar – the wise and gentle teacher, in whom I had placed my confidence, and even perhaps my every hope – was heavily, grotesquely drunk.

LXVIX

We read the world wrong and say that it deceives us.
Rabindranath Tagore

My confusion overwhelmed me.

I clasped the entrance arch with both hands, nauseous, trembling, unable to decide what I should do. The hurt and fury I felt bore down so hard that every breath constricted to a strained, asthmatic rasp.

The man whom I had grown to trust without reserve, to whose well-being I would have dedicated myself had he but asked, was now lying behind me in the darkness, foul-mouthed, ugly and inebriated.

I slammed my fists against the post in rage.

How dare he display such pathetic human frailty and excess! How dare he shatter my trust not only in him, but in the integrity of the Tradition! For in one moment, the man in whom I believed with all my heart had revealed himself no different to the innumerable chicken-*gurus*, hotel-*swamis* and hypocritical priests against whom he himself had advised.

So what did that make me? Another naive Westerner, so eager to be 'enlightened' by the mystic wisdom of the exotic East that I would cling to anyone who mumbled mantras and spouted consciousness and liberation? Another self-seeking foreigner, whose fantasy of some spiritual quest was just a further expression of my own culture's endemic hedonism?

I turned back to look at the fallen figure now making intermittent burbles in the blackness and felt a ferocious anger rise in me that I had allowed myself not only to be deceived, but that I had humiliated myself by affording this man the role of exemplary friend and teacher.

My impulse was to denounce him in the very place where he had once taught me *yamas* and *niyamas*. To turn away and leave him to his pitiable drunken squalor and find my own way back through the jackal-hunted forest.

But then I paused.

This did not fit.

Far below me on the hillside was a young man I knew and loved, who had repeatedly proven that his instincts into the true nature of a person were so acute as to be uncanny. Samuel would not tolerate, nor in any way be party to, such deceit.

Likewise, Kushal Magar had only ever shown fraternal care and generosity from the moment we had met. I knew him to be honourable and self-disciplined – and not a drunkard.

Even if he were, it was not for me to stand in judgement because of my own bruised pride, to reject him because of my own thwarted expectations. Rather, whatever his private conflicts or secret habits, and whatever their expression, it was for me to summon my own humanity and offer assistance in his plight, if only to watch over and protect him until dawn restored sobriety.

I crouched and leant against the entrance arch to ensure my composure. Only then did I stand again and make my way back to the drunken figure on the floor – to find him gone.

Alarmed, I searched the courtyard, but it was empty. Even the tiffin tins had vanished from their spot. I peered towards the forest's margin, but in such darkness that I could no longer discern the trees.

Looking back to scan the rock-face, my eyes were drawn

to a subtle glow of lamplight that had only now begun to flicker deep within a crevice.

I tiptoed up and peered in.

Kushal Magar was sitting with his hands resting quietly in his lap, his eyes closed and face becalmed. The dinner Jai Kumari had intended us to share was laid before him in neat display.

I slipped into the narrow cave without a word, leaning over him to smell for alcohol and urine.

'Welcome, brother,' he said with clear and steady speech. 'No need to sniff. All that is left outside.'

'But *jhankri-dajoo!*' I stammered.

'You have once again proven to yourself that you are a worthy student,' he announced.

I stared at him in dismay.

'And this,' he added, opening one eye to peer at me with cheerful kindness, 'even after I twice called you a monkey's bottom.'

LXX

Where the old tracks are lost,
new country is revealed with its wonders.
Rabindranath Tagore

My astonishment had turned to relief and laughter.

Kushal Magar chuckled too, reassured, it seemed to me, that I had passed this latest initiation. He offered to pour water from a bottle to rinse my fingers, then indicated that I should tuck into the dinner Jai Kumari had prepared. It felt like a reward.

'So what was all that for?' I asked, hungrily mushing lentils, rice and potato pickle into a mouth-sized ball.

'To enable you to prove to yourself that your compassion is greater than both your anger and your disappointment at what you first perceived to be my failure,' he replied. 'You have shown yourself ready for yet new learning.'

I watched him deftly gather spicy vegetables with his right hand, and wondered what might have happened had I not turned back at the temple gate.

'Must all your students endure the "drunken teacher" test?' I asked. 'Which was very convincing, by the way.'

'Not necessarily,' he replied with a smile. 'Some are instructed to refrain from meat, then find their teacher chewing on a strip of pork fat. Others, to abstain from all sexual stimulation, only to find their teacher' – he made an unambiguous action with his hand – 'as you might imagine.'

He again tucked into the vegetables and pickle, whilst I gave silent thanks that, considering his last example, I had escaped relatively lightly.

'Of course, this is nothing compared to the old *lamas* of the Tibetan form of the Tradition,' he revealed, 'who have been known to thrash, scald and exhaust their students. Even urinating on them and beating their poor penises with stones!'

We both looked up from our food to wince at one other.

'Many students could not tolerate such abuse – or bruises – and would limp off in disgust. It was only the rare few who would remain, and thus prove themselves ready for whatever challenging lessons the teacher had yet to impart.'

He pushed the tin of lentils towards me with the back of

his hand to indicate that I was welcome to finish them, but I declined. My appetite was sated.

Instead, I leant back against the cold cave wall, stared into the gutter of the lamplight in the *linga* niche and wondered for what new lessons I had unwittingly declared myself prepared.

LXXI

We must always change, renew, rejuvenate ourselves, otherwise we harden.
Johann von Goethe

'Are we staying here tonight?' I asked in surprise.

Kushal Magar had begun to unroll blankets I had not noticed tucked behind him.

'After such a meal, the body needs rest,' he casually replied, handing me a thick woollen bundle of my own that was lightly greasy to the touch and smelled of lanolin.

'Do Jai Kumari and Samuel know we won't be back?'

Kushal Magar offered nothing more than a tip of his head in response. He was busy removing a familiar collection of knotted cloths and little tins from his bag, one of which revealed a colour-stained figure of the elephant-headed god of new beginnings.

'Ganesha *puja* at night?' I asked. 'Before we sleep?'

'A reminder to be receptive to new learning. To choose freedom from all those ordinary thoughts and assumptions through which we normally experience the world – and ourselves.'

'But we've only ever used the symbolism of Ganesha at first light,' I declared, 'when determining the new day's intention.'

'You think wisdom may only be learnt in sunshine?' was all he offered in reply.

Kushal Magar placed the clay figure in an empty niche and indicated with a jut of his chin that I was to light a mustard oil lamp. Together we repeated the Ganesha mantra he had previously taught me. He marked the miniature elephantine forehead with crimson *sidur* pigment, then marked the pale pink breadth of mine.

He touched his heart, then reached forwards to place a palm against my chest. He looked into my eyes, as though making one last imperative appraisal, and took from the pocket of his heavy winter waistcoat a length of thick, black cloth.

'So are you ready, brother?' he asked. 'Are you willing for new wisdom?'

LXXII

One does not discover new lands
without consenting to lose sight of the shore.
André Gide

'*Jhankri-dajoo*, are you there?'
I had opened my eyes to blackness and lay quite still. I strained to listen for any sign of life through the thick wrap of cloth around my ears – but could hear nothing. For a moment I thought I caught the muffled

sound of birdsong, but could not be sure as it did not last.

When I had agreed to have my eyes bound before I went to sleep, I had not anticipated that I would also limit my hearing to little more than the rumble of my circulatory system and my sinuses' internal whistle.

I stretched out my hands towards the rough rock walls to confirm my bearings, then felt for Kushal Magar's bedding. Both it and he were gone.

I slipped from my blanket and on all fours aimed for the entrance of the cave. I twice knocked my head before I could finally feel the moistness of a new morning's breeze against my skin.

'*Jhankri-dajoo?*' I called again. 'Are you there?'

I cautiously turned back to explore the cave, where I discovered the water bottle and took a swig. I also found a feast of four small oranges beside a tin containing *puri* breads; a paper twist of fiercesome salted chillies; and a foil-wrapped pack of *aloo achar* potato pickle. Someone had only recently delivered them. The *puris* were still warm.

I sat back on my bedding to undertake my usual morning *sadhana* of mantra and mindful breathing to afford new mental focus. I followed this with the dedication of my day to *Ahimsa*'s principle of non-harm to myself or others. Only then did I begin my breakfast, clumsily stuffing *puris* with spiced potato and failing to judge what I had meant to be the merest smear of tongue-numbing *dalle khursani* chilli.

I found myself overeating to make up for the lack of company, and had to remind myself that this apparent madness had a purpose. In fact, as Kushal Magar and I had settled down to sleep the night before, he had described how higher in the hills some students required no blindfolds for this *Tapa* practice. Instead, their teachers placed them in caves so deep and dark that they had neither sound nor light for orientation or solace. Some were even reported to remain in sensory deprivation for as many as six weeks at a time – a custom he considered not only an excess, but in direct contradiction to the principle of *Ahimsa*. As he had insisted, such an extended period of isolation and withdrawal could too easily prove detrimental to both physical and mental well-being, even for the most hardy and well prepared.

'Why then, *jhankri-dajoo*,' I had had to ask, 'are you doing this to me?'

'Your time will not be so long,' he had offered in reassurance. 'If willing, you'll keep your eyes bound in bed, so that you awake in darkness. And as such you will remain until the following morning – or the next day – or perhaps a day or two after that, when you will be invited to remove it with the sunrise.'

'But for what purpose?'

'That you might experience a reduction of the external stimuli by which, at every moment of your waking hours, your mind remains transfixed. A reduction of the stimuli on which you depend to think your ordinary thoughts, to speak your ordinary words, to repeat all your ordinary habitual patterns by which you normally determine who and what you are.'

So here I had been left alone, uncomfortable, unsettled – and wondering whether if family and friends were to know that I had travelled so far after a year's hard work and sacrifice, only to sit inside a mountain in solitary darkness, they would call me mad?

Perhaps I was.

And Kushal Magar too.

LXXIII

Love! when you come with the burning lamp of pain in your
hand, I can see your face and know you as bliss.
Rabindranath Tagore

As the hours passed, it was not darkness that closed tight around my mind and chest, but an acute and painful loneliness that I had not acknowledged since my boyhood.

Such was its refusal to diminish that I again braved the entrance to the cave on hands and knees to listen for the possibility of an approach, for surely Kushal Magar or Samuel would soon check on me with a delivery of fresh food and water.

This set me thinking of the people I had left behind across those figurative Seven Rivers. Siblings and their children to whom I was a distant, barely known uncle. My plethora of English cousins, once childhood playmates, now changed by the passing of the years into adult strangers. The friends, once treasured, intimate companions, who had come and gone, and were now mostly blurred by time's indifference into virtual anonymity.

With neither sound nor sight to dissuade me from the passage of my thoughts, I drifted back into the tangle of lips and limbs through which I had gradually matured from boy to man and learnt my way of loving. It had proved a slow, demanding lesson and one I only now acknowledged had been realised as much through deceit as through devotion.

These re-materialising phantoms I now assembled into a list of names, of real faces, and found to my surprise that there were some whose imagined eyes I could not meet in recognition of both pain inflicted and pain endured. And in so doing, I recalled with unsettling precision contrasting legacies of both emboldening self-confidence and emasculating self-doubt, resentment and remorse, the echoes of which still lingered and retained their influence.

However, it was perhaps the enforced darkness that afforded new clarity, enabling me to see for the first time that there was no real blame to assign. We had all been clumsy innocents, misinterpreting our maddening draught of youthful hormones as nothing less than true and lasting love.

Of course our errors had been imprudent, the hurt we had caused unwise. But I could now see that such mistakes had been entirely natural and no less worthy of forgiveness than the repeated tumbles taken when we each had learnt to walk. There was, therefore, neither guilt to pamper nor bitterness to bear.

Indeed, for the first time I could clearly see that for all the pain and folly, in truth my life had been enriched by the loves that had been lost. And that all had had their place in what Kushal Magar called the lifelong, sunlit path to wisdom.

LXXIV

Those that have expanded vision see the light everywhere.
Thirumandiram

I awoke gasping from vivid, fierce dreams of labyrinths of locking and unlocking doors. Each unpredictable unfastening had revealed infinite regiments of men and women who, in rhythmic unison, had removed perpetual layers of clothes, their fingers, teeth and faces.

However, whether I had slept an hour, a day, or one whole night, I could not tell. Without my sight and with hearing muffled, I had lost all sense of time. Traversing the fathoms of my mind's immeasurable marine, I had begun to feel myself almost dangerously adrift.

I rolled on to all fours and made my way towards the entrance of the cave. I suddenly craved sunlight, the sight of trees, the song of birds. Any stimulation beyond the senses of my skin. Any interaction beyond the ramblings of what had started to seem the unravelling of my reason.

I doubted I could play this game much longer, bound in darkness and alone.

This unconstructive thought provoked a surge of claustrophobia of such force that I grasped the cloth around my head in readiness to liberate my ears and eyes.

But then I thought of Kushal Magar. The constant kindness of his eyes. The unfaltering compassion of his voice. The unfailing devotion he had shown to me in his role as my Bright Being.

I dropped my hands to hug my knees, to steady the fitful measure of my breath, until I was prepared to stare back into the restless, starless cosmos of my mind.

I first determined that my fear was more than merely for my safety, for I was certain that jackals, snakes and bears would keep their distance, whilst tigers – if any had survived the years of unchecked poaching – would rarely venture to this altitude.

Rather, the fear I fought in my sightless, near soundless state was of finally facing myself and thereby meeting the emptiness that so frequently consumed me. The grief retained for errors made and loved ones lost. The despair that I had so long wrestled with and yet denied. The conceit through which I deceived myself that no one else could really understand, nor ever truly know the complexity or measure of my self-defeating doubts.

I pushed my chin hard into my knees. I deplored my tendency to self-pitying passivity. And this when I had been introduced to the Tradition as a means whereby I might become the most effective and contented I could be. A method that in time might set me free, with will and effort, from the limitations of the mindless thought and action that I had unwittingly adopted as my ordinary habit.

And what of the momentary insight I had known on the garden's brink, when I had acknowledged a self unconfined by conditioning or form? A self inseparable from that sudden, blissful spate of unreasoned joy?

How long, then, before I truly grasped the opportunity to make that choice to change? Finally to choose *sukha* – a balanced, prosperous, liberating life, wholly 'happy from within' – over my usual choice of *dukha*'s 'constriction around the heart'?

How long before, for all my good intentions, I finally chose a life of wisdom, compassion and integrity, devoid of limiting self-interested indulgence? For had not Kushal Magar's teaching only ever meant to guide me to choose to free myself from what he had defined as the principal origins of mankind's collective fears, frustrations, anxieties and suffering?

First, our mistaken sense of separation, inaccurately imagining there exists a distinction between ourselves and our fellow man, nature and the cosmos.

Second, the erroneous belief that the impermanence of our senses, learnt emotional responses, physical appearance, material possessions or social status define who or what we are.

Third, the fiction – largely propagated by patriarchal hierarchies for their profit – that there exists a difference between the self and the 'divine', whether in the form of our culturally determined notions of a god or some abstract Universal Power to which we are beholden, and by which our wishes may be fulfilled, our 'sins' forgiven, our destiny ultimately determined.

And last, the misguided notion that we must each seek our own 'salvation' by any ritual, priest or creed.

I ran through these four now familiar concepts again and heard the calm of Kushal Magar's voice recount them. And in the seclusion of that silent, sooty cave determined I would find my way to truly live this learning, that I might at last dispel my fear of loss, my fear of both success and failure, my fear of what was and what might yet be.

And this that I might finally choose freedom from the misgivings I held about myself, by which my life had been long injured, my mind diminished, and my capacity to live and love fully, fearlessly, wisely and without condition so unreasonably restrained.

LXXV

The mind is the cause of both bondage and liberation.
Tripura Rahasya

I had been vividly, violently dreaming again. Or so it seemed, although I was certain I had remained awake.

I had found myself shouting out in panic as the internal, lightless night into which I stared had revealed in full holographic solidity my 'demons': disquieting mirages that lingered far beyond their customary term, even as my open eyes blinked within the blackness of my blindfold.

Was this, I thought, a taste of madness?

To settle my panting I reached out to find the solidity of walls and floor, and checked the wrap around my head was firmly in place. I needed to confirm that my nightmares were not the corporeal realities they seemed.

Yet still the fierce ghosts of my past, the distorted self-image of my present, lingered in the periphery of my vision.

I told myself I understood, at least in part, the psychological process I was undergoing. Sensory deprivation had been employed with purpose throughout the history of humankind. In the solitude of caves, cells and mountain-tops, generations of mystics and prophets had imagined self-originating revelations to be gifts from their version of the divine. In truth, I knew the lack of external sensory stimulation was simply amplifying the imagery within my mind, my subconscious now playing out before me as though externally projected.

I was, then, learning for myself an obvious, yet no less remarkable, truth: my version of reality was solely determined by my own memories, beliefs and metaphors. That even in my ordinary life, this normally unnoticed background noise of collected fears and griefs, neuroses, assumptions and self-doubts was directing my perception.

It was a fact that Kushal Magar had been careful to explain on completion of our last Ganesha *puja*, that I might be prepared for any likely provocations resulting from the blindfold.

'Brother, we have talked before about the filter we each set in place from our earliest years,' he had begun. 'The filter of *samskaras*, as we call them – acquired ideas, beliefs, guilt, pain and emotional responses we gather through attachment to the past, and through which we for ever identify ourselves and thereby experience the external world. Do you remember?'

I had – but had also known I did not yet fully grasp its meaning.

'Even what you call the "mind" is simply an accumulation of such *samskaras*. A series of learnt parameters we project on to a reality that is by nature limitless, and that can thereby lead to chronic inhibitions, habits, phobias, addictions and even illnesses – until we no longer see life as it is, but rather only as *we* are.'

'But I don't want a partial, blunted life that is only a limited reflection of my own history and neuroses!' I had protested. 'I choose an abundant life of unlimited thought, unlimited awareness, unlimited possibility!'

'It is this desire in you that confirms your readiness for the *abhinaddha diksha*,' he had announced, raising the thick, black cloth towards me, 'the "blindfold initiation" by which you might know for yourself the *samskaras* through which you perceive your world. For by removing ordinary, external distractions, the nature of your fears and obsessions will be revealed with greater clarity, exposing the petty cycles of thought and unmindful reaction by which you normally identify yourself – and thereby live your life.'

Only now, after all these long, dark hours at the mercy of my own, self-induced commotion, had I begun to understand his promise.

'But what of new *samskaras*?' I had asked, for it was obvious that the amassing of impressions and memories would never cease until my final breath. Therefore what I interpreted as my experience of life threatened always to remain merely a series of repeated reactions to my biography.

'Herein lies an opportunity for new wisdom,' he had assured me. 'Learn from your past and seek out uplifting, enlightening memories with which to replace the adverse and the obsolete.'

I had thought of the media, on which I largely depended for my underlying view of reality, with its predominantly cynical and sensationalist version of the world. Of films and books I had indiscriminately allowed to flood my mind with disproportionate extremes of banality and sentimentality, cruelty and destruction. What new and unconstructive *samskaras*, then, was I unwittingly choosing to amass?

'Maintain the *sadhana* you are learning,' Kushal Magar had advised in conclusion. 'Remain attentive to your choices. And in time you will find you no longer identify yourself solely through the compulsive, learnt reactions to which you were once attached, but will be able finally to know the freedom of choosing to push wide the boundaries, to live honestly, abundantly, joyfully – "by daylight".'

LXXVI

Give what cannot be taken.
Idries Shah

I had been practising a series of *bija* 'seed sounds' Kushal
Magar had taught me, exploring subtle shifts of sensation
and awareness with each change in *hasta mudra* hand
position, when I suddenly become aware of the scent of
ginger and garlic, cardamom and black pepper in the
closeness of the cave.

'*Jhankri-dajoo?*' I called out. 'Samuel? Are you there?'

I strained to listen for any sound. But all was still.

I stretched out my numb crossed legs and stumbled
towards the entrance with as much haste as I dared, hitting
head and shoulder on the uneven walls before I tumbled out
into the open.

But whoever had delivered my provisions had already
slipped away.

'How much longer?' I cried out towards the trees and
temple courtyard. 'Please, just tell me how much longer!'

I waited. But received nothing in reply.

I slumped back into the cave and grumpily felt for the
new supply of tiffin tins. I opened one to inhale the sweet,
straw-like scent of hot rice, and suddenly found myself in
tears, for I had realised that this simple food bore within
its preparation and delivery a priceless gift – a gift that has
the power to comfort, cheer and even change us: the sure
knowledge that out in that vast, tumultuous, inscrutable
world, there is someone who is on our side.

There is somebody who cares.

LXXVII

*Like the centre of a cloudless sky, the self-luminous mind is
impossible to express . . . like the moon on water.*
Lodro Thaye

I lost count of the times I roused myself by shouts and
tears from what could only have been '*samskaric*' visions.
Occasionally I woke from foetal sleep, huddled tight
beneath the blanket. But mostly, I found myself sitting
upright and wide awake, despite the disorientating surreality
that rioted through my head.

Between these real and imagined 'sleeps', I contemplated
my internal version of the world that played behind the
blindfold: the memories and impressions by which I
unwittingly experienced my ordinary, outer life.

This demented flux of thoughts often proved distressing.
In order to prevent myself from tearing off the blindfold
in what at times still threatened to become claustrophobic
panic, I continued to explore the range of techniques I had
been taught by Kushal Magar.

To dissipate the unhelpful emotional responses, for
example, I would sit comfortably on my blanket and observe
the pattern of each breath as it ascended and descended
between my navel and my throat; my perineum and pubic
bone; my hands and heart; between the sensory 'switchboard'
thalamus at the very centre of my brain and the open space
beyond my forehead.

I would watch without analysis or attachment as thoughts
emerged and just as fleetingly dissolved.

I would then experiment with what Kushal Magar
called *Unmesha* – the opening of the eye: the 'blossoming'

or 'expansion' of consciousness. This required that I focused on the gaps between my thoughts, which normally passed unnoticed. I would then lengthen these momentary pauses, creating ever greater space not only between the thoughts themselves, but between their varied stimuli and my learnt responses to them.

I would explore visualising internal *yantras*, each one a geometric shape associated with a traditional *mahabhut* or 'element'. These I would then apply to my body as a means to stabilise the workings of my mind, focusing thought to remarkable effect, whilst guiding me to relax my grasp on a perception based solely on the limits of my senses.

First, I drew my attention to my sense of smell, visualising a bright yellow square on which I saw and felt myself sitting: *Kshiti*, earth – all mountains, trees, animals and cities.

Second, my sense of taste, visualising a brilliant white circle: *Ap*, water – all oceans, rivers, fish, dreams and healing herbs.

Third, my sense of sight, visualising a scarlet, upward-pointing triangle placed from knees to forehead: *Tej*, fire – all lightning, stars, stones and intellect.

Fourth, my sense of touch, visualising at the level of my chest two triangles combined to create a six-pointed star as deep and dark as the night's sky: *Vyom*, air – all weather, birds and intuition.

And finally, I settled all attention on my sense of hearing, visualising at my forehead a crescent moon on its back, light-filled and crystalline: *Marut*, space – pure, shining consciousness, devoid of limitations.

I deepened the experience of these same *yantras* by next visualising each planate shape around me in three dimensions: the yellow square became a cube, the white circle a perfect sphere, the scarlet triangle a pyramid, the star a stellated octahedron, the crescent moon an 'orange segment' spherical lune. This required not only engagement of my mind's physical perception, but also its senses of place and motion: a skill I found required practice, even having to imagine tracing the varied surfaces of each form with my hands.

In conclusion, I visualised directly above my head *Chamkilo Tara* – the brilliant star – which, with all the nuclear force and brilliance of a supernova, was imagined reducing all the body's elements, shapes and senses, from the feet up to the crown, to searing cinders.

All that then remained was the experience of *ka*, the 'space between' – *antar mauna*, the 'inner silence', that reveals a consciousness more fundamental than matter, time or space.

An unimpeded consciousness, which, as Kushal Magar had described, enables us to reach out and know beyond the limits of our limbs and skin not only an intimate union with fields, forest and sky with no horizon, but – most importantly of all by far – with each other.

LXXVIII

Conflict causes pain in the mind . . .
Because of it, the whole world is in bondage.
Tripura Rahasya

Something was wrong.
By my calculation – of what I judged proper sleeps, the bouts of thirst and hunger, the need to relieve

myself by following the pre-laid line of stones that led to my make-do forest loo – at least another day had passed since I last ate. Yet still the tiffin tins sat empty in their stack, my water unreplenished.

Was this, perhaps, another test? Another way to prove to myself the depth of my dedication?

Yet as more hours passed I grew to doubt it. Kushal Magar would never leave me here so long untended, to suffer hunger and steadily dehydrate. It went against *Ahimsa*.

To be quite sure the routine had not been changed without my knowing, I made my way outside and in a broadening sweep explored the ground. But there was nothing. Only the still, sweet moistness of mountain trees. The cool, distinctive damp that marks a mountain morning.

And then, even through the binding of my ears, a sudden noise. An indistinct, protracted rumble.

Then three fierce bangs that echoed through hills and trees.

I listened hard, but heard no more, so carefully found my way back into the cave and sat on my bedding.

And there I stayed.

Quiet.

Unnerved.

And waiting.

You manifest compassion even towards your enemies.
Durga-Saptasati

'*Aung Aing Kring Kling . . .*'

I awoke with such a start that I reached out to grasp the wall, to confirm that I was still where I thought I was.

I had vividly imagined my nose was filled with the scent of smoky, mustard oil wicks and that a woman was chanting Durga mantras. A woman voicing 'seed' sounds of transformation, self-liberation, which keepers of the Tradition consider intrinsic to the very matrix of the universe.

'*Chamundaye vichey-aung.*'

I sat bolt upright, tense in sudden realisation that my companion was no internally projected fantasy. The woman was real and at my bedside.

'Who are you?' I gasped.

'Hello, *dajoo*,' Jai Kumari's muffled voice replied.

'*Bhaini?*' I laughed, wanting to break decorum by reaching out to hug her.

'It's time, brother,' she announced flatly, without further explanation. Her determined hands took hold to reposition me. 'You need your back against the light. Now keep your eyes closed – tightly closed – and repeat the mantra with me.'

A hurried movement at the back of my head – and at last the blindfold slipped its hold to fall about my shoulders.

I sat with eyes tight shut, yet grinning with relief at a sense of space around my ears I had never before noticed. The subtle sound of a breeze among the trees beyond the cliff-face. The unpredicted pleasure of another's breathing.

'*Aung Aing Kring Kling . . .*'

So was this really it? I wondered. No concluding teachings from Kushal Magar? No enlightening 'debrief'?

'*Chamundaye vichey-aung.*'

'Brother, keep your eyes low,' she instructed. 'Now slowly open them.'

By the uncharacteristic tension in her voice, I might have thought her anxious or impatient.

I gasped aloud at the flush of unfocused light. The myriad colours, shapes and movement. My hands more plump and pink than I remembered. My bare feet filthy, blackened and beautiful.

Before me rose a vermilion-stained wall of rippling, golden brilliance, each niche alive with *diya* oil lamps and marked with *sidur* pigment of such intensity that they caused my newly liberated eyes to run with tears. For at that moment, it seemed as though nothing in my life had ever been as wondrous as this.

And in the central recess, an image of Durga astride the once wild, unfettered tiger mind. The goddess who symbolised the restoration of universal, and thereby personal, order. Arms raised high with weapons to express the ascendancy of self-knowledge over the ignorance of self-defeating thought and behaviour.

'Thank you for this, *bhaini*,' I choked, examining the delicate features of her face, the reflected lamplight in her eyes. It was as though it had been not mere days, but weeks since I had last seen my own kind. 'Sister, thank you.'

'It is my honour,' she replied, bowing to me in *pranam*.

We paused and looked at one another.

'Then what's wrong?' I asked, my newly liberated senses instinctively alarmed.

Jai Kumari dropped her eyes.

'Forgive me, *dajoo*' – her voice faded to a whisper – 'but you have to go.'

'Go where?' I asked, a new, confusing trepidation rising with every breath.

'Whilst you've been here, an agitation has been called, a general strike ordered from Darjeeling. They've cut the power. They're closing roads. Special Forces are already here and roaming.'

She slowly raised her eyes back to me, her voice constricting with emotion.

'You have to leave today, right now. It's no longer safe. They've reached the village. They've beaten some and taken others.'

'But where's your father?' I demanded, quickly looking back to squint at the brightness beyond the opening of the cave. 'Is Samuel here with you?'

'Oh, *dajoo*!' Jai Kumari burst out, tears suddenly spilling down her cheeks. 'Please, brother, you must leave now. Both my father and Samuel-*bhai* have already been arrested!'

PART EIGHT

LXXX

Dazzling light, the darkness of the abyss, the cold impassivity of infinite space and time, and the uncanny grotesqueness of the irrational world of chance. 'God' for me was everything.
Carl Jung

I stared blankly at the ceiling fan as another tired tear sank into an already sodden pillow.

The room was hot and bright. Even with the wooden shutters down, a fierce Calcutta sun scorched jagged lines across frayed rugs, slack wallpaper and a mould-mapped ceiling.

My journey south across Bengal had been long and slow, made interminable by the undimmed fury and frustration that consumed me. Of course, I could have applied a variety of techniques taught by Kushal Magar to calm my heart and mind, but I chose not to. Instead, I felt fully justified in letting the ferment rage, not only on behalf of my unlawfully detained teacher, my cousin–brother and their companions, but with bitter guilt at my inability to intervene, to mediate, to set them free.

And this despite the desperate appeals I had made at military, police and municipal offices alike, where every man-behind-a-desk had insisted the situation was far more complex than an outsider could ever be expected to comprehend. There was therefore no choice, they had all asserted, but for me to comply with Emergency Orders by relinquishing my precious District Pass and leaving the hills without delay.

It had taken two days before I had finally been afforded a gruff police escort to the Central Bus Stand. They said it was for my own safety, when it was obvious that the authorities were panicking and paranoid. Every hill village was now seen as a potential hotbed of neo-Maoist revolution, every camera-bearing foreigner a potential journalist when no one wanted witnesses.

The resulting descent through precipitous jungle to the Plains – normally a matter of some four hours – had taken an entire day. The monsoon-broken roads had been obstructed at every bend by checkpoints blocked by army trucks, cars and public buses piled high with anxious passengers clinging to hurriedly assembled luggage.

The jeep into which I had been forced by unnecessarily aggressive Special Forces contained two earnest Swedes studying Tibetan for their theses; a fretful French woman with the shaven-headed son she had determined for a Gelukpa monastery; and two American missionaries, bags stuffed with Good News Bibles and 'He Died for You' ballpoint pens.

On the Gangtok road, yet more armed policemen had flagged us down to recheck our papers. They had also filched the missionaries' boiled sweets and Biros, insisting we made room for a further three companions: a Dutch backpacker emaciated by dysentery, and two jovial Swiss nuns. The latter had insisted we join them in a rousing Sunday school rendition of 'Telephone to Jesus', of which only the Americans knew the words.

Part Eight

I had made the evening train by minutes, and only then because it was running hours late due to flooding in Assam. There had followed a sleepless night on an unforgiving carriage bunk, during which, in an effort to dull the sound of wheels on rails and others' snores, I covered my head with a towel. This immediately returned me to the last moments of quiet in the cave, before Jai Kumari's news had caused the internal hinterland into which I had ventured behind the blindfold to implode.

The memory had not only renewed my sickening fear for Kushal Magar and Samuel, but brought a new anxiety: that in my urgency to leap to my feet and run down through the forest back to a Lapu harvested of men, I had lost my peace, my balance, my sense of self. Perhaps even any benefit of the Tradition's teachings that the previous years had afforded. For once again I had found myself despairing and adrift.

And with that thought there had surged such over-whelming anguish for two friends so easily swept away, for rare kindness, gentleness, innocence laid waste by soldier convoys, that I had had to pull the towel from my eyes and press it hard across my mouth to stifle an inconsolable grief.

LXXXI

It is all the same whether we live in a hut in retreat, or in
a house with many kinsfolk,
for the true self is as ever free from the multitude as from solitude.
Avadhut Gita

It had not been until lunchtime of the next day that the night train had finally delivered me to the miles of slum and shanty that led to Howrah Station.

I already knew and loved Calcutta, one of my favourite places in the world for the romance of its history and architecture, sophisticated literary and culinary culture; its cheerful chaos and the humanity of a people who, above all else, disdain insincerity.

However, this time the tumultuous crowds, persistent beggars and copulating pye-dogs inside the station, in addition to the toxic weight of static traffic beyond the forecourt, had felt brutally assaulting. No doubt a heightened sensitivity after the days of seclusion in Kushal Magar's cave, a reaction I had needed to delay in my efforts to find my friends and, as I had so hoped, fight for their freedom.

I had therefore sought out the only place I could think of to escape the intense press of people, where I might restore my poise and prepare to brave the intensity of the city. However, my plan to take stock and clean my hands and face in the Gents' First-Class Rest Room had been foiled by the backwash from the drains that had flooded the floor, through which two rats the size of toy terriers paddled towards my toes.

My last visit to Calcutta had been to meet another tribe of relations who still clung to the fading vestiges of their old life in what had once been an Anglo-Indian quarter that clustered around a near-collapsing parish church. They had even held out against the installation of a telephone, as though line rental from the Indian Telecommunications Service might threaten their nostalgia with the urban anarchy from which the older generation at least preferred to hide.

I did, however, have the number of an aged neighbour, though when I called from an unsanitary booth beside a stall selling deep-fried *puri-sabzi*, she had informed me that my cousins were presently 'out of station'. I knew another set of relations had recently taken over management of a vast, Victorian jute mill on the Hooghly River, but with no family member to hurry down stairs and across landings to answer my enquiries, I had no means of finding them.

Instead, I had breached the wall of rickshaw-*wallahs* tussling for my custom, and began a long and smoggy hike across the city's cantilevered bridge. I had cut through the old flower market's marigold mountains to walk among derelict warehouses and clamber over forsaken tram tracks. I had followed the river's wrestling and bathing *ghats*, to pass crumbling stone pavilions shading priests who proffered *puja* for the dead, until I reached the tree-lined quays of rusting boats.

And then inland, past vagabond cricketers with their make-do bats and scavenged balls, and skinny urban shepherds with their raw-boned flocks. Past soap-sudded bathers in the public tanks, faded Raj-time tennis clubs and plinths where once a bronze-cast Minto, Kitchener and Canning surveyed the Maidan's vast and dusty plain, around which the colonial Paris of the East now declines.

I had been heartened to find that the old, backstreet hotel I had previously frequented maintained its reputation for shameless eccentricity and erratic service. It even still promoted its set menu of inclusive meals, evidently inspired by the Spartan fare of some pre-war minor British boarding school.

The desk clerk had smiled in recognition at my arrival and had tutted at my tale of expulsion from the hills. He already knew of the rising trouble in the north and was eager to bemoan the sudden rash of cancellations by 'incomers' who, until now, had been intent upon Darjeeling tea, Ghoom monastery, Windermere gin, and tiger in the Duars.

'The way foreigners are running in panic to their fax machines, you'd think the lounge bar overrun by kukri-wielding Gurkhas!' he exclaimed, even as the Xerox beneath his counter had relaunched its drone and putter to deepen his dejection.

All this, of course, had proved to my advantage for rooms were unexpectedly available. So it was that I found myself in familiar, naphthalene and boiled mutton-scented surroundings, on the very bed of chalky sheets and crocus candlewick in which I had slept before. There was the same wardrobe door that needed a chair to keep it shut. The mantelpiece piled with silverfish-infested Fleming, Narayan and Highsmith. The wobbly standard-lamp with what could well have been the very same blown bulb. And then the hospital tiles, verdigris brass and cockroach traps of the bathroom, from which opened a narrow private balcony that overlooked so much decomposing Neo-classicism I might have believed myself in Ostrogothic Rome.

However, the complimentary brew and biscuits delivered to my door in welcome remained untouched, my shoes and filthy shirt cast on the floor, my rucksack left unpacked. All I could manage was to curl around my pillows in the heat and search for sleep, whilst the street below rang with the touting sleigh-bell chime of barefoot rickshaw-*wallahs*.

And as I lay there, I ached at the thought of what might at that very moment be being meted out to loved ones I had been forced to leave in the now unimaginable chill and mist of far, far too distant mountains.

LXXXII

To believe that one is in bondage is the greatest of all bondages.
It is like a child's self-imagined fear.
Tripura Rahasya

I woke to the smell of oily eggs and blackening lamb sausage – a dirty stench compared to the sweet scent of food so lovingly made and stealthily delivered to that distant hillside cave.

I was convinced I had slept for little more than an hour or two. The laddered lines of sunbeams about the room seemed quite unchanged, although the ceiling fan had finally expired. Only as I peered with slow-to-focus eyes towards my travel clock did I discover, with disbelief, that I had slept for fourteen hours and that this bright light was the morning of another day.

I hurriedly bathed in shallow, gritty water, then descended to find a corner of the dining room in which to brave the breakfast.

Just four of the cotton-topped tables were taken, from which curious eyes were raised to meet the new arrival in their midst. I sat down and wrote a list of state offices I might telephone to discover something of the situation in the hills, whilst around me I caught sight of cautious proddings of food on the serving plates, comparative sniffings of milk jugs and looks exchanged of nervous doubt.

I attempted to divert my thoughts from the commotion of the last few days by deciding that my fellow guests were a Scottish pastor and his wife, here to deliver a donation raised by a summer's worth of parish fêtes. A budget-travel journalist and his recently acquired boyfriend, whose mutual frostiness suggested they had already had a tiff. A pair of floaty yoga girls, who thought they were in search of something 'spiritual' when all they really wanted was lasting love. And a trio of charity workers recuperating from some far-flung project that would seem to have depleted their vigour and scorched their skin.

As smoky toast arrived with papaya and the *Calcutta Telegraph*, I scoured the headlines, but found little reference to the unrest in the north. There was a passing mention of a hill *bandh* general strike, uncertain reports of communal conflict, and a fuzzy picture of the burning of a lumpy Guy Fawkes-like effigy of either the District Magistrate or his deputy.

All I knew for certain was that heavy-handed overreaction had become the official stance since the troubles had first exploded just a few years before, when the National Gorkha Liberation Front had commenced its agitation for independence from the state of West Bengal.

The issue had been born as long ago as 1815, when the British East India Company had taken Sikkim as a colonial protectorate in order to defend the Himalayan kingdom from the aggressive attentions of Nepal. Twenty years later, Sikkim's reinstated Chogyal king had been 'encouraged' to express his gratitude by gifting his foreign liberators the district of Darjeeling. At this, Tibet had not merely protested, but had threatened war, which had been taken as sufficient justification by the British to annex all of South Sikkim, from its western borders down to the Plains.

Just three decades later, the British had been back in battle with another Himalayan realm. This time, their regimental guns had been turned against Bhutanese arrowheads, catapults and chainmail. Once again the interfering foreigners had been victorious, whereupon the resulting treaty had ceded to them both the hill district of Kalimpong and the plains territory of the Duars.

Between these Himalayan campaigns, the British had been waging Opium Wars, and in so doing had damaged their own lucrative trade in Chinese tea. They had therefore begun to pioneer planting across their newly acquired territory in the foothills of Kanchenjunga. For such ventures to succeed, an army of pluckers had been required. However, the indigenous Lepcha tribe had proved impossible to discipline, for as soon as British backs were turned, they would remove their clothes and skip back into the forest. The *sahib* planters had therefore shipped across the border so many compliant Nepalis, predominantly from the Gorkha tribe, that their culture and language had soon come to dominate the region.

Decades had then passed, until at the beginning of the twentieth century, during a time of civil unrest and the attempted partition of Bengal by a nervous Raj, a council of these same, imported hillmen had first appealed to the British government for semi-independence. Their petition of 1907, however, had been refused.

When forty years later India had finally gained its freedom from centuries of foreign rule, all British-administered territory had been automatically incorporated into what had become the world's largest democracy. In so doing, Sikkim's historic southern reaches, in addition to the territories that had been surrendered by Bhutan, had been absorbed into the newly demarcated India and claimed by the state of West Bengal.

However, whilst the state government in Calcutta had taken all the benefits of foothill tea and mountain timber, the hill peoples had found themselves without the compensation of proper subsidies or prospects, good roads or sufficient power. To add to their discontent, the native tongue of some 10 million Indian Nepalis had been disregarded by their new administrators in preference for the dominant languages of the Plains: Hindi and Bengali.

Too many years of frustration had finally forged a political movement that demanded not only self-determination for the hills, but an independent state called Gorkhaland, with its capital in Darjeeling. When general strikes and boycotts had been called to force resistant bureaucratic hands, the armed Central Reserve Police Force had been sent in to quell the 'agitation'. As the death toll had risen to some twelve hundred – one my own relation, summarily executed outside his own home – a Gorkha Hill Council had finally been established in a compromise for peace.

Yet still this conflict of both deep cultural and political interest seemed unlikely to find any easy or immediate resolution – a fact the new outbreak of unrest and its violent suppression had only gone to prove.

What this meant for the entirely apolitical village men, so roughly rounded up by government forces to intimidate those tempted to fresh protest, I could well imagine. I had seen for myself the ready force applied to backs and limbs by Indian policemen with their metal-tipped *lathi* batons: indiscriminate violence meted out to offenders and innocent bystanders alike, until legs were broken, skulls were cracked and lives were even lost.

The thought of where Samuel and Kushal Magar might be, therefore, and in what condition filled my heart with almost overwhelming dread.

All I had to hold on to was the hope that telephone lines to the hill districts might fast be reinstated, by which time, in usual Indian fashion, the commotion would have swiftly passed and normality be restored.

A sudden, snapped command to staff brought me back to the hotel dining room and the arrival of a robust woman of both an age and extraction made indistinct by her liberally applied foundation. She bore down on the only table marked 'Reserved' and a breakfast delivered to its setting by servants in soiled service wear, whereupon she battled with hands plump and weightily adorned to adjust the balance of her coiffure, so tall and teased with lacquer she might have claimed top billing as a Circassian Beauty in a Barnam sideshow.

Thus considering herself prepared to invite communal notice, she rumbled formal greetings to us all, wafted winsome fingers towards me with an introductory, 'You're new!' and signalled for her attendant to douse in brown sauce a greasy onion omelette with side servings of bubble and squeak and cheesy soldiers.

We had been joined by our proprietress: the doughty Miss Balbilla Floye.

LXXXIII

The world puts off its mask of vastness to its lover.
It becomes small as one song, as one kiss of the eternal.
Rabindranath Tagore

I spent the first hour after breakfast perspiring in an unventilated cupboard at the back of a gentleman's outfitters that reeked of unwashed feet.

As shop assistants stared through the door in shameless curiosity, I clasped the sticky earpiece of a public telephone and endeavoured to charm my way past a barricade of receptionists and secretaries whose collective aim seemed only to keep me from my target. I tried the British High Commission, the Hill Council office in Shakespeare Sarani, both state and private tourist boards, and even the Department for Panchayats and Rural Development. But no one could tell me anything I did not already know: all communication had been cut and foreigners in the hills were now forbidden.

Back out in sunlight, I avoided the savvy gangs of women with pillow pregnancies aggressively begging for money for 'hopitul check-in', and slumped beside a street-side shrine to smiling gods. I tried to guess what Kushal Magar would now advise – a thought that suddenly reminded me that with all the anxious drama of the past few days I had not opened my notepad since the evening he had offered me the blindfold.

I turned quickly to dig into my backpack, unzipped its 'secret' pocket and withdrew the book. I flicked through pages dense with my erratic script and still infused with wood smoke, and struggled to accept I had so recently been sitting in that mountain cave with Kushal Magar as I had attempted to record his every word.

These transcripts I now scoured, hungry for his counsel and his comfort. It struck me how often he had impressed on me that we all have a duty to resolve conflict and ease suffering – not only in others, but in ourselves; and that we must take responsibility for our own thoughts, our words and actions, for they contribute directly to the world's accord or discord.

'Seek out uplifting, enlightening memories with which to replace the adverse and the obsolete,' he had encouraged on that last night together. 'Choose to live honestly, abundantly, joyfully. By daylight.'

The only way I could think to follow his guidance and relieve the world of at least one more discordant heart, was finally to concede that there was really nothing I could do but wait for others to find a way to settle the situation in the hills – and to trust that sanity would ultimately prevail. And if I was now to choose to replace the 'adverse' with the 'uplifting' and 'enlightening', then I would spend the coming days in celebration of this extraordinary city and its people by revisiting a choice selection of my favourite haunts.

There was the rambling home of childhood hero Rabindranath Tagore, its rooms still echoing the poet through piped recordings of his songs and recitations. The family graves of my forebears among dilapidated mausoleums and obelisks webbed with washing lines that seemed to sustain Park Street Cemetery's very fabric in their polypropylene embrace.

The Burne-Jones stained glass of St Paul's Cathedral, its Canterbury 'Bell Harry' Tower radiant with whitewash against a sky of smog-tempered blue. The lofty corridors of books that line the pavements towards the celebrated Coffee House in which Sens, Chattopadhyays and Boses once sparred in intellectual *adda*.

The weathered art deco bulks of once-British banks and businesses. The replica of Curzon's Kedleston, its Palladian proportions raised to ensure patrician governors and viceroys would always feel at home. The elevated *rawk* verandahs of Indian-gothic merchants' mansions, and all the wonders of the Marble Palace skulking in the sparrow-spattered dark and damp of its lofty halls' decay.

And between them all, street markets, monuments and temples; churches, synagogues and tenements. The Giant Banyan on its crutches, the Burmese Pavilion in its park. The cookery on every corner; the communal bathing at every pump. The tailors able to judge a man's measure with nothing but a practised glance. The sculptors raising gods in splendour from river mud, straw and donated hair. The pimps, pastry chefs, rent-boys and poets. The pavement dentists, doctors, *dhobis*, letter-writers and haberdashers. The barbers, beggars, magicians and general mischief-makers.

I decided first to walk towards the dusty glories of the Indian Museum – far more suitably known by Calcuttans as the Jadughar, or House of Magic – where I might escape the noise, the rising heat and tireless pluck of unshod rickshaw-*wallahs*. To my surprise, I found the building virtually empty of all staff. In fact, I met on my unhurried tour only a father and son blinking at a balding tiger in its papier-mâché wasteland, and two college boys in respectful hush before what a yellowed label vowed to be the Buddha's ashes.

I took the opportunity of this unexpected quiet to settle on a corner seat, where I pulled out my notepad again, and finally started recording the most significant events of the past two weeks. I began with Kushal Magar's Drunken Teacher Test, a memory that, for the first time in far too many days, induced a smile – and with it that same fierce longing to sit with him, Samuel at my side, and again know the comfort of their kindness.

I next tried to outline the days and nights spent in the cave alone with eyes and ears bound, but no words could do them justice. And yet in my attempts to describe that initiating plunge into the hidden eddies of my mind, I was struck by a new understanding: it is not in the experience itself, but in subsequent reflection that its true value is found, its inherent wisdom gained.

My slow note-making was eventually interrupted by the excited chatter of the college boys, who had joined forces with the father and his son to hunt out the museum's only mummy. I therefore tucked away my pad and pen, and wandered on in search of new solitude, through halls lined with neglected cases of meteors and coins, gums and resins, dyes and tans.

It was not until I reached the great sculpture galleries of ancient deities, bodhisattvas and tirthankaras that my heart brightened at the sight of iconography I recognised from distant mountains and the little scarlet temple. Goddesses with benign smiles, orbicular breasts and abundant arms. Gods with *trishul* tridents, fearless phalluses and lotus legs.

I paused first before an antique image of Ganesha in festive frolic, his stone-cut trunk tempted into a tangled twist by a bowl of sweets, and his companion rat trotting dog-like around his dainty, dancing, elephantine toes.

'Lord of Wisdom and New Learning,' a startlingly familiar voice suddenly announced behind me. 'Where better to start your day?'

I spun around, convinced beyond a doubt I was deceived – to face the beam of a strikingly beautiful and immediately recognisable young man.

'Well, well, British-cous',' my cousin Jasper grinned. 'Who ever would have thought?'

LXXXIV

The self that hovers in between
Is neither man nor woman.

Devara Dasimayya

Cousin Jasper seemed far less astonished to find me where I was not meant to be, than I was to be discovered by him.

I gasped aloud in disbelief, throwing my arms around the delicacy of his bones to be quite sure he was no heat-induced illusion.

'How can you be here?' I exclaimed, pressing out his breath in my enthusiasm. 'I rang your neighbour yesterday, but she said you were all away!'

'They are,' he wheezed into my ear. 'But now I'm not!'

'Then how did you find me?'

'Oh, you're easy,' he replied. 'I guessed you'd be staying in that same crazy place as last time. And of course you'd be spending your first morning in the Jadughar sculpture galleries. You're just too predictable, cous'!'

For the first time in many days I laughed, prompting in him a hearty effort at outdoing the tightness of my squeeze.

Almost a year older than me, Jasper was a relation by

marriage, an only child whose parents had drowned in a ferry sinking in the Hooghly when he had been just seven years old. He had been taken in by his mother's sister, wife of one of my blood-cousins, and had thereby been welcomed as a full member of my already eclectic family of Anglo-Indian stock. Unlike Samuel, however, Jasper bore no mountain blood. He was descended from a Scottish adventurer who had made his fortune in silk, and the daughter of a *zamindar* Bengali baron, who had once picked a fight with the Tagores only to be trounced with bankruptcy.

'Okay, okay, you win!' Jasper spluttered. 'Now let me go, so I can examine you properly. I could recognise you from behind, no problem. Now I need to see if I still recognise you from the front.'

I let Jasper pull away to scrutinise me in unnerving detail.

'You're older,' he said.

'And you're not!' I replied.

Nor was this flattery. Jasper's graceful build, his flawless complexion, screen-worthy cheekbones and blue eyes fringed by dark lashes were unchanged since the time I had first made my way to Calcutta after my initial meeting with Kushal Magar. The only difference was that he had now grown his thick hair beyond his collar, which was most unusual in the midst of Indian men's customary conservatism.

But then, this was no ordinary Indian man.

My arrestingly beautiful cousin Jasper had been born hermaphrodite.

LXXXIV

In reality, consciousness is everything. All that is seen here, there,
and everywhere, in all forms, is . . . Consciousness.
Tripura Rahasya

J asper and I were sitting on a wooden bench in a shady
corner of the museum's central courtyard.

I had asked after his family, to learn that every
member was attending a relation's week-long wedding
celebration south of the city, along the Matla River. He
had only just returned for two days of university tuition,
before he travelled to Orissa for a field-trip course on *dakini*
temple sculpture. We discussed his incongruous passions for
cookery and traditional *kushti* wrestling, and the thesis on
'Gender Identity and the Tantric Androgen' he was writing
for his degree. I learnt that he now volunteered in his spare
time at the city's first sexual health education charity, and
that the offices had twice been raided by the police with
accusations of 'polluting society by encouraging young
persons to commit unnatural offences', he recounted with a
dismissive laugh.

Jasper, in turn, had listened in alarm to the details of
my unscheduled arrival in Calcutta; of violence in the
hills, of gunfire, mass arrests and hasty foreign expulsion.
He had sympathised with the distress I showed at the
mention of Samuel and Kushal Magar by grasping my
hands to declare with confidence that all would ultimately
be well, the peace restored, our shared family and my
friends unharmed.

'You know how it is in India,' he said with a shrug.
'Politicians whip up mobs into the usual frenzy and then a

236

week later everyone's chatting about the latest test match at the same *chai* stall.'

To cheer me up, Jasper announced that we would celebrate our unexpected reunion by lunching together before he had regretfully to spend the remainder of his day in tutorials and lectures. However, we still had a wait before his preferred eatery unlatched its doors to '*ghee*-fried *luchi* with sweet *cholar daal* of yellow gram, green chillies and crunchy coconut, and of course *begun bhaja* fried aubergine with plenty of late-season *anaras* pineapple chutney!' After a meagre breakfast of parched toast and tart papaya, his proposed menu had already set my stomach rumbling.

'So, how to spend our hungry hours?' he asked. 'Any sights you haven't seen? Remember how you gave my mother the willies last time, wandering backstreets and alleyways until you'd discovered yet another ruin the guidebooks never mention?'

I had many delightful memories of my weeks spent in this teeming city, but today was happy to forgo all sightseeing that I might relish this rare privacy with Jasper. Although we had maintained a lively correspondence over the past few years, there was much about him and his life that I had never had the opportunity to ask freely in person, as we had only ever met with a close assemblage of relations within eager earshot.

However, even in the courtyard's shade, the humid heat was fast becoming oppressive. I therefore suggested that as we had already paid our museum entrance fees, we return to the cooler interior in which he had first found me.

'You just want to get back to those sculpture galleries' he said, flashing his life-brightening smile as he drew me up to stand. 'As I said, way too predictable, cous'.'

Of course he was right. The recent years of travel in India, the myths I had heard recounted, the insights offered by Kushal Magar and my own studious efforts, had all seeded in me a fascination for tantric iconography. In addition, Jasper had both an academic and practical understanding of Bengali history and culture, which over recent years I had encouraged him to share, turning his every letter into an informative and insightful essay. Now that he was here in person, I was eager to glean all I could of his extensive and intriguing knowledge.

So we returned to halls of multi-limbed monoliths, where Jasper led me first towards the rock-hewn figure of a solitary man of perfect proportion, four-armed, serene and ithyphallic.

The *trishul* trident in his hand and the humped bull with dangly dewlap at his side announced this to be an image venerated for generations as the metaphorical 'male' aspect of the universe: Shiva, whose name means 'welfare, happiness, prosperity, liberation' – the intrinsic consciousness, the order of the cosmos personified, to whom myth attributes the imparting to humankind of music, medicine and, of course, the Tradition.

As I had learnt over the years, the names bestowed on India's Ancient One were innumerable, each epithet another way to reflect upon the nature of both the material universe and ourselves. For there is nothing in the cosmos that the idea of Shiva does not express: all light and darkness, tranquillity and turmoil, asceticism and eroticism, all life, all death.

Despite his apparent maleness, in tantric iconography Shiva always reveals the integral presence of 'female' Shakti. In the image before which we now stood, this androgyny was indicated by a *tatanka* woman's earring in his left ear, whilst the three-line *tripundraka* with which Shiva's forehead and phallus were marked revealed the 'male, female and other' of humankind's true nature.

Both Jasper and I stepped back to reflect upon the statue's supple musculature and geometric faultlessness, its empathetic humanity. The sculptor had displayed remarkable skill in his interpretation of Shiva's names of Sudarshana, He who is Good to Look Upon; and Charu, the Beloved, Intelligent and Beautiful.

'No wonder it was said the gods were so overwhelmed by Shiva's comeliness that they were unable to praise him without a quiver in their voices!' Jasper laughed quietly.

I agreed. And yet, not unlike my childhood hero ancient Greeks who had embodied in sculptural form their aspirational idiom *kalos kagathos* – handsome and honourable – Shiva's outward beauty had as its purpose the expression of the inner qualities of benevolence, compassion, stability and non-judgement. And this, Kushal Magar had repeatedly impressed on me, was so that we too might learn to give of ourselves without thought of reward and live by a love that is fearless, impersonal, dynamic, unfailingly humane and without condition.

'Of all his names, I think I most like Sakha, True Friend. And Sarvashubhamkara, He who Does Good to All,' Jasper revealed. 'Reminders that we each have a moral responsibility to one another.'

I nodded, still transfixed by the sensuous androgyny of the narrow stone-cut waist, pitched hips, broad shoulders, strong chest – and a pair of granite eyes that seemed to gaze with equanimity into both an internal and external universe devoid of limitation.

LXXXVI

Each one of us is the universe,
as miraculous and beautiful as the stars.
Kushal Magar

The almost reverential hush into which we seemed to slip reminded me of my instinctive response when seated outside the little scarlet temple with mountains in perpetual drift above.

This brought to mind a time when Kushal Magar had impressed on me that the primary difference between the orthodox understanding of the Hindu pantheon and that of the Tradition is that in the former, under priesthoods, the gods are contained and superior, unapproachable and inaccessible except through sacerdotal intervention. This, in turn, maintains an unchallengeable hierarchy of self-serving men. The Tradition, in contrast, holds that gods and humankind are not only equal but indivisible, the divine available to all because the divine *is* all. And this, in turn, requires no form of priestly intercession.

The Tradition therefore markedly differs from devotional Indian convention in its understanding that neither the term Shiva, nor its associated iconography, describes a personality. For Shiva is not a 'god in heaven' from which we mortals are kept as a result of our inherent 'imperfection'. Rather, his image and symbols express the tantric recognition of a remarkable disposition to order in the cosmos, a vital equilibrium of which the myriad material patterns of the universe – all animate life and inanimate matter – are an expression.

'This is the reason that keepers of the Tradition look

out into the world and see only interconnection, kinship and unity,' Kushal Magar had once said to me. 'A reality far greater than the mere bounds of our limiting self-interest.'

The bright memory of his voice renewed my dread of the deprivations he and Samuel might be enduring at this very moment, when here was I doing little more than wandering the city as though on holiday.

'Siva – embodiment of the reconciliation of all paradoxes and polarities, the union of all opposites!' Jasper declared, interrupting the darkening of my thoughts. 'You know, I could even say it's been through my understanding of his symbols and mythology that I've come to understand and accept myself.'

I turned to study the beguiling beauty of my cousin's face. His open, fearless manner revealed nothing of the profound self-doubts he must have wrestled with in his upbringing. To have lost both his parents and to have had to accept adoption into a new family must have been challenging enough. But then he had had to come to terms with a genetic condition for which, at least in most cultures outside India that only recognise two sexes, he would have been stigmatised, coerced to conform to others' experience of 'normality'.

However, Jasper had known the benefit of growing up in a country where people who are other than ordinary are considered closer to the truth of reality than the rest of us. Even Indian passport application forms and voter identity cards offer three gender options: male, female and an all-embracing third.

Jasper had also been raised in tantrically inclined Bengal, with its enduring affection for traditional Baul singers who hymn of expanding their consciousness by no longer identifying themselves as either wholly male or female, masculine or feminine. A further advantage had been that

Jasper had passed his summers in the same hills where I now spent my winters, and had therefore been nurtured by another fundamentally tantric culture that actively embraced difference, notably in matters of gender.

And yet, despite this largely constructive cultural reception, it still could not have been easy for Jasper to welcome the fact that he was at such variance with the norm, and thereby to accept himself fully.

'But then of course, aren't we all fundamentally androgynous?' Jasper asked, his eyes still holding to the figure in which he evidently found himself reflected. 'Because despite our bodies' apparent physicality and the way we constantly identify ourselves and each other through them, we're none of us a solid reality.'

I smiled at the memories of bright mountains and a Bright Being that his words stirred.

'After all, we're just a passing, precious, momentary event, aren't we, cous'?' he asked, reaching out to take my hand. 'All just a brief, complex, beautiful interaction.'

LXXXVII

Eternal, stable, steady and unchanging . . .
neither man, nor woman, nor eunuch.
Vayaviya Samhita

'Look, there's me!' Jasper declared, as he approached the time-worn toes of a white sandstone sculpture: an exquisite figure in a sensual, *tribhanga* dance-like posture. Half ithyphallic male – coiled serpent of knowledge around his muscular right arm; bull-headed boy expressing the balance of nature, the order of the universe, dancing around his right shin. And half plump-breasted female – lotus in her left hand as symbol of unlimited possibility; a tiger, ancient symbol of tantric initiation and the unfettered mind, playing kitten-like at her left foot.

I stood silent in the face of beauty that had an indefinable, tangible force all of its own. And yet I knew this likeness well. It was an image upon which *sadhana* was focused during initial learning in the mountains, for it represented the 'deep structure' of universal consciousness and energy in perfect combination.

'Ardhanarishvara!' announced Jasper. 'Understand the name? *Ardha* means "half", *nari/nara* "woman/man". Then *Ishvara,* a word usually interpreted as "an accessible expression of the unlimited, the unconditional", but which in the hills originally meant a person who'd gained self-knowledge and self-mastery through the Tradition. You see, truth unravelled in just this one image that embodies far more than our ordinary dualism!'

I smiled at Jasper's pride at finding himself reflected in this stone-worked expression of an irrepressibly diverse universe. An internal and external cosmos devoid of limits, in which all potential imbalance, all conflict, can be resolved, reconciled and once again made harmonious.

'Of course, ancient Egypt had hermaphrodite deities too,' he continued. 'As did ancient Greece and the Old Americas. Even your European Norse gods had Loki, who shifted between sexes. And Tibetans have their Avalokiteshvara, hermaphrodite bodhisattva of compassion and wisdom, whose image is back there, against the wall.'

I heard his every word, but my gaze was still held by the curvaceous lines of arms and necks, hips and legs, the serenity of face and benevolence of a mixed-gender smile, free from self-interest, that curved above us.

'Even the Brahmin's own Vishnu is described as shifting between his male and female forms,' Jasper revealed. 'One legend, for example, tells how Shiva set his sights on Vishnu in such a state of excitement that his dripping seed caused *lingas* to spring spontaneously from the ground. He then led Vishnu to the shade of a chalam tree beside the sea, where they passionately united. And this is why Shiva's names include Vishnukshetra, He whose Wife – literally "whose fertile womb" – is Vishnu; and Vishnukalatra, He with Vishnu as his Bride – literally "as his hips and loins".'

I looked at Jasper with surprise.

'The story goes that the "sap" they spilled as a result of this god-on-god action transformed into a rushing torrent, which took the name of Ganga – Ganges in English – hence Shiva's name Retahkulya, He whose Virile Semen is a River. And from this flood a handsome son was born called Harihara, who was credited with the ability not only to relieve famine and plague, but to tame lions and milk tigers!'

Jasper explained that this tale of such an unlikely union marked a moment in India's history when attempts were being made by the priest caste to merge the unorthodox and orthodox traditions through the creation of a new mythology. However, he admitted that in modern times this story was rarely narrated, and that it is usually qualified with the note that to simplify the procedure beneath the chalam tree Vishnu took on his female form, Mohini the Seductress.

Always eager for Jasper's invariably keen insight, I asked him how he understood the variety of myths of hermaphroditism and gender shifts that were to be found in so many cultures.

'Well, such legends and images were used as a way for

people to understand the wholeness of things – and of themselves, of course,' he reflected. 'Which may be a reason Ardhanarishvara is described as presiding over *adbhuta rasa*, the "aesthetic emotion" in humankind of awe and wonder.'

My gaze lingered on Jasper with an almost enchanted fascination, as he reached out to take my hand again and squeeze my fingers.

'And it is wondrous, isn't it?' he said, with a broadening smile. 'All this. All you, British cous'. All me.'

LXXXVIII

The Linga is . . .
the sun which gives birth to the world and upholds it.
Shiva Purana

There was one aspect of the mixed-sex image before which we stood that was less ambiguous in its gender and impossible to ignore: an enraptured phallus, or *linga*, extending to the limits of a neat navel. In fact, such was Shiva's association with this singular appendage that he was sometimes simply known as Sundarshishna, He whose Phallus is Beautiful.

'Good to know our largest sex organ is the brain,' Jasper muttered, 'or some of us might be left feeling a little lacking.'

I laughed, even as the memory of the hillside *linga* at Lapu-*basti* instantly returned me to Samuel and Kushal Magar – and with them the resurgence of an anxious constriction in my chest and belly.

Jasper distracted me by emphasising that whilst the

Occidental mind often struggled to disassociate any phallic image from the bawdiness of juvenile humour or the banality of pornography, for millennia in India the *linga* has been the primary symbol of universal order: consciousness without limitation.

Similarly, he explained, the disquiet provoked in some by the *linga's* apparent eroticism would be mollified if detractors understood that Shiva's phallus is *svayambhu*, 'self-stirred'. This adjective denotes that Shiva's state of permanent arousal does not indicate a libidinous mien, but rather self-mastery. The celestial erection therefore embodies the surpassing of all desire, for Shiva is considered the primordial *tantrika*, epitome of expansive inner freedom.

I had learnt for myself over recent years that shamanic trances were often associated with erections. Indeed, I knew that in the hills a *thankieko laro* – Nepali for a 'lengthened firm penis' – is honoured as the very 'presence' of the Supreme Shaman, Shiva being the principal figurative deity of the *jhankri*. It is a notion that extends far beyond the merely ritualistic, however, affording all mindful sexual intimacy, whether alone or with a partner, a wholly positive, enriching, even 'sacred' quality for the *shaiva tantrika*. So it is that all those born with a penis traditionally earn the honorific epithet of *Linga-dhara*, Bearer of the Divine Phallus.

I had also discovered, more than once when travelling in the mountains or wandering the shores of the great rivers of the subcontinent, that it is still possible to meet a male *tantrika* using his own *uddhapana* 'upright measure' as the focus of *pratyahara*: the withdrawal of self-identification through the intellect and senses, as a means to induce a spontaneous state of meditation. Such men will sit in quiet practice, first stirring and then directing the 'enlightening' force of sexual arousal through the body–mind. Those unable to maintain tumescence in such a practice will typically employ instead a portable mini-*linga*, or even the perkiness of a symbolic, up-standing thumb.

'Cous', I'm a *linga-dhara* too,' Jasper said, interrupting my internal exposition, 'in case you've ever wondered.'

Of course I had. Jasper had an ethereal beauty I still struggled to define. Except to say that his genetic gift – the presence of both testicular and ovarian tissue in his body – had created a person who was not less, but distinctly *more* than male. A reason, perhaps, why his approach to the world often seemed so much more considered and insightful.

And yet Jasper did not consider himself to be especially unusual. As he took pleasure in explaining, around one in every 150 births can be classed as intersex to some degree – although there are authorities that quote a far less conservative figure of about one in every 59.

'It's even prompted some experts in the field to suggest we humans would be more accurately identified as having at least five definable sexes, instead of just the standard two,' he declared. 'After all, isn't it the birthright of every one of us – whoever and whatever we may be – to know ourselves complete just as we are, worthy to love and be loved, of benefit to the balance of the world, free-spirited and happy-hearted?'

I enthusiastically agreed.

And I smiled at the thought that Cousin Jasper once again sounded as though he too had had the benefit of Kushal Magar's teaching.

LXXXV.IX

We do not know of anything that You are not.
Shiva Mahimna Strota

Jasper's next tug was in the direction of a display case from which the majority of exhibits had been removed, leaving only pale geometric shapes in the dust and a scattering of faded labels to show where and what they had once been.

His purpose was to point out a solitary cast-metal ellipse mounted on a pair of legs with dimpled knees and two sets of neatly nailed toes. On closer scrutiny, the peculiar object proved artfully incised with symbols of a mouth and tongue, a pair of open hands, eyes, ears and genitals.

'The female equivalent to Shiva's *linga*,' Jasper announced. 'The *yoni*, or divine vulva. Symbolises the forces of creation and dissolution inherent in every aspect of existence, from which everything comes and to which everything inevitably returns.'

I turned to scan the gallery, seeking out images of goddesses I knew to be personifications of the principles embodied in this *yoni* – goddesses that not only embraced every hue and demeanour, but even defied cultural aesthetics and conventional morality. And there they were: Parvati, Tara, Lakshmi, Durga, Chinnamasta, Kali – all figurative expressions of *Para Shakti*.

Ever since Kushal Magar had first explained the symbolism of the tantric goddesses, I had been fascinated by the term *Para Shakti*. Its first word bears the sense of ancient and initiatory sound: the inaugural big bang. *Para* was also an idiom for the number 'ten thousand million', a figure that was itself a general expression of limitless multiplicity, in the way we might use 'billions'. The second word, *Shakti*, energy, derives from the root *shak*, meaning 'that which is powerful, that which has the strength to act', for it describes both essential cause and effect: the elemental vibration that literally animates the universe – all space, time and matter – into existence.

For keepers of the Tradition, every representation of the *yoni* or image of a goddess therefore conveys the essential intimacy of all that exists in the cosmos. It is an insight that has profoundly affected the *shaiva tantrika*'s sense of the value of every form of life and, thereby, their personal responsibility to them.

This recognition that energy *is* everything also means that Shakti is expressed in innumerable forms across the subcontinent. Not only are idiosyncratic village deities almost invariably female, but on my travels through rural India I had been surprised to discover that these goddesses were often represented by the simplicity of a geometric *yantra*, or even nothing more than three equal-sized stones. This trio, it had been explained to me, were named Mahalakshmi, 'Abundance', denoting Shakti as the essential energy of the universe; Mahasaraswati, 'Knowledge', denoting Shakti as *Prakrti*, nature; and Mahakali, 'Power', denoting Shakti as *Maya*, all life, and thereby the intrinsic 'divine' value of all experience.

I had seen for myself such tripartite symbols honoured daily with flicks of vermilion pigment, the colour traditionally associated with Shakti; a flame, to express commitment to the lifelong quest for self-knowledge; incense, as a vow to master detrimental thoughts; milk, to express commitment to master selfish desires; fragrant paste, as a vow to master detrimental behaviour; and flowers, in recognition that all the qualities conventional culture deem 'divine' are in truth already our own.

'But perhaps the most important thing to grasp is found in the little pictures around this *yoni*'s opening,' Jasper concluded, drawing my attention back to the legged ellipse in its dusty case. 'For they represent the senses, reminding us that we already have all the tools we need to pursue our own 'enlightenment' by using them to learn fully and freely, and to engage benevolently with the world – and, of course, each other.'

His words prompted from me another smile for the memories they sparked – and then with them the return of a fierce, pressing anxiety for another too distant place and people.

XC

Shiva embraced Skanda, kissed him, and . . . for a moment,
the entire universe danced.
Linga Purana

Our momentary hush was interrupted by a man in squeaky sandals, who trailed his wife and mother, and two daughters decked out in frilly socks and petticoated party dresses. I listened to the long, soft consonants of what I recognised to be Oriya, the distinctive language of Bengal's neighbouring state of Orissa, as Granny paused to pronounce the names of gods I did not know and offer details so remarkable that the eyes of adults and children alike grew wide with wonder.

As they moved on, Jasper guided me towards the muscular youth the family had last examined.

'This is Skanda,' he announced.

'Of course.' I nodded. 'The Spurt of Semen.'

'So you already know the myth?'

'You mean Shiva's seduction by the gods of love and springtime, Kama and Vasanta, which leads the god of fire, Agni, to give Shiva what the Puranas describe as "supreme bliss", taking in his mouth Shiva's "jasmine-perfumed" emission "like a man tortured by thirst swallows water"?'

'That's the one!' he replied, with a laugh. 'So tell me how it ends.'

'Well, Shiva shoots so much that it spurts out the side of Agni's mouth into the Ganges. But the divine semen proves so potent that the river begins to boil and has to deposit it where Varanasi now stands. And there it stays, glowing in the dark, until it's absorbed into the buttocks of six wise women – who then give communal birth to Skanda!'

'Then maybe you also know that, as the god of male beauty, Skanda is also known as Kanta the Handsome, or Murugan the Beautiful One,' Jasper said. 'Though my favourite of his names comes from the south: Subrahmaniam, the Beloved of Seekers of Wisdom. That's because he represents the understanding of hidden meanings, and thereby the defeat of even the most subtle detrimental instincts that bind the consciousness of man.'

I looked up to study the bold, curly-headed youth who sat astride a fan-tailed peacock – symbol of both impatient desire and India's monsoon, traditionally considered the season of fertility and love. Peacocks are also known as snake-eaters in India, so with such a *vahana* vehicle under his command Skanda protects Nagas, those mythical serpent divinities that are the guardians of knowledge that leads to wisdom.

'Of course another name for Skanda is Kumaraswami, the Unmarried God,' Jasper continued, 'the eternal "happy bachelor". It's probably the main reason he's regarded as the symbolic patron of men who reject conventional marriage in preference for the love of another man.'

I was astonished.

'In fact, although it's not talked about much these days, male intimacy has always been shared at initiation into Skanda's *achara*, the traditional sect that employs his image. Such *pujas* are normally undertaken in forests or open fields, where male *shaiva tantrikas* together use his symbolism as a means to overcome internal chaos and mental darkness, so that they might, like Skanda himself, become *shukraja*, as they say – a light-filled, "spurt-of-semen-produced" son of Shiva.'

I looked from smiling Jasper to stone-cut Skanda again. And wondered whether I really understood anything at all.

XCI

Mutual friction . . . is great sadhana.
Yoni Tantra

The rumble of Jasper's stomach declared itself with such resonance around the sculpture gallery that we sniggered like miscreant schoolboys, prompting his eyes to linger on his wristwatch as though if he waited long enough the hands might hurry him to the hot, puffed *luchis* for which he longed.

And yet, however hard he stared, we still had to wait until the restaurant opened.

It was therefore with a hungry sigh that Jasper led me to the figure of a flute-playing youth I easily recognised as Krishna, his name the term for the dark half of the lunar month since his skin was the colour of storm clouds. It was a choice that surprised me, for I had only ever associated this cheerful deity with the highly sentimentalised religious zeal performed on urban pavements across the West by shaven-headed Hare Krishnas, devotees of a monastic-worthy morality that had fetishised celibacy and condemned same-sex intimacy since the organisation's founding in New York, back in 1966.

'You know Krishna, of course,' Jasper began. 'But maybe not that his image and mythology we recognise today is largely that of an ancient, pastoral protector named Mal, He who can be Embraced, who was originally entreated for defence against forest fires, torrential rains and dangerous animals.'

This was new to me.

'Naturally, as with so many of the old gods, when the priest caste first came upon him, Mal-Krishna, as he could more correctly be called, was declared an "unclean earth spirit" – a *yaksha*, like the tantric goddesses. And yet, in time he too was absorbed into the conservative pantheon, even being claimed as another incarnation of the Brahmins' Vishnu. Of course, he still maintains his original association with the husbandry of cows and horses, although nowadays his earlier pastoral attributes are usually assigned to a brother named Balarama – *bala* meaning both "power" and "semen", *rama* meaning "dark-coloured" and "pleasure" – whose symbols are the plough and pestle.'

'Then why were the orthodox so keen to acquire him?' I asked.

'Simply because, like all those other non-Vedic deities, Mal-Krishna was so popular among the rural people whom the Brahmins wanted to dominate. You see, he was originally considered more like a trusty friend, a heroic teacher who shared his knowledge with the common folk without prejudice – or priests. He was also loved for his long association with the joy of life and the celebration of *lila*, or playfulness, with early myths describing him as pleasure-loving, a quality represented by his legendary passion for butter.'

'Butter?' I asked, knowing that there were no random symbols in Indian iconography, and that, besides Kushal Magar, it seemed no one could unravel such hidden meanings like my erudite Bengali cousin.

'The Sanskrit word *rasa*, with which Mal-Krishna is especially associated, means not only "melted butter", but "love", "desire", "pleasure" and "male seed". Not an obvious connection perhaps. And yet there's another term, *tejas*, which is similarly applied not only to fresh butter, but brilliant light, the self-illumined body – and, once again, semen.'

I could not see where this was leading.

'Put all this together and you begin to understand why Mal-Krishna was long the symbol of "auto-eroticism", as we like to say in highbrow academic circles. Any mindful act of *hasta-maithuna*, literally "hand intercourse", dedicated to him is therefore regarded as much a "spiritual" rite as any act of *puja* or *sadhana* in the daily round of domestic life.'

'Are you serious?' I laughed.

'Of course. In fact, one form of *hasta-maithuna* is undertaken to the rhythm of a particular mantra, using only the thumb and index finger. In the hills, this is called

Shivako Haat, the hand of Shiva. The resulting *sukravisrshti* "resplendent emission" is then taken between thumb and fourth finger, and dabbed on the centre of the chest and between the eyes, or those of a partner, as a mark of respect and devotion.'

India – and Jasper – never ceased to surprise and delight me. Nor could a contrast be more starkly exposed than between the humane and liberal traditions he described and the guilt-inflicting censure to which I had been raised.

'Of course, Mal-Krishna's original, earthy and overtly sexual character has been largely reduced to a wholly asexual nature by the modern *Vaishnava bhakti* cults. And yet, even his modernised, sanitised version still wears the peacock feather of impatient desire in his hair, and holds in his hands a *murali*, or bamboo flute – slang here for a "stiffie" and traditional symbol of the divine *linga*. But significantly, his right foot is shown crossed over and pointing to his left, which indicates that liberating self-knowledge may be found within the many pleasures of material, sensual life.'

'So how does Krishna, or Mal-Krishna, fit into the androgyny we have been discussing?' I asked.

'Well, to begin with, there are myths that describe him expressing himself as Durga,' he explained, 'whilst various old Tantras and our celebrated Baul singers refer to Krishna as a male form of Kali, who, having enchanted so many men, wished to experience pleasure in the arms of women. But, cous', that's only where it starts to get interesting . . .'

Through enjoyment one gains liberation . . .
Hence the wise who wish to conquer [themselves] should
experience all pleasures.
Kularvana Samhita

Jasper next directed my attention to an elaborate frieze cut into pink sandstone. Its weathered length bore evidence of a busy and theatrical narrative, at the centre of which I recognised the unmistakable crossed-ankled stance and raised flute of the customary Krishna.

'Just as "male" Shiva is also "female" Shakti,' he began, 'so Krishna's female self is Radha, meaning 'prosperity, success and lightning'. Unusually, legend describes Radha as Krishna's older, married lover, for theirs is a mystical intimacy known as *parakiya rati* – the erotic passion for one who belongs to another. Myth even tells how they'd meet beneath the moon, beyond the village boundary, to make love protectively encircled by milkmaids, the *Maha Ras* – those who yearn to taste.'

At this, Jasper pointed towards a carved gathering of sari-clad women in illustration.

'Now, such are Krishna's erotic associations that even the most conservative Vaishnava cannot ignore them. Even priestly mythology recounts how Krishna once took the form of Prince Rama, the Pleasing One, a mortal hero whose beauty was such that on entering a forest to save sages from assault, every plant, tree, bird and beast ached to touch his body as he passed.'

I was sure I had witnessed a not dissimilar response, more than once, when Jasper had entered a room.

'In fact, so handsome was Rama that the very fiends he had intended to destroy were enchanted the moment they rested their impish eyes on him. Even the sages, who had lived as austere a life as any man could, were seduced by the sight of Rama and, being naked, could not hide the perky protrusions of their irrepressible arousal.'

'Perky protrusions?' I winced.

'Naturally, Rama was deeply touched by this group display of appreciation. However, he had to apologise that even if through the sages' own yogic powers they were able to express their female forms, he still couldn't give himself to them as he had vowed fidelity to his wife, Sita. Instead, Prince Rama offered an extraordinary promise: the day he returned to his form of Krishna to tend Shiva's cows in a magical place called Goloka, they would join him as *gopis*, or cowherdesses. They could then make love with him for just as long as they desired.'

Jasper again indicated to the frieze, and figures clasped in an embrace.

'Of course, in time this vow was fulfilled when, in the pastoral idyll of the divine Cow Land, Krishna, aroused "like a bull elephant in rut", as the old texts say, explored his passion with no fewer than sixteen thousand *gopis* – one of whom, legend likes to tease, was Shiva himself disguised as a cow-girl that he too might know the delights of intimacy with the Dark One who can be Embraced.'

'Your myths are so much more fun than our Noah's Ark or Robin Hood!'

'Oh, but there's more! You see Krishna was not only loved by cowherdess *gopis*, but by cowherd *gopas* who'd spend their days playfully wrestling, cuddling and holding hands, singing sweet melodies as they massaged each other, or just laying their heads in each others' laps. Now, as you might have gathered, these lads were of a what you might call a "sensitive disposition". So much so that when Krishna was tending to Radha and the girl *gopis*, the boy *gopas* found separation from their *nayaka* "heroic lover" unbearable. They'd weep, turn pale with longing and lose their appetites. They'd forget their songs, neglect their herds and, if Krishna were away too long, simply lie very still in the dust, breathing shallowly.'

'You're making this up!' I laughed.

'Not at all!' he insisted. 'Each time Krishna returned, the lads were jubilant, overwhelmed by *vipralambha sringara* – a term that describes the intense erotic desire ignited by separation from a lover that then leads to "mutual enjoyment". They'd dance, sigh and become giddy. They'd get fits of the hiccups, joyfully "disregard all popular opinion" and feel themselves mere wisps of cotton floating across the meadows on a warm breeze. In fact, we're told that the bliss experienced by Krishna's *priya-narma-sakhas* – his "most beloved, intimate boyfriends" – was comparable to the ecstasy of sexual union, a rapturous love only shared in cherished friendship that is called *sthayi*, literally "the action of standing erect".'

With this final flourish, Jasper led me to another carving to prove that if such androgynous tendencies needed more candid declaration, Krishna and Radha are sometimes depicted wearing each other's clothes. As promised, whilst the image of Radha was wrapped in her lover's robes, Krishna had donned her silk sari and golden ornaments, having already lightened his complexion, Jasper assured me, with fermented cassava pulp.

It was this playful androgyny, he explained, that had long ago inspired throughout Bengal, Orissa and Uttar Pradesh a devotional ascetic cult of men known as Sakhi–bekhis, which still survives today. In a form of extreme devotional *bhakti*, they explore the sensuality of these myths at a very personal level by cross-dressing as living embodiments of Radha and the *gopis*. And this that they might experience 'spiritual emotion' with *cudadharis* – 'plume-bearing' men dressed as Krishna, who sport a crown of peacock feathers – and thereby know for themselves the deeper truths that both his iconography and mythology represent.

'So you see, it's this association of sensual pleasure and spiritual illumination that is the very essence and purpose of Mal-Krishna in the pantheon,' Jasper stated, bringing vividly to my mind the day Kushal Magar first introduced me to Kama as the third Aim of Life. 'For Mal-Krishna's image and mythology reveal that, in accordance with the teachings of Bengali Vidya – our tantric Tradition of Bengal – the truth we seek is found not in denial and withdrawal, but in the union of both worldly delights and wise and mindful living.'

XCIII

No difference shall be thought of between the two
as between the moon and moonlight.
Vayaviya Samhita

Jasper and I wandered out into a sudden blaze of sunlight, accompanied by the toot and rumble of the city's traffic as it struggled along Chowringhee Road.

He took my arm and, with a hunger-prompted skip, hurried us through feeding throngs at street stalls and over gutters piled with discarded leaf and paper plates, clay and plastic cups. He paused to consider the local delicacy of a fish-head curry that bubbled among the smog, dust and flies of a crowded street corner, but I took one look at the opaque, piscine eyeballs staring blindly from their steaming, spicy sea and tugged my cousin away.

Fortunately, the restaurant stood nearby, a fan-breezed, low-lit relic of a time when even Calcutta had a jazz age. Our morning's wait had been well worth it, for the table was soon spread with all the tasty fare that Jasper had intended.

With our first mouthfuls, talk returned to our iconographic tour. This prompted Jasper to recount another tale of Krishna from a version of the *Mahabharata* recorded in the twelfth-century *Padma Purana*, yet which may still be heard in a culture that esteems *sakhya*, intimate friendship, above all other relationships.

'Arjuna, the Bright One, was a great and good king,' he began. 'However, his family of Pandavas had long been at war with their treacherous cousins, the Kauravas. The conflict might have threatened to annihilate them all had Arjuna not had Krishna as his *sakha*, his dearest friend, whose heart was gladdened simply by his company – as, of course, mine is by yours,' Jasper added, offering me another spoon of fresh pineapple chutney as though to prove it.

'Unfortunately, the family feud soon reached its violent climax when the Pandavas and Kauravas finally stood face to face at Kurukshetra. Now with Krishna in their midst, the Pandavas were at an undeniable advantage. He even made the sun set and rise again in the heat of battle just to confuse the enemy, an intervention he justified by declaring that all he did was born of his love for Arjuna, a love that surpassed all others. "For he is half my body," Krishna announced, "and I am half of his." '

'Water, sir?' our waiter interrupted, thrusting a bottle of Bisleri towards me, his eyes not once breaking their gaze on Jasper.

'Now, as the war reached its climax, the Pandavas made a vow that if they were to prevail then, as was the custom in those days, a perfect male would be sacrificed at dawn in atonement. However, once they'd actually won, they realised that among the victorious Pandavas there were only three perfect men from whom to choose: raven-haired Krishna, mighty Arjuna himself, and Arjuna's son Aravan the Stallion. There was little discussion, for the young prince insisted that for the sake of their clan none but he could die.'

Jasper's account was proving so gripping that our waiter remained standing in mesmerised attendance.

'Such was Krishna's compassion for the boy that as dusk fell he gave himself to Aravan as though he were his wife, that the courageous youth might know true ecstasy before he died. So it was that as they made love all night long, sweet Aravan discovered the most blissful pleasure that any man might bear.'

At this Jasper paused to take another *luchi*, as though for dramatic effect, before continuing.

'And then, as the sun again began to reclaim the darkness, the young prince rose from his dishevelled bed, stepped out into the new dawn to be bathed, anointed and then beheaded, leaving Krishna to weep in grief for the noble youth who had been his "husband" for only one brief, exquisite night. Indeed, Krishna chose to remain in mourning, as if he were a widow, for the full period that social custom demanded.'

As though to offer comfort, our waiter burst back into life to top up our glasses.

'Time passed and peace settled across the land, so Arjuna and Krishna again journeyed high into the mountains. Arjuna took the opportunity to ask Krishna as to the nature of his light-filled divinity. Krishna's reply was to direct Arjuna to bathe in a lake, where lotuses – symbols of unlimited possibility and the inherent joy in life – grew most profusely. When Arjuna rose from the waters, he found he had changed into his female self and thus transformed approached the love of his heart. However, the sight of Krishna's dark, curly hair, his beautiful mouth, his perfect nose and cheeks; his broad shoulders and his slender waist; his *linga* barely covered by the saffron cloth around his loins; his strong and slender legs, proved so overwhelming that Arjuna fell to the ground in a faint.'

I glanced up at our waiter, who was now leaning forwards in anticipation.

'Krishna looked upon his quivering companion with such love that his very skin shone with *rasa*, the "juice joy" of pure sexual union – pleasure without desire, judgement, need or attachment. For *rasa* is the bliss that allows man to glimpse the unknown, and is in itself a beam of light through which to comprehend it. And so Krishna lifted Arjuna into his arms and carried him into the forest, where together they spent hours exploring the most exquisite pleasures that any man can know.'

It was a revelation that caused our audience of one to gasp aloud.

'When Krishna eventually withdrew, he asked his maidservant to bathe Arjuna, whereupon he became his male self again. Krishna then took him in his arms once more and whispered into his ear, "I bless you, my beloved Arjuna, that you alone might know my secret – which is also yours." And at that moment the king could suddenly perceive that, like each one of us, he was all that was wise and all that was foolish. He was all directions and seasons. All rivers and fires, all suns and moons. All men and women. All gods. He was all that is and was and will be. And having come to recognise the limitless quality of his true nature, Arjuna was thereafter known as Savyasachin, the Ambidextrous, signifying his ability to unite his male with his female self.'

'One more plate of *luchis* for you, sir?' our flushed waiter interrupted. 'All fresh and hot. And most complimentary.'

XCIV

I do not wish to see those faces
With mouths that have never plunged into mouths.
I do not have time for men who are born
In this world but are dead to love.

Bengali Baul song

Despite the fact that Jasper's afternoon was already booked with tutorials and his evening with manning a helpline at the charity office, he seemed in no hurry to give me leave to return to the hospitality of the bewigged Miss Floye.

Instead, as our meal concluded with *gokul pitha* coconut cakes for him and *aam kheer* mango custard for me, he delivered an unexpected postscript to the mythical night of love shared by Krishna and the perfect prince, for he revealed that the event is still celebrated every year, during a late spring festival called Chittirai-Pournami.

'For seventeen nights preceding the full moon in April, tens of thousands of men gather at the village of Koovagam in Tamil Nadu, to explore with one another the unbridled passion of *shringara rasa* – the erotic emotion of mutual pleasure as shared by Krishna and Aravan.'

'So have you?' I had to ask.

'Of course,' he replied with a laugh. 'Though only in my role of safe-sex-educating charity worker, handing out leaflets, condoms and sensible advice!'

'But what exactly do all those men do?' I asked, puzzling to imagine the possibility of any annual, devotional event with such a premise.

'Well, they divide into those who wish to take the role of "husband" prince, called *panthis*, for the night and those who prefer to take the role of "wife" Krishna. These last include *alis*, men regarded as "sexless" in that they defy all ordinary definitions, such as *hijras* from the north, *jogappas* from the south – and biological hermaphrodites, like me! Then there are *kothis*, men who live like other males in society, even marrying and having children, and yet who are sexually receptive to other men, hence their nicknames *do parathas* or *dublas*, meaning "double-deckers". And lastly *dangas*, men whose instinct is wholly towards women, yet choose to give themselves as "brides" to Aravan for that one, sacred night. In fact, these *dangas* are often attended by their spouses and even their children, who assist them in this ritual transformation into Krishna.'

I sat staring at him across the table, feeling as though, even after these years of intimate interaction with India, I had just landed on quite another planet.

'For the duration of the festival, all three "wifely" categories will marry their Aravans by having yellow *thali* threads tied around their necks. At the same time, some of the *alis* and *kothis* take the opportunity to marry their long-term male partners. And then, on the night of the full moon itself, their wildly erotic celebrations culminate in the sacrifice of the image of Prince Aravan on the village cremation ground. A great cry rents the air as all the *alis*, *kothis* and *dangas* break their glass bangles, tear off their *thalis*, wrench the jasmine flowers from their hair; beat their chests, wipe the kohl from around their eyes, and smudge the "marriage" vermilion on their foreheads in mourning for their "husband" – just as myth tells us Krishna once did.'

'And the benefit of all these histrionics?' I asked a little breathlessly.

'A playful and powerful way not merely to acknowledge, but to experience both within themselves and out into the universe the masculine and feminine as interdependent, opposite and yet equal forces.'

As our eavesdropping waiter delivered the bill and Jasper checked the notes I had placed on the table, I stared out beyond the smoked-glass window and wondered at the veneer of so-called liberality that we boldly award ourselves in the West.

And at a world far more surprising, a humanity more diverse, and routes to self-knowledge far more extraordinary than I could ever have dared imagine.

XCV

Earth's crammed with heaven . . .
but only those who see take off their shoes.
Elizabeth Barrett Browning

A full morning of enthralling lectures, close followed by the heartiest of lunches and an afternoon of humid heat had left me drained.

Jasper wanted me to move into the empty family flat, but as the remainder of his day would be occupied with tutorials, followed by his night-shift duties on the helpline phones, I preferred to stay where I was and meet him in the morning. It was therefore with regret that we went our separate ways.

As Jasper caught his bus to the university, I returned to the hotel, where I squandered the remainder of the day in sleep that was sporadically interrupted by vivid visions of wailing cross-dressers, hyperventilating cowherds and fiery *lingas*.

When I eventually stirred, I lay staring at the dead ceiling fan, agonising again over where Samuel and Kushal Magar might be and in what condition. And then, just as I had finally determined to walk off my anxiety by rousing myself for a dusk-time stroll to temple and busy market, a furtive tapping on my door revealed a waiter I recognised by his grin as the young man who had served me toast at breakfast. He told me Madame had sent him up with a tray of complimentary 'tea and biscuit' and that his name was Dhirendra-dhirendro – 'at your servicing'. I was, however, 'most welcoming' to call him Bobby.

At the close of a day of surprises, I should not have been unsettled when Bobby refused to let me take the tea-tray, but instead stepped with mannered stealth into my room and quietly shut the door behind him.

'So now I do sir good-good massage for good-good sleeping,' he announced, as he added an alarming quantity of sugar to the cup of tea he was taking the liberty of pouring.

Before I could think how to respond, he had removed a small bottle from his pocket and had promptly begun to undress.

I ordered him to stop, but Bobby flashed his shiny grin, folded both shirt and trousers on the tub-chair's faded tick-ing, and in a moment stood before me in nothing but lean, dark-skinned muscle and a fraying pair of turquoise briefs.

In spite of this unconventional approach, the unexpected promise of ease in aching limbs and neck, from what I hoped might be practised fingers, held undeniable appeal. However, I had travelled far and long enough to know that 'massage' did not always imply the innocence of a mere shoulder-rub – and considering the subject of the day's discussions I wanted to make clear to him that I was not interested in any Hand of Shiva 'happy ending'.

'No worries, sir,' he countered, a pronounced Bengali trill in every 'r'. 'Just good-good massage and no-no hunky-punkies.'

I considered the incessant throbbing in my temples that I had been enduring since the overnight train journey from the hills and decided that, despite a niggling trepidation, I would accept his offer.

'So, sir, now please be doing the same,' he instructed, indicating towards his own state of undress. 'And please be lying on sir's good face,' he added, signalling with lifted chin and eyebrows towards the bed.

The single-sided wrestle I subsequently endured, on what fast became an oil-drenched counterpane, hurt. However, as Bobby repeatedly climbed over me to drive his thumbs, his elbows and, at one point, his knees into my flesh, I considered how beautifully at ease he was with both his body and with mine; a fearless, uncomplicated sensuality with which I was still largely unfamiliar in myself or my culture, and yet which had filled my day with Jasper.

Upon the flourish of his final clout, I hobbled to the tub-chair, placed a copy of the *Calcutta Post* to protect its seat before I sat, and doubted that by tomorrow I would be able to walk so far again.

Bobby padded to the bathroom, where he soaped and

splashed with the same fearless gusto with which he had attacked my muscles. I, meanwhile, attempted to steady a dizzy head by sniffing the sweetly pungent slick that glistened on my skin. No doubt an exotic, ancient recipe of fine spices, I imagined – cinnamon, ginger, perhaps a little pepper. A blend to seep its magic into bullied limbs throughout the night to deliver me relaxed and tranquil by the morning.

'What is this oil you use?' I asked, inadvertently drawing him from the bathroom tiles to towel his skin boldly before me with a disco-worthy shimmy. 'It has a strangely familiar scent.'

'Oh most special-special mixture, sir,' he announced, proudly proffering a small, red, plastic bottle that bore a distinctive clipper ship I had not set eyes on since I had first explored my father's side of the bathroom cabinet in about 1973.

'You've been rubbing me with Old Spice?' I laughed.

'Oh yes, sir,' he replied with a grin, taking my amusement as an invitation to drop into an agile squat and place his hands on my greasy knees. 'Now, sir like Big-Big Finish, when Bobby show his shapes and do his good-good loving?'

PART NINE

XCVI

There is no other happiness in this world
Than to be free of the thought
That I am different from you.
Shiva Strotra Avali

Bobby was not in attendance at breakfast.

'Out for special *puja*,' I was informed by a grumpy fellow waiter as he attempted to press on me a serving of someone else's rejected mutton rissoles.

In truth, I felt relieved at my impromptu masseur's absence, for he would have seen me wincing as I hobbled down the stairs.

The measured descent of Miss Balbilla Floye into the public rooms was heralded by a flurry of activity on the staircase as two maids and an elderly retainer clucked contradictory instructions at her every step. She, however, ignored them all, dispensing indiscreet financial directives to the accountant who was standing to attention below beside the bell-desk.

As the procession finally delivered its charge to her table, I was tempted to duck behind the *Calcutta Times* that I was examining for news from the hills. However, I could not ignore yesterday's unexpected refreshment, so stood to offer Miss Floye my courteous thanks. She scrutinised my gratitude through the tint of two-tone spectacles and slipped a manicured nail beneath the unnatural darkness of her elasticated hairline for an absent-minded scratch. There had evidently been some misunderstanding, she insisted. As the busy proprietress of a popular establishment run to an exacting budget she was not in the habit of 'handing out free tea willy-nilly'. What, then, could her 'Naughty Bobby' have been thinking?

As the full truth of the previous evening's exchange began to dawn on me, Miss Floye patted the worn padding of the neighbouring seat and proclaimed that she would be 'terribly tickled' if I would join her.

In a moment, my place setting and newspaper had been transferred by the grumpy waiter, and a fresh pot of tea for two delivered to our table, whereupon Miss Floye employed the excuse of 'being mother' to draw her heavily painted face uncomfortably close to mine as she poured a cup of single-estate Assam.

'Young man, this is a red-letter day!' she announced, with an unsettlingly coquettish giggle perfumed by the nauseating waft of sweet scent. 'First thing this morning, my accountant announces he's found a new tax break to my benefit – and then at breakfast I hook myself a toy-boy!'

XCVII

Keep ever at your side a mate that is your equal.
Theocritus

Jasper was already waiting at the entrance when I reached the Jadughar, House of Magic.

I apologised for having been delayed by my repeated efforts to discover the latest on the situation in the north. Immediately after breakfast, I had telephoned the same offices as the previous morning, with the addition of the news-desk of the *Calcutta Telegraph*. As with all my previous efforts, my enquiries had remained impeded by a citadel of secretaries, whose singular defence had been to place me on interminable 'hold'.

Jasper's response was to hug me, initially in fraternal encouragement – and subsequently in sympathy for the massage-inflicted limp I had acquired, even as he hooted at my account of Bobby's energetic efforts at an inventive, if ultimately foiled, seduction.

His evening had been far less eventful. The helpline phones had been quiet enough for him to take sporadic naps, disturbed only by a confessional call that should have been directed to the police, and two wrong numbers.

'Such a waste of an evening,' he groaned, 'when I could have been spending it with you.'

I had anticipated we would pass a second instructive morning in the museum's sculpture galleries, but Jasper led me instead towards the dusty trees and dusty shepherds of the park-like Maidan.

We had to risk our lives between the insanity of traffic on Chowringhee Road, before we could commence our stroll among soldiers jogging in tight lines, white-clad 'sporties' on their club tennis courts, and destitute families washing clothing and themselves in grimy public tanks. It was not until we were in sight of the towering dome of the Victoria Monument – a silhouetted mirage in the gritty haze of Calcutta's polluted heart – that Jasper finally chose a tree for us to sit beneath on calico squares, which he drew from his trouser pockets with a prestidigitator's flourish.

'So when did you first know?' he asked, digging into his cloth satchel for a pack of Chat Patta biscuits.

'About you?'

'No, no,' he said, laughing. 'The whole family talks about that as though I'm some prize heifer! I mean about you, British cous'.'

It was odd that throughout our years of letter-writing this was a subject we had never found the need to broach. Now that he had, I admitted that my story was comparatively simple. I had always known that my emotional and physical inclination was to bond with my own sex. In fact, one of my very earliest memories was the truly heartfelt wish that I would find a best male mate with whom to spend my days in high adventure and to share my bed at night.

'If I were to tell you my first love was a girl called Moumita, for no other reason than that she owned an imported Sindy doll with its own mini ironing-board and roller-skates,' Jasper confessed, 'then would you tell me yours?'

'Oh that's easy,' I replied. 'His name was Ian.'

My glory was I had such friends.
W.B. Yeats

The very mention of Ian's name, even after all these years, still brought a smile.

In fact, I was surprised to find I could recall every detail as though it had been last summer, when I had actually been in the first year of my infants' school and Ian had been in his third. I could even remember the curious, unnamable response I had felt at the first sight of his handsome knees and suntanned shins between the hem of shorts and tops of grey school socks.

Indeed, such was the flame he had ignited in my six-year-old chest that the toll of every break-time bell would speed my heart in readiness to stand in bold defiance of the bully boys who spent their time in playground persecution, just so that I might watch Ian in the company of his chums who laughed at every joke and did everything he told them.

I had looked on in secret wonder and understood. I would have done anything he had told me too.

After weeks imagining that the boy I did not dare speak to might share my joy in furry caterpillars, foraged fruits and frog spawn, I had disclosed Ian to my Monday Diary. With conscientious colouring I had drawn his uniform in blue and grey, his sunny curls, his long strong legs, that confident, carefree smile I had yearned to win one day. And then beneath, in my best pencil: 'This is Ian. He is in class 3B. I would like to be his friend.'

Tired perhaps by others' ordinary efforts at crayon cars and trains, stickmen Noggin and Pogle's Pippin, my teacher had shown an interest. I had earned a red-ink tick, a silver star, a drawing-in so near that I could smell her breakfast Sugar Puffs, and see up close the blink of eyes so kohled they looked like zips. And then had come the startling instruction that I was to walk to Ian's class and make my portrait public.

Class 3B had first been charged to lay down fountain pens to see a picture the 'little chap from Miss Ormiston's' had brought them. The teacher had then called the subject of my art – and my first love – to stand.

Blond and gently blushing, Ian had appeared from among the bob of heads and, for the first time beyond my hope-filled dreams, rested his sunshine smile on me.

The teacher asked that he escort me back to the pre-fab hut they called the Starter Class, but I dared not speak for fear of sounding foolish and had instead fought a reckless whim to pitch into his chest and sniff his jumper.

The next day's playtime, Ian had sought me out beyond the Bulldog, Tag and Marbles. He led me to his patch to place hands around my waist and sit me on a wall for introductions. His friends gathered to shake my hand, to laugh at my dad's jokes, to learn to suck nectar from fen-nettle and read weather from the clouds.

Every breakfast thereafter, I had eaten my eggy Marmite soldiers in a rush and run to what had once been days of lonely longing. Even the rusty railway bridge I had to mount no longer scared me, for in my sleep Ian had hurdled tumbling planks and girders to save me from electric lines that sparked in threat below. And all the while, his handsome knees had remained on full display – for in my dreams my champion had worn nothing but his grey school socks.

Ian had even once attended church to sit with us and sing our hymns, and see me through the sermons with Battleships and Hangman. Afterwards, as parents gathered in their gossip and boys had chased then caught their giggly girls, I stood on tiptoe behind a tree to press my lips to his. Such was my awe at this first kiss that when we joined the grown-ups congregating in the porch, my hand firmly fixed in his, and announced that he and I were now married, I had thought it meant for ever.

Instead, Ian had never again been allowed to come round and play, to potato print, string soup-tin phones, or pass me secrets penned in lemon.

And when autumn came, with heart aflame I had run once again to begin the new school year, I had found to my dismay – and then despair – that Ian and his sunny curls, his smiling chums and their whole year, had gone.

XCVIX

The universe shines undivided and unbroken . . .
Then why do you, who embody all, grieve in your heart?
Tripura Rahasya

'Do you think my life is lessened for never having learnt to suck a fen-nettle?' Jasper laughed.

We were on the move.

Our solitude had been imposed upon by a herd of wiry sheep destined for the mutton *biryanis* and *kosha mangsho* curries of the city's celebrated street stalls and kitchens. Jasper had therefore been prompted to lead me on a zigzag course between the shade of pigeon wood, teak and sausage tree, until we reached a leafy path that led to one of the many *ghats* that sink their broad stone steps into the Hooghly.

Arriving at a shoreline packed tight with boats, we found the river sediment scattered with flotsam and naked boys, the latter honouring our arrival with a display of dives and back-flips in the scum of dirty, oily waters.

To my surprise, we also found ourselves confronted by a row of dishevelled goddesses propped against a retaining wall, their original pigments still forming vivid stains down every river step. These, Jasper explained, were survivors of the previous autumn's Durga Puja, when the city erupts into a festival to surpass all others as lovingly dressed and bewigged versions of Shakti are borne through the madding throngs to be slipped beneath the surface of the river. However, when the Hooghly's notorious tidal bore returns some of these deities to daylight, they are again respectfully honoured until the ferocity of the Bengal rains liquefies their pigment, blazing sun disintegrates their clay, and crows pilfer strand by strand their tarnished tinsel trim.

We chose a step that rose a safe distance from the water's edge, where we might settle in the shade of a bedraggled Durga and her tiger whose festive dip had smudged his stripes. Sitting back on reinstated calico squares, we deliberated over Bengali Marxism and the decline of Calcutta's once-famed fashion for *adda*, intellectual debate. We discussed the politics of a notional Gorkhaland in Bengal's northern limits and tried to guess how soon the ban on foreigners might be lifted in the hills.

'There's really nothing that can be done,' Jasper insisted. 'Except to keep your mind busy and your hope alive.'

I nodded, as though I agreed.

'So come on, I want to hear what happened after Ian,' he said, in an effort to distract me.

Jasper's question brought to mind the years of taunts and violence I had subsequently endured, not only at school but even when walking into town or through the local park. I had understood neither the reason for my physical persecution nor the terms I had been called, but they had impressed on me that by some inexplicable failing on my part I was not who or what I was supposed to be.

As the years had passed, I had determined to prove myself on the rugby field. But all to no avail. Even the games teacher enhanced his popularity by joining in the general sport, referring to me only as the Pouf, the Batty-boy, the Bender.

The deep self-loathing that defined my adolescence had only intensified, until the decision to end my life had been born of its own calm, bleak logic. Suicide had not merely promised deliverance from relentless unhappiness and isolation, but had seemed a fully justified conclusion for a mind and heart that lay too far beyond the familial and social pale – or any god's redemption.

It was during those weeks of final, fatal preparations that an unexpected multitude of saviours had suddenly appeared: eternally paired names of heroic ancients discovered in the classical studies page-notes of my school's defiantly outmoded curriculum. Alexander the Great and his beloved Hephaestion had been the first stars in my secret firmament. They had soon been joined by Hercules and Iolaus, Achilles and Patroclus, Pausanius and Agathon, Zeno and Parmenides. However, it had been the Sacred Band of Thebes that had afforded the most marked and lasting impact. To learn that two and a half millennia ago there had been a celebrated battalion of soldier-lovers, whose courage on the battlefield and devotion in each other's arms had been extolled throughout the ancient world, had begun the rehabilitation of what had long been a deeply damaged self-image.

There had soon followed torch-lit readings beneath the

bedcovers of Petronius and Plato, Forster, Gide, Cocteau and Carpenter. The significance of these texts had been immense, for they proved to me that I was not, nor ever had been, alone – nor mentally ill, morally depraved, nor demonically possessed, as some around me had taken perverse pleasure in insisting. My natural instincts, my congenital sensibility for which I had been so despised – and in turn had learnt to despise myself – had instead won me an honourable, if yet still hidden, brotherhood. This in turn had afforded me a brightening, and quite literally life-saving hope that, like so many had evidently done before me, I too might meet a noble, heroic heart that also sought the tantalising promise of Whitman's 'intense and loving comradeship', the 'personal and passionate attachment of man to man'.

'Might all have been so different if we'd only known each other sooner,' Jasper said, reaching out to touch my arm as I concluded my account.

'Undoubtedly.' I nodded, resting my hand on his. 'And yet, you know, I've come to see it was those years of conflict with myself that somehow led me to the *jhankri*'s hut in the first place – where, of course, I've had revealed to me the humanity of a Tradition that unreservedly honours all of who and what I am, in ways certainly no religion I have ever come across has been able to.'

Nor was this exaggeration, for my interactions with Kushal Magar had offered me far more than the condescending 'tolerance' of too many individuals and systems that liked to imagine themselves liberal. Instead, I had discovered a people and a way of being that acknowledged my natural inclinations as not only a valid expression of the universe's illimitable wonder, but an opportunity for insights and reflection from which they too would wish to learn. In those distant hills, I had found myself honestly and openly embraced without censure or condition – an experience so radical, so transformative that my heart had finally found freedom from deep conflicts that over time had grown so dark and dangerous.

'The Tradition has also enabled me to recognise that all those years of unkindness and rejection prompted me to demand questions of myself and of the world that I would never otherwise have thought to ask,' I revealed. 'And after all, isn't it our questions – or sometimes lack of them – that somehow ultimately determine the direction of our lives?'

Jasper turned the summer sky of his eyes to look at me with understanding.

'So you see, all is well' – I smiled, in recognition that I had instinctively quoted Kushal Magar – 'because mine have ultimately brought me here to sit with you.'

C

*Can sandal paste blended with cool camphor or snowflakes,
delightfully cool, compare with the refreshing touch of a friend's
body? They are not a sixteenth part of this delight.*
Pañchatantra

The bathing boys were back and raucously challenging us to join them in their swim.

We offered our excuses through a mutual grimace at the thought of the dark, polluted slick that sped its poisons towards marine dilution. Instead, Jasper offered them the remaining pack of biscuits in his bag, prompting the tallest swimmer to spring up the *ghat* on stick-thin shins and bow on their behalf before bounding back to distribute the spoils. In appreciation, we were treated to another volley of dives, back-flips and renewed beckonings for us to strip off our clothes and join them.

'What else do you have in there?' I asked Jasper, only now noticing the over-packing of his satchel.

'Oh, books for this afternoon's last tutorials for the field trip. And oranges to see us through till lunchtime. Ever read this?' he asked, pulling out a volume from his library. 'The *Kamasutra*, The Thread of Desire?'

'Never,' I admitted.

'I only mention it because, considering yesterday's discussions, legend attributes the text's original compilation to Dattaka, who was changed into his female form by Shiva. And when he was later made male again, Dattaka found himself fully conversant in the sexual habits, arts and needs of both sexes, which he then promptly transcribed!'

Jasper handed me the book, which proved to have been translated by a French scholar whose works on Indian culture, history and mythology I already admired.

'It was collated in this form about eighteen hundred years ago, yet this is the only translation to date that has not been expurgated,' he impressed. 'So shame on the suffocating sexual conservatism that we Indians foolishly continue to impose on ourselves, even after half a century of self-rule, that it had to be undertaken by a francophone foreigner!'

I scanned the pages with curiosity, admitting that I knew nothing more than its reputation as a treatise on sexual acrobatics.

'Oh, but it's so much more than that,' he insisted. 'You see, it's not just one of the primary texts in an ancient and extensive tradition of erotic Shaiva literature in India, which flourished well up to the sixteenth century. The *Kamasutra* is essentially a tolerant and humane textbook of instructions in the exploration and fulfilment of the third Aim of Life, Kama – the expansion of consciousness through sensual pleasure.'

It was the first time I had heard this phrase from someone other than Kushal Magar.

'But as far as its general reputation goes, the *Kamasutra*'s central premise is that the snug union of opposite sets of genitalia is only one of many pleasurable forms of human intimacy. Nor is the text only concerned with the varied arts of love, but also of manners and etiquette. It advises, for example, that to be attractive both men and women should not just take care of their appearance, but learn to sing, play instruments, dance, sew, cook, garden, do woodwork, write poetry, flower-arrange and even undertake a little compassionate veterinary surgery.'

'But how does all this fit into your thesis on "Gender Identity and the Tantric Androgen"?' I asked.

'Because the *Kamasutra* describes human sexuality in every variation, accommodating all humankind in three basic categories according to their differing natures and affections – *pums-prakrti* men, *stri-prakrti* women, and *tritiya-prakrti*, which translates as "third nature". However, none of these titles was as limitingly rigid as today's pedestrian "heterosexual" and "homosexual".'

'And they're only Victorian psychiatric labels,' I grumbled, 'invented to categorise, and thereby either authorise or legislate against, human nature.'

'Precisely!' he declared. 'For example, whilst the *pums-* and *stri-prakrti* categories were applied respectively to men inclined to women and women inclined to men, they also included the intimacy of *kami* and *kamini* – male and female "bisexuality", as the modern West would choose to identify it.'

Jasper paused to pass me a clementine.

'Peel it in one, cous',' he challenged.

'And the third category?' I asked.

'Ah,' he said with a smile. 'Now that requires a little more explanation.'

CI

The way to happiness . . . lies in fulfilling the behests of Love, and each finding for himself the mate who properly belongs to him.

Plato

'As I said, in old India those who did not by nature engage in procreative sex were termed *tritiya-prakrti*, the third sex, whose protection under the law was esteemed an important social principle,' Jasper began. 'Now, these *tritiya-prakrti* included the elderly infirm, those who for whatever reason chose to be celibate, the congenitally asexual, and impotent men, who were termed *budbudayaazu*, meaning "one whose semen is but a bubble".'

This last made us both laugh so loud the urchin swimmers turned to wave again.

'And then there were those whose natural instinct was primarily towards their own sex, traditionally divided into further categories according to their appearance and inclination. There were *svairini*, for example – women whose instinct was to their own kind and who were able to earn their own living wholly independent of a man, under full protection of the law. There were *stripumsa* – masculine women, though not necessarily also *svairini*. And *sandha* – transgender men or biological hermaphrodites. Ta-da!'

'Amazing how humane at least parts of old India were,' I remarked, 'especially compared to its contemporary Christian Europe and America, where people who did not fit were either outcast, declared insane, possessed by demons, or simply put to death!'

'Well, just think how long it has taken the Western medical model to reach the conclusion that something as straightforward as same-sex attraction is biologically determined and not an illness that can be cured!' he exclaimed. 'Especially when you compare it to the *Sushruta Samhita*, one of India's most celebrated medical texts, which stated over a thousand years ago that sexual orientation is innate and not acquired, with both biological sex and inclination being determined at conception, and therefore entirely natural.'

'So under which category would I have been included?' I asked.

'Not looking for a new label are you, cous'?' he asked, scowling in playful reprimand. 'Well, the *Kamasutra* applies the grammatically neuter term *napumsaka* to men whose nature is for personal and passionate attachments with their own sex. Although I must say my favourite term is *samlingrati*, which can be literally translated as either "joined-together amorous enjoyment" – or "equal penis pleasure".'

'I'm adopting it immediately!' I laughed.

'And you know, before colonial Christian notions of "morality" were imposed on the subcontinent, such "joined together" men were able to live in *samlingik sambandh* – same-sex relationships once recognised by civil law as a bond of love and cohabitation that required only mutual agreement, and neither parental consent nor religious ceremony.'

Jasper took the *Kamasutra* from my hands, flicking through to find a passage marked by pencil underlinings.

'See here,' he announced, 'it says that citizens with this kind of inclination get married together because they love each other, "bound by a deep and trusting friendship". And even that "because it is based on love, the *gandharva* marriage is the best"!'

The significance of the term *gandharva* I understood. Originally the name of a Himalayan tribe, folk memory had transformed them over generations into irresistibly handsome men born from the fragrance of flowers, from whence they were said to have derived their nourishment. In time, myth had even attributed to them the very secrets of heaven, hailing Gandharvas as experts in healing, music, drama and the arts of love.

However, the application of their name to marriages between men was founded in the fact that a defining quality of the Gandharvas was that they were so 'completely submerged in the ocean of pleasure' and so 'heroic in sexual dalliance' that every woman and man who looked upon them was said to have become aroused. Even Shiva was said to have been 'mysteriously fascinated' by them, unable to draw his eyes away when they were in his presence. So it is that with their legendary eloquence in all forms of erotic intimacy, in India the art of giving and receiving pleasure is still termed *Gandharva Vidya*, the knowledge of the Gandharvas.

'Of course things are no longer as they used to be,' Jasper admitted with disappointment. 'North India's liberalism really began to wane after the death of Emperor Akbar in the early seventeenth century. And increasingly so after the fall of the Mughal Empire in 1857, which brought the imposition of British law with all its censorious Victorian attitudes.'

It was one of many destructive colonial legacies of which I had frequently despaired.

'Yet even Gandhi-*ji* – the man who liked to imagine that "religion, medical science and commonsense alike forbid sexual intercourse" – lived for a couple of years, in his thirties, in what some have termed a "*gandharva* marriage",' Jasper said to my astonishment. 'Gandhi-*ji*'s "soul mate", as he called him, was a German-Jewish architect and activist called Hermann Kallenbach, to whom he wrote passionate letters, describing how Hermann had completely "taken possession" of his body, saying "this is slavery with a vengeance", whilst pledging to him "more love, and yet more love . . . such love as the world has not yet seen". Rather beautiful, isn't it? Particularly from the pen of a man who spent his remaining years preaching that it was the "duty of every thoughtful Indian not to marry" and that nothing was "as ugly as the intercourse of men and women"!'

I shook my head, hardly able to believe that what he was telling me about India's supreme, loincloth-draped ascetic could possibly be true.

'But it's among ordinary folk, rather than celebrities and politicians, that the old ways survive. Like the Bengali custom of lads exchanging flowers and thereafter referring to each other as "*aamaara phula*" – "my flower" – as public proof of their intimacy and devotion,' Jasper said with pride. 'Although, of course, it's really only the last remnants of the true tantric tradition that still recognise in the unconditional union of kindred partners the "enlightening" liberation so many talk about and believe themselves seeking. You know, when egos dissolve and all sense of biological sex or socially defined gender finally merges into one.'

Not knowing that the truth lies within one's Self, the deluded are confused by searching for it in scriptures [when in reality] there are no commands; there are no prohibitions . . . neither merit nor fall; no heaven and truly no hell.

Kularnava Tantra

J asper was looking at his watch.

'Sorry to say it's about time we found our farewell lunch,' he announced. 'I have two lectures and a bag to repack before I catch the bus this evening.'

We stood to take our leave of the rumpled goddesses and returned the farewell waves of the skinny boys at their wallow. Back on the river path, we paused at the ferry pier to scan the other, palm-fronded shore with its Victorian jute factories that led to the railway sheds of Howrah Station. And in between, all the busyness of trade along the Hooghly, borne by rusting tankers and their tugs, leviathan cargo ships and dredgers, punted wooden rice-boats, and the fantastical floating haystacks of old straw-barges.

'It's hard to think of any modern society that, like early India, would consider the presence of *tritiya-prakrti* third sex people to be especially auspicious,' I admitted. 'Or where, beyond the liberal minority, the sort of protection once offered to them is upheld as an essential social principle.'

'And yet in some parts of India today, men who prefer their own kind are still considered an auspicious gift. And this is because they're seen to embody the essential wholeness of the universal. In fact, there are people in rural districts and in the hills who honour the sensibility of their *tritiya-prakrti* children by encouraging them to take pastoral and ritual roles in temples, or to adopt the role of compassionate "holy man" teacher, reconciler or healer. Like our gentle *jhankris*.'

I had seen this for myself in my relations' foothills, where the main Shiva temple was attended by a tall and beautiful *napumsaka pujari* – 'same-sex-loving officiant' – bewitching to observe as he glided about the complex performing his duties with quiet nobility. I had also learnt that whilst certain Buddhist sects forbade their monks '*dharma*-sex' with women, which could lead to progeny, non-procreative '*kama*-sex' with each other was considered no obstacle to monastic life. In fact, it was even encouraged to ensure not only physical and mental health, but to develop emotional maturity and empathy, and to dissipate the potential conflicts that can arise when men live in such intense proximity.

Similarly, during my travels through south India I had spent time with *velichapadus*, 'revealers of light', the highly respected ritual male dancers, advisers and healers of Kerala, who are commonly 'third nature', as are the members of their entourages. Indeed, *velichapadus* often take another man as their lifelong partner, the nature of their intimacy being commonly considered to be the very act that enables them to sustain their legendary gifts.

'So historically, has there really been no proscription in India against love between the same sex?' I asked.

'Not until Victorian Britishers introduced their Section 377 legislation in 1862,[2] I'm sorry to say,' he replied with a wince, as though in apology for exposing the bigotry of my ancestral countrymen. 'Prior to that, the only "divinely

---

[2] This colonial legislation was finally repealed in 2009, only to be reinstated by the Indian Supreme Court in 2013.

directed" prohibition regarding human intimacy was a single verse from the Mahabharata, in which the voice of Shiva tells Parvati that some "foolish pums-prakrti" – meaning men whose natural inclination is towards women – are "of evil conduct" because they take "advantage of viyoni". Now this refers to very specific sexual crimes, as viyoni is the term for the five "improper wombs": that of another man's wife – adultery; of one's mother or sister – incest; of an animal – bestiality; of a child – paedophilia; or when against another's will – rape. So you see, unlike your Judaeo-Christian culture, we have never seen same-sex love as an issue.'

'The fact that so many in the world still do certainly seems a poor measure of our humanity,' I mumbled, as we continued our stroll along the riverside.

'Then let's spread this old book's wise and compassionate conclusion!' he exclaimed, thrusting the *Kamasutra* above his head as though a new revolutionary standard. 'Because it not only embraces all humankind, but emphasises that personal integrity surpasses all imposed moral systems. Here, there's a closing passage you should read.'

He flicked through its pages as we walked, then paused to direct my attention to lines again already marked in pencil.

'Opinions differ on the matter of purity between the authority of the moral codes, occasional local customs, and one's own feelings,' I read aloud. 'One should therefore behave according to one's own inclinations . . . according to one's own convictions.'

I looked up to meet the eyes of an elderly man, smartly dressed and with a newspaper folded beneath his arm, who had stopped to stand before me on the path.

'Very well put, young man,' he said warmly. 'And welcome to my country.'

CIII

*Joy begets Love
and Love begets Joy.*
Mountain saying

J asper and I were again sitting in the window seat.

The same welcoming waiters had laid before us a gunmetal *thala* plate bearing a mound of steaming rice and six small *bati* bowls filled with an array of such excitingly unfamiliar dishes as crisp *khosha chorchori* vegetable peels, *chhanar kalia* curried cheese and *lauer mishti dalna* sweet marrow. These, I was informed, we were to eat in strict order, from left to right, progressively to 'tantalise the palate'.

We had returned to Jasper's favourite restaurant by rickshaw, our barefoot *wallah* having deftly cut a circuitous route among the congestion of Strand Road to slip us down a side street and through warrens of dilapidating wonder, below which spread villages of the homeless, sleeping, cooking, washing, playing and loving in encampments on the pavements.

We sat and talked of politics again, of texts he recommended that I read – and of his deepest wish to meet someone with whom to spend his life.

'You know, a friend who could love me as I am,' he confided, 'yet who would encourage me to see the world in ways that had never once occurred to me. The sort of friend in whose company I might always wish to strive to become all that I can be.'

Before I could respond, a dish of sweetmeats was delivered to our table with the compliments of the manager.

'They like you here,' I noted.

'That's because I've brought a foreign customer. Always good for business. And, of course, because by birth I'm really rather auspicious!' he said with a smile. 'You see, everything we've talked about these last two days is much more than mere theory here.'

I had certainly attempted throughout our discussions to seek out practical meanings beyond abstract philosophising, as Kushal Magar always encouraged me to do. I had thereby come to understand better that the notions to which many of us mindlessly cling our entire lives of 'I am this and not that', 'I love this sort of person and not that sort of person', *ad infinitum*, do not enrich, expand or liberate, but rather limit and diminish us. Accordingly, I had begun to perceive how these unnatural limitations often left us frustrated with our lives, our relationships and our capacity for true intimacy, without us ever allowing ourselves to recognise the reasons why.

'You'll still be here when I get back next week, won't you?' Jasper asked, as he beckoned for the bill. 'By then my parents and brothers will be back too.'

'I'd like to say yes – but I still don't know what the best thing is for me to do.'

'Then join me on the field trip!' he insisted. 'If I ask they'll certainly make room!'

Ordinarily, I would have leapt at the opportunity of travelling with him, especially when it was to explore rural tantric iconography in the hinterlands of a largely unspoilt tribal state. However, I felt I could not possibly leave the city unless it was to go back up to the hills, or at least with some sort of confirmation that Samuel and Kushal Magar had been released from captivity and were unharmed.

Then what exactly did I now intend? To run up hefty hotel bills whilst anxiously awaiting a restoration of peace and communication in the northernmost reaches of Bengal? Or could I accept that it might well take many weeks, or even months, before foreigners would again be permitted to return, and instead book a flight back to London, where no doubt I would only fret and spend the money saved on hotel bills on persistent long-distance phone calls?

It was a decision I felt unable even to begin to make, as we lingered amid the jostle of the restaurant pavement.

'Then promise we'll be together soon,' he insisted, pressing his face into my chest as he hugged me tightly in farewell.

'I promise,' I replied. 'And thank you for finding me. These two days have been a gift.'

'As are you, British cous',' he mumbled in return.

CIV

*The things that set you free are the very
things that now bind you.*
Kularnava Tantra

Back through my bedroom door, I delayed a seemingly impossible decision by flopping across the Old Spice-scented candlewick to jot notes on what had felt like my morning's lessons.

However, the infinite diversity I was attempting to describe made me question my dilemma: to stay or go? It was a quandary between two opposing choices that seemed over-simplistic in a dynamic, living universe, that − for all our determined efforts to reduce its qualities to 'male' and 'female', 'right' and 'wrong', 'them' and 'us' – was at its very essence an inexpressible, irrepressible multiplicity.

I had still reached no conclusion when my eyes demanded rest, at least until the harshness of the city's heat had eased its rigour. I determined first to scour the grime from my skin, only to have my plan scuppered by the dry, asthmatic wheeze which was all the bathroom taps could produce.

With the hotel devoid of life – guests, staff and proprietress seeming to have already retired for a collective nap – I padded down towards the kitchen in the hope of finding a member of staff willing to provide water for a simple wash-down with a bucket.

My tentative rap on the breakfast serving-hatch revealed that only one attendant had maintained his watch.

'No problem, sir.' Bobby grinned through his sing-song syllables. 'And then,' he added, dropping his voice and flashing his lashes, 'may I do honouring to sir with good-good bubbly scrubbing?'

I insisted that a half-filled pail was all I would require of his faultless hospitality.

'But if sir is leaving before breakfast,' he pressed, 'may Bobby do knocking after dinner-service to give good-good rubbing for goodbye friendliness?'

The offer of another oily tussle across the counterpane held no appeal, but I had to question his belief that I was checking out when I had not yet made any such decision for myself.

'Please be forgiving' – he smiled a length of bright, white teeth – 'but good sir must be where good heart is most wishing.'

And there, at that moment, my resolve was set.

I would take any available seat on any train leaving northwards in the morning, and travel as close to those vast and verdant foothills as I could before politics and Rapid Action Force policemen curtailed my passage. And there, in sight of the mounting expanse where those for whom I most yearned were being held, I would wait until any means of determining their welfare and security became apparent.

It was thus, in relief at my restored purpose – and in apology for thwarting his final wish for a bubble-based farewell – that I took intuitive, bright-and-shiny Bobby firmly in my arms. And felt him tremble.

PART TEN

CV

Man barricades against himself.
Rabindranath Tagore

I awoke to dew-damp air sweetened by the scent of tilled earth, lush vegetation and burning dung.

My tired eyes blinked through barred train windows to watch Bengal rouse by a myriad lamplights' gutter. Village women were honouring goddesses beneath boughs of trees garlanded with marigolds and tinsel. Daughters were feeding kitchen fires with rice stalks in readiness for the return of youths still squatting in ablution over field furrows. Shawl-shrouded men on spindly limbs were leading flocks and herds into the morning's mist. Dusty eagle owls were taking flight from fruiting tamarinds, as cockerels and peacocks gave vocal welcome to the rufous dawn in canon.

I had waited a long, hot Calcutta day for my precious Tourist Quota seat on an evening train that had been largely requisitioned by the army. The wasted hours had at least given me time to post a letter to Jasper explaining my unplanned disappearance. I had also promised that on my return I would stay at his family home, as he had asked. I now worried that my message might not reach him and

regretted that the neighbour had not been home both times
I had tried to ring.

The railway clerk behind the ticket window marked
'Handicapped, Foreigners & Freedom Fighters' had assured
me that the journey north would take fourteen hours, 'or
sometimes more', but we had already been stationary for at
least an extra two. Engine trouble, the young soldier lying
opposite confidently informed me.

Pravir and a pair of fellow privates, both of whom still
snored in the bunks above our heads, were rejoining their
regiment in the hills after an extended weekend's leave.
Pravir had been back to his home village, where his parents
had chosen for him a wife of whose youth and compliant
nature he wholeheartedly approved. Next furlough they
would be married, he announced with pride, and by the
end of harvest she would deliver the first of many sons. A
Brahmin's horoscope, for which he had saved many months,
had categorically confirmed it.

When, at his enquiry, I revealed that I was neither a father
nor espoused, Pravir's forehead concertinaed to a scowl. Had
I better not hurry, he insisted, for once my sisters married
and my mother and aunts were gone, who would cook my
food and scrub my clothes? And if I had no wife to provide
that all-essential 'manly release', and no children as evidence
of my 'manly duties', was I not already a source of shame for
my good parents, the butt of mockery from both family and
neighbours?

'After all, friend,' he hissed, as though his very words
might prove a fatal invitation, 'death is coming!'

The train's irritable rasp back into life, followed by a series
of petulant jolts, finally forced our two companions awake.
They peered down at us from the billows of their bedding
like drowsy, dry-lipped seraphs. They yawned and stretched,

then, clad only in regulation khaki vests and shorts, swung down dark legs to share a *tiffin-wallah*'s flask of Catering Corps sweet tea.

Such was their initial affability that I offered to share Bobby's farewell gift of mint leaves and tomato ketchup sandwiches as a means to brave the subject of the unrest they were returning to subdue. I was especially keen to know whether any of them had been previously assigned to, or had any knowledge of, a village known as Lapu?

Whilst the offer of my eccentric snack was emphatically declined, Anik, who bore a boxer's nose and the incongruous eyelashes of a chital doe, confirmed he had served with a Special Forces transport transferring 'agitators' from the area around Lapu into a *dak* bungalow hastily converted from travellers' rest-house into military 'interrogation centre'.

I flinched at the brutality suggested by such a term, but pressed for the location and condition of his charges. Had he, for example, come across an Anglo-Indian lad named Samuel? Or a *jhankri* of the Magar tribe? Did he know if they were still detained? Did he know if either of them had been hurt?

The soldier shrugged dismissively. These hill types all looked alike and were all troublemakers, he asserted, eager to describe how his troop had quickly identified and 'dealt with' the ringleaders, teaching 'the rest of those *junglies* their lessons' before driving them back 'to their fellow forest monkeys'. At this admission he swiped the air as though to demonstrate delivery of cruel clouts and kicks – violent charades that made me wince, whilst prompting his smirking companions to pull illustrative 'chinky' eyes and squeal like a pantomime girls' chorus.

I suddenly felt sick.

'But no foreigners allowed beyond Siliguri!' the third

soldier interjected as though in threat. Of all of them, he had shown suspicion both at my interest and my lack of amusement at their ugly jests. 'And as it's always unmarried men who are drug-dealing and gun-running in the hills, you just keep going east to Assam! Go spend your dollars on cheap chicks in Guwhati!'

'No, better you types all go south!' chipped in Anik. 'Join those other idiot foreigners playing *swami-guru* yoga and lying naked on the beaches like dying cattle in the sunshine!'

'Or better still, just go back home, grow a 'tache and get yourself married like a proper man!' Pravir declared, a proposal that prompted such hilarity both he and Anik spilt their tea.

But I had already drifted back to palm-frond huts and flag-topped shrines beyond the glassless window of the train. I was focusing on slow-motion buffalo carts in convoy through fields of sugar cane.

I was swallowing to restrain my nausea at the thought that I might be sitting with sneering men who had inflicted harm, not only on Samuel and Kushal Magar, but on others of those people with whom I most longed to be, in hills from which it seemed I would yet be kept for far too long.

CVI

Since I know nothing at all,
I shall simply do whatever occurs to me.
Carl Jung

The train station appeared to have been transformed into the film-set of some Bollywood war epic.

Each platform, stair and concourse was choked with rifle-bearing soldiers and their kit. Quartermasters' colossal stock in crate and sack. Shoe-shine boys and *tiffin-wallahs* competing among the milling crowd for custom. And clustered close around mounds of string-tied boxes and stripy zipper-bags, families who by their anxious bewilderment I took to be new refugees.

Gazing at the fray to which I had been finally delivered, I could see no way of reaching the official exit without a battle of will and elbows. Instead, I wound my way through teams of porters piling coffin-like black trunks into towers according to regiment and rank, until I reached the distant side of the railway buildings. I winced at the stench of dehydrated urine in which the ground and end walls were drenched, then turned the corner to discover, to my great surprise, a party of a dozen Lepchas – Mutanchi Rong Kup, the Beloved of the Great Mother, as the indigenous tribe of the hills prefer – all of whom were squatting beneath the shade of an advertising hoarding.

I offered a cheerful '*Kahmri!*' in greeting as I approached, causing their faces to widen in astonishment. '*Aket do?*' I persisted, asking after their well-being.

At this, they could no longer contain themselves, clapping their hands and crying out in delight to hear an approximation of their own tongue attempted by a foreigner. The truth was that over the years I had learnt but a few words of their Tibeto-Burman Rongring language from the cook who produced endless treats in her mud-walled kitchen at the home of Samuel's parents, themselves proud bearers of Lepcha blood amid their already exotic blend of Indo-European genes.

In honour of my effort, the family beckoned me to join them in a pre-packed stock of food that instantly appeared from woven bags and metal canisters, such precious rations that I only allowed myself to pick politely. However, as I began to question them about the village from which they had descended, and heard of homes ransacked, farmland torched and brutal beatings – even of their transgender *mun* wise-'woman' – my appetite fast waned.

I shared in their distress, and told of cousins and the *jhankri* to whom I had determined to return, but they simply shook their heads. 'Most sorry, brother' – they grimaced, pinching tongues between teeth to express regret – 'no foreigners allowed.'

I felt my heart sinking again – a self-defeating indulgence, I decided, when others' homes and lives were being lost in hills that rose so near to where we sat, yet which remained hidden by a haze of dusty heat and wholly inaccessible.

In less than two days since leaving Calcutta, I already found myself unable to decide what I should do for the best.

I imagined Kushal Magar might have reminded me of my Purushartha duties to find a means by which the equilibrium we too easily lose through our self-interest might be restored. For whilst it was beyond my means to resolve the violent politics of this present conflict, I could at least restore *my* balance and thereby render myself of benefit to those in far greater need of comfort and protection.

It was with this new clarity and, perhaps, a less self-absorbed intention that I turned back towards the bank of oblique eyes beneath the signboard to ask what, in small return for their precious food and welcome, I could do for them.

This question induced excitable discussion, silenced only when the eldest of the women stepped forwards to request I do nothing more than accompany them in their day's journey to the river, where they intended to meet others of their tribe. They then planned to camp together, until safe passage might be secured back to their plundered villages.

'We were waiting until darkness. But with a Britisher as a brother, the soldiers will not be causing us more trouble,' her translator, Tingbo, whom I guessed to be her grandson, explained.

'Well then, of course I will,' I replied. 'Especially as it was those same soldiers who forced me out of your hills last week. It would therefore be nothing less than a privilege to accompany you back towards them!'

'*Achulay! Achulay!*' the family chorused. 'Hurrah! Hurrah!'

My response had evidently been wholeheartedly approved.

Self-surrender is the surest of all methods . . . the best of means.
If it is not used, other means do not avail.
Tripura Rahasya

The walk eastwards, keeping close to railway tracks in preference to roads lined with canvas-topped army trucks and the bored young men in uniform of whom my new companions were so wary, was long and slow, yet joyful.

The little band proved their people's reputation for light-heartedness, easy laughter and *apra-vam* impromptu song. Indeed, the Lepcha were widely known as much for their sincere, generous and co-operative natures, and their culture devoid of caste or creed, as for their affording authority only to those with the wisdom of age, and their fondness for merrymaking sprees. I also knew them to be noted for their remarkably free and playful sexual expression – a fact reflected in the total lack of linguistic taboos in their witty, metaphor-filled tongue – and for being neither aggressive, nor quarrelsome, nor personally ambitious, the only three qualities their culture deemed 'immoral'.

As the steel rails swung southwards, we cut away through grain and mustard, through butterflies in tumble, to skirt farmhouses tucked beneath tall bamboo and banana thickets. We traversed in single file the labyrinthine banks of paddy fields, through the glint of dragonflies, the grump of frogs in flight from hungry herons, until we reached the river's drift, in which pied kingfishers hunted.

It was with relief that I eased my rucksack and the shawl-bound provisions I had insisted I help carry on to sandy banks.

I stretched my sodden back, washed arms and face, then helped light fires to double-boil water in readiness for food, whilst young men stripped to wade beyond the sparkling shallows in search of fish. However, with the pleasures of raucous swimming all too quickly found, the boys eventually returned to land still laughing, at ease with their undress – and empty-handed.

I joined the communal laughter as failed fishers next snatched each other's clothes and ran around in circles, revealing, to my surprise, dark bruises on their bodies. And yet, despite the general jollity, I had to face the sobering fact that beyond today's assignment and camping at the foothills' base in daily hope of news, I still had no means of locating Samuel and Kushal Magar.

I expressed my quandary to Tingbo, who had settled close beside me as he dressed. His solution was simple: 'Stay with us!' he insisted. 'You keep safe. We keep safe!'

As proof, he called out to his grandmother, who concurred that I was 'most welcome', for the Lepcha considered the British had saved their people from extinction under the oppressive rule of the Bhutanese.

'You-people honoured we-people, and in our great gratitude it is our turn to honour you!' she explained.

'You see!' Tingbo laughed. 'Our food, your food. Our family, your family.'

I touched my heart to show gratitude, vowing to remain until I saw them settled with their fellow Lepcha refugees.

And so, with wet boys re-clothed, tea drunk and our meal of rice, lentils and oil-preserved chillies consumed, the fires were extinguished and our trek northwards along shoreline shingle resumed with a communal song, as what would unexpectedly prove to be our only day together began to fade to dusk.

CVIII

Whatever is desired and made a dedication to becomes reality.
Paratrimshika

The sight of smoke plumes spiralling in the day's last light prompted more boisterous cheers of '*Achulay!*' My companions were certain we approached the other camp.

It was not, however, until we forded the river where it curved, split, widened and ran low that we could finally determine a second group of some twenty Lepchas settled beneath a broad-boughed banyan.

Through the joyful clamour of their reunion and the misplaced honour they afforded me, Tingbo introduced our new companions as more relations from their village. Whilst his family had run across the fields during the attack, these others had escaped the soldiers' sweep by climbing into trees. It was only when he and others of the older boys had returned to collect more provisions that they had been caught and beaten.

'We Rongpa are gentle people,' he said, unconsciously touching the marks on his cheek and forehead. 'No hurting. No hitting.'

Our evening was spent around new fires sharing more food and tea, recounting more stories and singing yet more songs. Thinking of the conversations I had had with Jasper, I took the opportunity to ask about the Lepchas' fascinating notion that mankind has three 'souls'. It was a question that prompted a lively discussion, which Tingbo summarised in translation.

First, he explained, there is the *apil*, man's individual

consciousness that returns to the ancestors at death. Second, the *mangkung*, which determines man's inner nature. Third, a 'soul' of opposite gender to the body's biological appearance, each man bearing a female self called Nandlen Nyu, each woman a male self called Kathong Fee. This third aspect is considered to have been given by the Mother-Creator, Itbu-moo, that mankind's amorous and sexual natures might be enlivened. Therefore, when a couple are attracted to one another or fall in love, they believe it is these opposite gender selves that are, in fact, responding – an essential 'hermaphrodite' aspect to human nature that embraces affection and intimacy between all combinations of genders.

When my companions invited me, in exchange, to share 'a myth, a truth or insight', I revealed that I had once had a Great-Aunt Isi who too had been a Lepcha, her father both the Raja of Phuptshering, below Darjeeling, and the Mudhal of Pachin, in the Kurseong Valley. This fact caused such excitement and so many communal cries of '*Achulay! Achulay!*' that I thought the soldiers we were so cautiously avoiding might be alerted to our presence and arrest us all.

'A Rongpa Grandmother-auntie!' Tingbo whispered in wonder once the entire camp had settled down beneath shared blankets. 'Then you truly are our brother!'

I thought Tingbo almost immediately asleep, whilst in my discomfort on bare ground and my mind busy, I stayed awake to stare at stars and bats and the final sliver of a crescent moon, listening to a wild world industrious in nocturnal animation.

I thought of my precious and extraordinary hours with Jasper, and reflected on the unexpected adventure of the last few days that had led to this incredible conclusion: lying at a forest's edge with Lepchas, in night air that bore such a peculiar, sweet smokiness that when I attempted to take too strong a sniff I started coughing.

'Not too deep, brother,' Tingbo mumbled. 'You know the smoke that led us to this banyan was not from our brothers' camp?'

It had not occurred to me that there had indeed been no fire lit on our arrival to produce those initial plumes.

'That smell is the cremation ground around the river's bend,' he explained from beneath his bedding. 'You're breathing in dead Hindus.'

I promptly drew my sleeping-bag to cover my nose, even though I knew it was too late to make a difference. I also knew that the Lepcha did not burn on pyres, but were buried sitting in a basket, or reclining with legs outstretched, head raised on a stone pillow. And this that their sightless eyes might 'look' towards Kanchenjunga's bright white peak, to which at their life's end they believed their essential *apil* consciousness returned.

Perhaps it was this thought and our unexpected proximity to death that provoked in me a new unease for those who lay beyond the army roadblocks and imported Russian rifles. It prompted fears that prevented me from sleep, despite the day's fatigue – until I accepted there was nothing I could do but again set my *bhavana*, determining with all my heart to ascertain by any means that those I loved were liberated and unharmed.

I tried sleeping on my other side, but only lay listening to the insects' steady measure, my companion Lepchas' snores, and the hurry of the river, until I could no longer deny what had become a pressing need. I unwrapped myself from bag and blanket, slipped on my shoes and tiptoed off to find a spot where I might attend a tea-caused urge.

The forest's edge seemed darker beyond the company of

the camp, the thoughts of snake and tiger more threatening without the snores of my companions. As I rummaged with my zip, I was reminded that Lepcha men are in the habit of exposing their penises when fearful in the solitude of the forest – especially in trepidation of meeting the huge and hairy *Sangrong mung*, who they believe is summoned if someone whistles after sunset, an act accordingly forbidden in Lepcha communities. I had even heard it said that to dispel such night-born dread, Lepcha men commonly shake their manhoods at the gloom and boldly declare, 'Take this!' before striding on with renewed courage.

It was as I looked up beyond the tree I had just dampened that my eyes fixed upon a figure that, at first glance, seemed suspended on the river. A figure whose white attire appeared an incompatible brightness beneath scattered stars and narrow moon. Indeed, so unlikely and alarming was this vision that I dared not move.

I stared again to ascertain that this apparition was neither fantasy nor soldier, determining it to be a man dressed in the white *daura-suruwal* of the mountain Nepalese, his hands held out in *mudras*, his chest adorned with strings of bones and beads.

I stumbled forwards into moonlight and released a trembling cry.

Standing in the middle of the ford and staring back at me was Kushal Magar.

CVIX

Out of the chaos would come bliss.
Dylan Thomas

I could not contain my tears.

Nor could I repress my impulse to run into the water, plunging in my hands to touch his feet. And then to break decorum and, for the first time in all these years, hug Kushal Magar to my heart.

Nor did he resist, but returned my affection with the tender strength of a long, reciprocal embrace.

And there we stood – pipistrelles in frenzied flight about our heads, river swirling round our shins – both tightly held. Both silent.

Until, unable to contain myself longer, I let loose a torrent of questions.

How could he be here, standing in this river in the middle of the night? So where was Samuel? Was Jai Kumari safe? In Lapu or Darjeeling? What had the soldiers done to them after the arrest? Had they burned the village? And what of Kalimpong? Was all the family unharmed? But how was this possible? Had I found him, or had he found me? Or was our being at the same place, at the same time just another remarkable coincidence?

All he offered in response was to draw back to study my barely moonlit features. He gave a pensive smile, which, perhaps for lack of light, I could not see reflected in his eyes.

'Come.' He indicated with his chin towards the bank. 'No benefit in us catching cold.'

It was not until we reached the forest shore, where my Lepcha friends still slept, that I noticed he was limping.

'They hurt you, didn't they?' I gasped, the very thought setting my chest and belly aflame with fury. 'Then where is Samuel? Did they hurt him too?'

'To restore the balance outside,' he replied, 'we must first restore our own within.'

I tried to focus on breathing in the cool night air, when a sudden movement beside us made me start.

'Samuel!' I cried out in relief.

'Brother?' Tingbo whispered in reply.

I made hurried introductions, both men responding to each other with tilts of heads and respectful touches of the heart.

'Then will you also join us, *jhankri*-brother?' Tingbo asked, indicating back towards the sleeping camp. 'You are most welcome.'

To my surprise, his invitation was respectfully declined.

'Would you instead permit me to take our brother away with me?' Kushal Magar requested.

I turned to him astonished, unable to imagine where we could possibly be going in the blackness of the night.

'But of course,' Tingbo replied. 'Our British brother has fulfilled his promise and has seen our family to safety. Now he has his own path to pursue.'

'What's going on?' I asked Kushal Magar as Tingbo vanished back to camp, insisting he would fetch my luggage. 'You haven't answered any of my questions. At least tell me where Samuel is!'

His only answer was to place an emphatic hand on my arm.

As I struggled to make sense of Kushal Magar's uncharacteristic reserve, Tingbo reappeared, his short mountain legs bearing the burden of my rucksack with apparent ease.

'I'm sorry to be leaving so suddenly,' I began, but did not know what else to say. The fact was I could not explain this peculiar spiriting-away in the middle of the night, not even to myself.

'No need for sorry-ness. You must be doing your new duty,' Tingbo replied, glancing back to Kushal Magar with no sign of misgiving. 'But before you leave,' he added, as I squeezed his narrow shoulders in farewell, 'I wish to tell you that, well, you know how after harvest when the paddies are dry and smell so sweet as we run barefoot through them?' He reached out to take my hand and press my palm against his heart. 'Well today, being with you, brother, I have been even happier than this.'

CX

Our final fear arises only when life is left unlived.
Bindra

We walked along the star-bright bank in silence as I turned and waved, turned and waved, until Tingbo subsided into shadow.

I followed Kushal Magar towards our unnamed destination, my mind a storm of questions, to none of which he yet seemed ready to attend. We skirted the darkness of the forest's edge, gradually rounding the broad curve of the river, where a steep bank appeared, the top of which seemed flat and almost clear of trees. As we climbed into dim moonlight, I turned to study his face in profile. It was evident that he was not himself. Withdrawn. Sullen even.

'What's happened?' I asked gently, unable to wait any longer.'What are you not telling me?'

Kushal Magar slowed to indicate that we should sit on a stretch of sandy ground. He positioned himself to face me, touched my knees and then his heart to indicate new teaching. And this when, until little more than an hour before, I had feared we might never meet again.

'Brother, life is a series of inevitable endings,' he began, his eyes holding fast to mine. 'Our sleep, work, meals, journeys, loves, our daily dusks. By each of these small finalities, we learn to set our sense of time and season in what is otherwise history's indifferent, annihilating span.'

Such was the unease his words provoked that I broke his gaze to look away to constellations whose myriad fiery stars, for all we knew, may long ago have been quenched.

'Our sense of who and what and why we are is largely determined by our response to these intimate conclusions. The fear of our own, however, has lain so heavily upon the human heart from the moment our forebears first knew themselves finite, that for millennia we have imagined all manner of myths, philosophies, rites and religions to comfort us in the face of that one decisive end.'

I nodded in uncomfortable agreement.

'Of course, no other animal or bird lives in the daily knowledge of its certain demise. This is the gift of none but self-conscious man. We alone know ourselves set upon an inescapable course towards that ultimate horizon. And it is herein that our silent suffering lies: not in the moment of death itself, but in its anticipation.'

I knew this to be true, for unless we chose to find solace in the belief of an impending reunion with loved ones in some sort of Afterlife – a Bardo, Sheol, Limbo of the Patriarchs, Spirit World or Summerland – or in being born again to resolve our 'issues' as though caught in some perpetual cosmic therapy, was not our 'silent suffering' in essence but a fear of unimaginable change? The ego's dread of its ultimate annihilation?

'And yet,' he continued, 'the personality that anticipates, fears and suffers is in truth but a momentary *bindu* – a knot of faculties that unties at or shortly after death.'

I did not respond, but felt a deep alarm rising as I wondered at the purpose of this subject when all I truly wanted to know was whether Samuel was also free from custody and safe.

'Here, people consider that due to man's attachment to the physical body for his sense of self, even after its demise, this *bindu* unties more quickly if the corpse is cremated and some small part buried in a riverbed, before the crows are fed.'

'*Jhankri-dajoo*, what are you trying to tell me?' I demanded, my heart now beating in my ears.

Kushal Magar drew his breath and paused, as with him the sky, the river, the dark forest with its unseen beasts all seemed momentarily suspended.

And then: 'Be strong and hear me, brother,' he said softly, reaching out to grasp my hands as though both to comfort and restrain me. 'Samuel-*bhai* is dead.'

CXI

I t was full light when I awoke to crows in chorus.

I lengthened my aching limbs, shielded my eyes from a brightening dawn – and then again lay still.

All was not well.

A commotion was raging in my head and chest, a violent confusion I could only attribute to what had seemed a night of startlingly vivid dreams of a *jhankri* walking on water. And then a burst of words I could not comprehend that had summoned crushing weight and searing pain from which I had been unable to find reprieve.

I seemed to think I had been writhing in my sleep, sobbing loud and shouting. I must have woken Tingbo.

I shook the snags of memory from my head to stretch again and turn to scan the camp.

To my dismay, it was no longer there. No Tingbo. No Lepchas. Not even the dark, defensive wall of trees.

Instead, before me lay a scene of desolation. Soot and cinder, smoulder and scorch.

'Hello?' I called towards a solitary, shawl-wrapped stranger, who stood away from me above the river's brink, his arms outstretched and moving, as though communing with the reel of crows above his head.

But when the figure turned to reveal a face I knew, of which I thought I had only dreamt, my chest compressed until it seemed I felt the splintering of my ribs and both lungs pierced.

And suddenly, every second of a night that had been no dream at all replayed in terrible lucidity.

'They took us all, but did not hold us long,' Kushal Magar had recounted with a tired, impassive voice, as I had crumpled forwards gasping. 'But before we were released, they made sure no limb or spine would forget our meeting. We Lapu men and Samuel-*bhai* made our way back together, well away from roads. It took two days as some needed to be carried. You might imagine our relief, then, to find only one farm burned and all the women – including Jai Kumari – unharmed.

'Samuel-*bhai* would not stay. He insisted he return to Kalimpong and his parents. I asked him to wait until one of us could lead him by a hidden route across the hills at dawn. But such was his anxiety he would not be persuaded, so our schoolmaster gave him his scooter to see him quickly home.

'As he made his way, Samuel-*bhai* met a woman by the roadside with an ailing child. Of course, what else was he to do but take them to the hospital? But the teacher's scooter was in poor repair, so when the petrol line kept clogging Samuel stopped and cleared it by sucking on the tube. Over and over again, sucking on the tube, sucking on the tube. And yet when they eventually reached the hospital, it was all too late. The child was already dead.

'By the time Samuel had returned to his parents, he was already confused and flushed. His speech had become so slurred they thought he must have been drinking millet *chang*, which they had never known him do. They took him to his bed and tucked him in. But he never woke again. A heart attack from petrol poisoning.

'The cremation was undertaken before next nightfall, when his father asked me to complete the rites – the burial of one remaining part in a riverbed, and then the feeding of the crows. But in the hills access to the river has been denied. Our crossings and cremation grounds are now guarded by soldiers, with the excuse that we *jhankri*-types are all agitators in disguise. I have since been walking down through the forest to reach this *masaan-ghat* to do my final duty.

'So do you understand me, brother? All is done, the rites complete. Samuel-*bhai*'s *bindu* is released and gone.'

His words had left me unable to speak.

Or to accept the true and dreadful nature of the sacrament at which I had first found him standing alone and silent in the river's drift.

CXII

> *My unfulfilled past clinging to me from behind,*
> *making death difficult.*
> Rabindranath Tagore

I had closed my eyes and curled up tight, not so much to sleep as to shut out the madness that threatened to overwhelm me.

Kushal Magar roused me periodically to offer a foul unguent of mountain herbs in fermented yak's milk. And with every proffering the promise: 'To ease your grief, brother, to ease your grief.'

It was not until another sun had begun to set that I finally woke to find the initial shock had eased and I was now in the fold of a numb stillness. Kushal Magar was boiling *daal-bhat* rice and lentils. Beyond us sat a naked man with his eyes closed, mind and body in meditative suspension, his *rudraksha* necklace, entangled locks and ash–stained skin all announcing him Aghori Baba, one of a radical sect of wandering, taboo-breaking *sadhus*. In the darkness of the previous night, I had had no sense that I had been led to the forest cremation ground.

'Jhankri-dajoo,' I murmured, my voice as lifeless as the charred, grey landscape before us. 'Why bring me to a burning *ghat* to tell me?'

'The loss of those who are our delight delivers us to pain beyond all measure,' he replied, his eyes intent upon me as he drew close. 'Pain for which only the passing of time and the company of those who share the same sorrow may afford a gradual easing.'

He paused to hand me a small bowl of steaming rice and lentils. He said nothing as I turned away. I could not face the thought of food.

'But why tell me here?' I asked again, my head and heart still so blunted by the account he had delivered that I could feel nothing but a remote and abstract bleakness.

'That you and I might stand together before death. That you might know for yourself that dissolution bears no moral quality of its own beyond that imposed by our own cultures and beliefs. For death is not an enemy to be feared or defeated, brother. It is essential to the very existence of the universe, releasing the energy that forms our shapes and minds, scattering us and the wisdom we have gained to reorganise as new life, enabling both the vital change and the stability that allows you and me – and all of this – to be.'

He had impressed this notion on me before, but never had the words so starkly contrasted with the beliefs in which

I had been raised: that destruction – whether flood or war, disease or mere accident – was a just punishment meted upon the 'sinner'; that death was either the long-awaited release from life's intractable vicissitudes, or the ultimate divine curse against man for Edenic disobedience.

'Do you see?' he asked. 'Life and death are inseparable. One is not good and the other bad, for both are necessary.'

I did not respond, but again looked out across the cremation ground, a place I knew held great meaning in the Indo-Nepali mind, in a way that was not always easy for outsiders to comprehend. The ancient death rituals – the *antyeshti*, last sacrifice – were so far removed from the sanitised funeral homes and municipal crematoria of the West that foreigners were often shocked at the scenes of ordinary life mingling with what proved to be in truth very ordinary death.

I well remembered my first sight some years before of Varanasi's pyres and priests, 'untouchable' *doms* along the shoreline sifting through the cinders for gold teeth, half-charred limbs protruding from Gangeatic scum. And yet those hours on the busy burning *ghats* had delivered me to a new dimension of perception; an awakening affirmation that the vast ocean of life demanded more than just dipping in a trepidatious toe. That its infinite depths were to be plunged into, its inestimable fathoms sounded, its boundless waters drunk.

'Of course, you already know our Nepali term for pyre is *chitaa*,' Kushal Magar said, 'a word that comes from *chit*, universal consciousness, for in both is everything dissolved. Not only our physical appearance, but all the fears, habits and hierarchies by which we limit and darken the experience of our lives.'

I scanned a cremation ground now busy with a final

flurry of ritual activity. Fires were either being fed to intensify the last incinerations, or raked to ensure that all significant remains were reduced to carbon before sunset.

'The burning of every pyre is therefore considered renewed learning for those of us who still have life to live in all its wonder.'

I noticed there had been two new deliveries, too late to burn, which would have to remain bound in their cerements and under the watch of the Aghori Baba, as guard against rats and jackals. Only at dawn would families return to undertake the final rites.

It was certainly undeniable that to sit in sight of the spectacle of cremation, among the all-pervasive sediment of the deceased, both prompted and intensified reflection. For where else might I have so starkly confronted the full, debilitating force of my grief for Samuel but by literally facing the inevitability, even mundanity, of death? How else might I have found another way to let him leave?

'But now you must eat,' Kushal Magar suddenly insisted, pressing a second bowl of hot *daal-bhat* towards me. 'You need your belly full. You need your strength. Tonight there will be no sleep.'

'Why no sleep?' I asked, mechanically taking the bowl and staring at its contents.

'Brother, tonight is *amavasya*, a dark moon,' he offered as though sufficient explanation. 'It is time to embrace new learning.'

CXIII

In death the many become one;
in life the one becomes many.
Rabindranath Tagore

The starlight had grown brilliant.

I watched Kushal Magar make his approach to the last remaining figure on the cremation ground: the Aghori Baba, who had already settled for the night beneath the branches of a scorched and leafless tree. They seemed to exchange little more than a single phrase before he beckoned me to join them beside the two corpses that awaited the coming day's fires.

I had been close to the dead before, not only in India, but back home in Europe. My first, when still a child, had been the discovery of a girl lying across a grassy verge beside her broken bicycle in Normandy. I had stared in fascination at her open yet unblinking eyes, her lips apart as though in silenced song, her cheeks as matt and white as soft-paste porcelain. I remembered how, despite my youth, I had felt neither fear nor repulsion, but quiet awe – a response to the presence of death that had ever remained with me.

It was for this reason that when Kushal Magar led me to the bodies beside the seared tree, I felt no trepidation. Nor when, after a touching of their hearts and the mumbling of mantra, I watched the Aghori Baba lift the feet of one of the sheet-bound bodies, whilst the *jhankri* bore the shoulders, to lay the head northwards on a stretch of open ground.

Once our ash-stained companion had withdrawn into the darkness, Kushal Magar began to intone in earnest, his hands moving through a series of gestural *mudras* to focus our intention. Yet still I felt myself an inert observer in what seemed the lunacy of someone else's dream. I watched him score a circle around the corpse through the earth's ash crust, into which he stepped to untie the shroud and spread its scented cloth.

And there we stood, silent sentinels at head and foot of the naked body of a young Nepali man of seemingly perfect form and health, except that he was lifeless – his slim limbs limp, neat ears and nose stuffed with untidy plugs of cotton, his penis tied tight with string.

I looked on impassively, struck only by the idea that this dead youth might have been Samuel – a thought so difficult not only to comprehend but to believe that I suddenly found myself questioning his loss. Was it really true? Or had all this just been some ultimate test of Kushal Magar's? Was Samuel in fact quite safe at home? Or was he concealed out there in the darkness, ready to surprise me once it had been judged that some new lesson had been learnt?

These doubts summoned a new and sickening anxiety in my heart. Could these two men, who I counted as my dearest friends, really perpetrate such an unpitying conspiracy?

I glanced about in sudden, maddened hope that a furtive movement or glint of lamplight might expose my cousin-brother in his hiding place, their mischief foiled.

'Samuel? Are you there?' I cried out. 'Because I can't do this any more! You have to stop! I've had enough!'

'Brother, brother!' Kushal Magar gently protested, raising his palms towards me in the traditional fear-dispelling *abhaya* gesture. 'Samuel-*bhai* is already gone to fire and river, crow and weather. It is done. The wisdom of his life has been shared.'

I shook my head, dizzy with new waves of nausea, and

stared back into the darkness. I refused to accept it could be true.

'Do you understand? He is gone,' he repeated. 'Yet Samuel-*bhai* is not lost.'

I looked back towards the benevolence of his eyes and knew Kushal Magar could never perpetrate such a merciless deception. He might challenge and provoke me, and always for my good – but never would he inflict such cruelty.

'Then who is this?' I muttered towards the mottled feet laid out before me.

'An unknown brother,' was all that he replied.

We stood in silence, as I tried to process the snarl of facts that stupefied my every sense.

'But, *jhankri-dajoo*,' I eventually asked, 'what are we doing here with him?'

'If you are willing, I am offering you your *shava-sadhana*,' Kushal Magar announced. 'Tonight, you are initiated by contemplation on a corpse.'

CXIV

For what is it to die
but to stand naked in the wind and to melt into the sun?
Kahlil Gibran

I knew of *shava-sadhana* in theory.

Aghori Babas and Tibetan *trapas* monks were all known to employ its practice at some stage of their training. I had heard that years of preparation were normally required to ensure the student was suitably mature and of sufficient emotional stability to face its provocation. Never, therefore, had I imagined that I would find myself presented with such an extreme initiation – and with it, the ultimate confrontation with my own mortality.

The custom, as I understood, required the selection of the fresh, unblemished body of a mature adult of the same sex as the student, in the company of which, and under a teacher's watchful guide, a night would be spent in contemplation. If no suitable corpse could be located, a dead animal, or even a life-sized effigy made from grass, might be presented as a substitute.

Whilst *shava-sadhana* was not advised for those titillated by the morbid or grotesque, students of an excessively sensitive disposition were more likely to be guided through nothing more challenging than a night-long yogic *sadhana* on the burning *ghat*, their *asana* postures and *pranayama* breath-retention practised to the dying light of smouldering pyres, culminating in *pratyahara* 'mental withdrawal' undertaken on the remaining bed of cold cinders.

However, whichever version was deemed best suited, this 'instruction from destruction', as it is called, was to enable the student to face their fears and self-doubts; their culturally ingrained notions of good and bad, pure and polluted, sacred and profane – and thereby to confront their ordinary motivation and conditioning. This in turn was to assist the student to dispel patterns of self-defeating greed, vanity, apathy, anger and resentment, that they might better replace habitual self-interest with self-awareness, and thus live and love more fully, fearlessly and joyfully.

Such was the nature of *shava-sadhana* that over the years I had heard recounted around the kitchen table all manner of fanciful mythologies in its regard. It was said, for example, that if the practice were effective the head of a corpse laid prone would spin around to voice esoteric secrets. Or even that by magical means a dead man's phallus alone might be resurrected, enabling his cold seed to be 'gathered' for purposes ever more arcane.

In contrast to such outlandish horrors, my Kalimpong aunts preferred to whisper, with that ghoulish delight peculiar to matronly relations, of 'meditation corpses' being ridden through the night like fairytale broomsticks, cadavers belching jet-engine flames from their dead mouths, whilst black sesame seeds – symbols of man's virile energy aroused – spluttered from their navels.

Where once I might have joined in the familial amusement at such gothic tales, I knew I never would again, for this moment was unlike anything I could ever have imagined. And so soon after the news of Samuel's death, from which I still felt myself peculiarly removed, that I now feared the painful turmoil it might provoke in both mind and heart.

I had been so consumed by the intensity of my thoughts that I had not noticed Kushal Magar empty his cloth bag to don the symbolic accoutrements of his craft: the strings of bone and dried-seed beads, the cotton sashes of white and scarlet, the headdress trimmed with peacock feathers and *kauri* shells.

Thus prepared, he voiced rhythmical mantras as he raised the *thurmi* ritual dagger before plunging its blade into the ground as though *linga* into *yoni*. And this, not only to represent the binding of elemental space to earth that stability might be symbolically assured throughout the coming practice, but to signify the forces of consciousness and energy that constitute both the animate and inanimate, the quickened and deceased.

And then the final act of preparation: lighting a flame through which I passed my hands, before pricking both thumbs with acacia spines. As custom demanded, the margin between the living and the dead had been defined with fire and thorn.

'Brother, are you ready?' he asked.

But I could find no means of answering him, for how could I ever be prepared for such a rite as this?

All I knew for certain was that this one man had never failed me. Nor did I believe he ever would. What else, then, was I to do but trust him?

I therefore looked into the rift of his dark eyes, raised both hands to my heart and bowed my head. At his instruction, I bent first to remove my shoes, then clothes, until I stood naked in the starlight.

'Then, it is time,' he said – and bade me step into the circle.

CXV

On the destruction of a jar,
the space within unites with all space.
Avadhut Gita

Hours had passed into the night, yet I was still awake with skin so chilled and mind so restless that sleep held very little threat.

When I had first looked down on the dead young man, his supine limbs and torso stretched out before me like an unresponsive star-cast shadow, Kushal Magar had offered choices. Some preferred to sit on the cadaver's chest to commence the meditative practice, he had revealed. Others rolled the corpse face down to straddle its pelvis, perineum pressed to sacrum.

At the suggestion of such intimacy, my numb bravado had suddenly failed in a fierce rush of repulsion and alarm. I had never before resisted Kushal Magar's teaching, but this one act I could not do. The very thought of resting my bare-skinned weight against dead flesh had provoked my every ingrained taboo. I could look – perhaps even touch – but no, I could not sit on a corpse.

Kushal Magar had watched and waited, as he always did, allowing me the time first to react and then contend with myself; to explore internally until I could find my own means of understanding or at least acceptance.

It had occurred to me that, whilst I knew there was obviously nothing to fear from the deceased themselves, I simply had too much knowledge of the hidden process of putrefaction already under way, of bloat and ooze soon to begin. I had, therefore, and with Kushal Magar's sanction, selected instead to sit cross-legged at the dead man's side – my only concession, to allow bare knees to touch cold hand and shoulder.

Once I had proven myself calm and yet engaged, Kushal Magar had guided me to draw in vermilion paste three straight lines between both the body's nipples and its pubis to form a downward-pointing triangle: the *traipura yantra*, a simple geometric figure representing to the tantric mind the elemental vibration that literally animates the universe into existence – *Para Shakti*.

I had next been instructed to mark in pigment the diminutive indentation of the navel, representing man's ordinary perception, limited by mindless habit and conditioning; petty self-interest, conceit, pessimism, fear. And then, to contrast this, a broad circle within the triangle to represent the all-inclusive awareness of an enlightened, 'sunlit' mind.

I had been instructed to place flowers upon this *yantra*, which Kushal Magar had ready in his bag: ritual recognition that all the qualities conventional culture deem 'divine' are in truth already our own.

He had then encouraged me to rest one hand on the lifeless chest, the other on the belly, that I might know for myself the true intimacy of life and death. The intertwining of creation and dissolution in both the cellular and cosmic. The indivisibility of subject and object, the inner and the outer, microcosm and macrocosm.

It was not easy.

Without the attentions of an undertaker's trocar, twine and needle, tissue plumpers, wax and pots of pigment, the day-long dead do not in truth look – or feel – as though they are merely sleeping. At such intimate proximity to the coldness and peculiar pallor of the deceased, my analytical mind had protested loudly, repeatedly reviewing the path that had led me to the seeming madness of this moment. Sitting on an isolated cremation ground in the middle of the night. Beside a corpse. Naked.

As the hours passed I knew, perhaps quite naturally, moments of intense revulsion that caused my head and stomach to reel with such force as very nearly to overwhelm my resolve. More than once, I prepared myself to call an end, to pull away hands and knees that I had begun to convince myself were absorbing the corpse's very chill – a deathly pall I fancifully imagined might extend its reach, stealthily ascend my limbs and still the drum of my own heart.

This in turn awoke in my mind all manner of folkloric nonsense: vampires, ghosts and zombies, by which, from my earliest years, my own culture had impressed on me its communal terror of our inevitable end. The reappearance of these foolish, childhood fears alarmed me to think that, even in an adult who considered himself rational and far beyond superstition's stupor, such fantastical mythologies could emerge from the subconscious to play upon senses already struggling to assimilate the truth of Samuel's loss.

However, even as I dismissed the folly of such ghosts, there arose the question of what might have caused this young man's death. Whilst his body appeared untarnished by either injury or infection, it was the possibility of contagion that made me envision some vile disease now seeping from his pores to mine, foul pathogens leaching their pollution into my veins.

And yet, as with time and determined concentration I eased into the rite, my thoughts eventually began to settle with increasing clarity on death's ever-present attendance, its inevitability and necessity, despite all our effort to disguise and deny it. For how could life be truly grasped, its unlimited wonders known, if we hide from a primary aspect of its experience for no better reason than its potential for stirring emotional distress?

This brought to mind my school-friend Tim, who had red hair, white legs, blue lips and a congenital heart condition that prevented him from playing sports. Throughout our junior school Tim was made to sit alone in all weathers at the sideline, to watch the rest of us inanely chasing balls across football, rugby and cricket pitches. Such had been my concern for his enforced solitude that I faked colds, headaches, even limps to sit beside him and keep him entertained with stories, jokes and Fruit Pastilles. Then came the morning assembly at which, slipped between the swimming gala scores and lists of house detentions, his sudden death was announced. I looked about in shock, desperately searching for his face as I rummaged through my pockets for the sweets I kept for him, as though the promise of his favourite blackcurrant gums might summon Tim to arrive late with an apologetic note from his mother, his red hair wild, his cheeky grin the colour of a winter sky.

Tim's had been the first real loss I had known, beyond those of elderly relations, whose long, rich lives had reached their natural conclusion. There had subsequently been many more close deaths, of course, throughout the years – family and friends taken by sickness, accident and suicide. Unexpected losses that left me fearful of what might similarly curtail my years with unforeseen haste.

But that Samuel was also gone, I still struggled to accept. Especially when he remained so alive, so vibrant in my inner senses that his removal from my external world simply made no sense. In addition, such was the speed of cremation in India, primarily due to climatic conditions and hygiene, that I had no personal evidence of Samuel's death. No body, no farewell rite. Only Kushal Magar's word, however incontestable.

And rather than the safe formality of a funeral at which to recognise his loss and share my grief for him with others he had loved, I had instead my knees and palms against flaccid skin – a corpse that he too had briefly been, and that I would also one day become.

This last fact proved just as challenging to accept as Samuel's loss, for the rhythm of my heart and breath, the vitality of my every cell, seemed invariable and eternal. That they too would fade and ultimately fail seemed, at this vibrant, life-filled moment, an impossibility.

Yet here it was, beneath my hands and eyes, the proof. For this dead stranger was my sure end – both inevitable and necessary.

In that moment, I understood the power of *shava-sadhana*, for never had I been so aware that I was breathing, thinking, feeling.

And with this realisation, I knew for myself beyond mere theory, as never before, the true absurdity of wasting any moment of our lives on judgemental attitudes, the irrationality of prejudice, on meaningless attachments to appearance, memories, possessions or reputation, on our self-interested acts of either aggrandisement or abasement, on our obsessions with soul-numbing conformity and habit – through all of which the majority of us function all our lives long.

I closed my eyes tight to let this new flurry of thoughts flare through the darkness of my head.

And with them came a new assuring peace.

A new dedication never again to take for granted, or even to forget, that I was alive!

A vow to honour Samuel by applying all I had learnt in his company, and by his example. And this that I might truly live and love fearlessly, joyfully, without condition – that no hour or opportunity might be wasted of a life that was, with every passing day, ever more brief and precious.

CXVI

That my learning might be limitless
My body, once restless as the waves,
He in calmness set.

Thirumandiram

When next I opened my eyes, I found a single smear of light had breached the eastern sky. The stars were waning.

Kushal Magar was sitting on the opposite side of the corpse, his gaze so intent upon me that I could believe he had willed me to rouse from my contemplation.

'*Jhankri-dajoo?*' I mumbled, my eyes and head slow to adjust to an external world from which I felt I had long been withdrawn.

'It is time,' he quietly replied. 'Dawn is come. The family will be returning.'

We touched our hands to our own foreheads, lips, hearts and pubic bones to mark a closing dedication, before he led me in the repetition of concluding mantras as we cleared the torso of its flowers and washed away all trace of vermilion. I placed my fingers on the darkened feet in last respect and stepped outside the circle to watch Kushal Magar sweep away his incised circle.

As I dressed, he rebound the cerement with new knots so that we might together return the corpse to its original position. The Aghori Baba, who still sat as sentry beneath the seared tree, said not a word, but opened one bloodshot eye as acknowledgement in parting.

'So what comes now?' I asked, as we made our way back to our camp on the far side of the cremation ground.

'It is the custom to refrain from singing, dancing and sexual intimacy for fifteen days following *shava-sadhana*,' Kushal Magar replied. 'And this that you might dedicate your time to contemplative *Svadhyaya* – you remember the fourth *niyama*?'

I nodded: the expansion of awareness through reflective study and mindful *sadhana*. It would certainly require many more days of careful consideration to begin to understand how our night's watch over a corpse could have left me feeling remarkably, even inexplicably, calm of heart and clear of head. And yet, whatever its psychological explanation, I found myself with a newly restored equanimity in which I hoped to come to terms, in time, with Samuel's sudden and unnecessary parting.

'You have also proven yourself *Vira*, a student worthy to be called "heroic",' he declared. 'For you have shown the depth of courage that is the foundation of true integrity, of "wholeness". You have shown that your love of life is greater than your fear.'

Kushal Magar directed my eyes towards a small gathering of white-clad men on the far side of the ground. They were pouring *ghee* across corpse, cloth, wood and strings of golden marigolds.

And then a flare of violent light, of spit and crackle, as hungry, tall, blue flames took hold of butter-basted cotton, bark and skin.

The young man with whom we had spent the night – whose lifeless form had afforded me unexpected opportunity to face my deepest fears not only of losing those I loved, but also myself – was, like Samuel, completing his return to fire and earth, sky and tree and rising sun.

CXVII

Whomsoever we love, in him we find . . . the final truth of our
existence . . . in [him] we have touched that great truth which
comprehends the whole universe.

Rabindranath Tagore

We waited a whole day until the pyre had burned its charge to embers and cast him windward.

'The last respect that we can give,' Kushal Magar had said.

And he was wise to wait. The passing hours, our faces blown with ash from wood and hair, skin and bone, allowed some consolidation in the convoluted course of thoughts prompted by my night beside the dead young man.

For as we waited, I came to see with ever greater clarity that in truth our end is already here, our hearts reckoning their steady ebb in rhythmic measure, each day's sun and moon in cadence counting out our years. The quell of one more conversation, the conclusion of another meal, the turning in, the turning off, the goodnight kiss, are all but draughts of death's finality diluted.

I then began to question what we humans grieve for to such depths that we have invented gods for comfort? Even to attribute to them complex theologies of promised afterlifes, resurrections or rebirths – imagined salvations from ourselves in conditional reward for what is always some degree of denial of our wonderfully imperfect humanity.

Instead, it seemed to me, this sure knowledge of our inescapable demise not only provides compelling impetus for us to reconsider our every attachment and priority –

that each moment might be valued, each day well and fully lived – but affords us freedom, here and now, from any need for resentment or indifference, inhibition, cowardice, apathy or greed.

For surely, by death's certain benevolence, is not our every moment – this present life, our loves, these limbs – made glorious?

The last, declining light of another day only confirmed to me the meanings I had begun to glean from my night on the cremation ground. I would always ache for Samuel, the memory of his kindness and his mischief ever vibrant in my mind. But now I chose not to allow his physical loss to darken and diminish my life, but rather to enhance it by rendering every interaction, word and intimacy worthy of my full attention – every new moment meaningful and significant, in celebration of him.

'Brother,' Kushal Magar said, dampening the fire and preparing his shawl-and-blanket bedding for another sleep, 'tomorrow we must part.'

'But aren't I coming with you?' I asked. It had not occurred to me to consider any possible alternative.

'In the morning I return to the hills, to which others still say you may not come,' he replied. 'My duty to Samuel-*bhai* is done. His family must be told. And there are yet others to whom I have responsibility.'

'Of course.' I nodded, my heart constricting at the thought of Samuel's parents. 'But, then, what am I to do?'

'Go home,' he answered. 'You have completed all that was needful here. So now return to do your duty to your family, your society – and thereby learn wisdom.'

I could only think that if the political unrest were to persist, as seemed the present threat, it could be a long time yet before foreigners would be permitted access to the hills again. I did not know that I was ready to accept such a separation.

Kushal Magar, however, had no misgivings.

'You are generous enough to think you still need me for guidance or for comfort,' he said. 'And yet you already have enough to find the knowledge and the peace you seek. You simply have not yet chosen to see it in yourself – when, in truth, your own heart is by far the greatest *jhankri* of them all.'

I remained unconvinced. It was not just his instruction I knew I would miss, the chance to explore subjects I could not share with any other, but the honesty of his friendship; his gentle nature; his clear, compassionate interaction with the world that never ceased to delight, inspire – and yes, he was quite right – comfort me.

'But now, time for sleep, brother,' he announced. 'We both have long journeys to begin at daybreak.'

As he settled down beside me, I tucked my shawl into my neck to make a pillow. I pulled the sleeping-bag around my chin and laid an arm across my rucksack as though Samuel were again close enough to keep me company and warm.

'But *jhankri-dajoo*, what if the troubles are not resolved?' I whispered in the darkness. 'What if I cannot reach you for many months – or even years – to come?'

'There is no benefit in "what ifs",' he replied, 'for could we know life's surprises and conclusions, there would be no daily adventure to pursue. There would be no need for the fearlessness you have shown here to embrace both life's pain and pleasure, its quiet and ferocity. There would be no new learning.'

He reached out in the dark to rest a hand against my shoulder.

'But however long it may yet be until we meet again,

you need only trust your heart, then live by it with courage and compassion. For you already have all you need to be an active man of honourable deeds.'

Even though I could not see him, I could hear the abiding smile in his voice.

'All I ask is that you remain benevolent in your thoughts, words and actions, never underestimating the difference each one of them can make, both to others and yourself. Stay curious, seeking out wisdom wherever and with whomever you may be. Restore balance and bring peace by starting with yourself. Live and love so fully, so joyfully that there is no time, no mind for fear. And engage with every day as though it were both your very first and very last.'

I turned my eyes towards stars that blazed above us in their thousands, and vowed to myself that I would honour his every word.

'But perhaps most of all, brother,' Kushal Magar said, reaching out to place his hand on my head in what I knew to be his final blessing, 'choose always to be happy.'

EPILOGUE

Despite the unrest and even violence that continues to disrupt life sporadically along the northern border of West Bengal, I returned to the hills as soon as foreigners were again permitted access.

Outside the little scarlet temple beneath Kanchenjunga, Kushal Magar's attentive guidance inspired me through a further eleven winters. Our lessons were interrupted only when all routes to Lapu were swept away by landslides after a devastating earthquake struck the region. Even then, we managed to exchange supportive messages, courtesy of an obliging relative who was working with a local rescue team.

During those years, Kushal Magar introduced me to ever more demanding physical practices, meditative techniques and challenges, all of which continue to inform, transform and undoubtedly brighten my daily life. I shall remain forever changed – happier, freer, braver, more accepting of myself and others – and deeply grateful.

It was Kushal Magar's own wish that the Tradition's initial teachings be shared. My hope therefore is that, as a mark of my respect for him and his culture, the introduction offered in these chapters might inspire others to free themselves from those thoughts, words and actions that perpetuate ill-will, harm and inhumanity. And that, in so doing, they might choose instead to engage more honestly, courageously, joyfully, benevolently and meaningfully not only with themselves and their fellow man, but with life in all its limitless variety and wonder.

GLOSSARY

(Listed in the order the Tradition is commonly taught, as presented in this book.)

p. 8   *Bhavana*   Mindful intent.

Choose to take responsibility for our own thoughts, words and actions, that we might learn to live with greater awareness, understanding, intensity and joy.

p. 9   *Shaiva Tantra Yoga*   A practical, experimental system of liberation from self-limitation; a guide to ways in which to live and love more fully, fearlessly and joyfully, without detriment to ourselves or others.

p. 17   *Sukha*   All that is prosperous, agreeable and liberating; 'freedom of the heart'.

In preference to *dukha* – suffering, 'constriction around the heart' – choose to pursue stable pleasures that are beneficial, improve both physical and mental stability, afford peace of heart and mind, and that brighten and expand consciousness.

p. 20   *Shaiva*   The adjective for Shiva, who symbolises the predisposition to order in the universe, consciousness without limitation, benevolence and *Sat*: truth that is a way of being.

Seek self-knowledge without self-interest.

p. 24 *Sadhana* The practical exploration of the Tradition's teachings, all of which guide us to take responsibility for the quality of our own consciousness and thereby our interaction with the world.

p. 31 *Tantra* A technique for the expansion of consciousness, heightening awareness beyond our normal waking state; the means by which to deliver ourselves from a limited, self-centred viewpoint, and thereby from our potential for inhumanity, both to ourselves and others.

p. 32 *Yoga* The active, practical 'technology' that enables us to perceive ourselves and our world more accurately, affording the freedom of heart and expansion of awareness that enable us to live and love more fully, effectively, justly and joyfully.

Avoid unproductive thoughts and behaviour. Find the good, the beneficial in whoever and whatever come our way. Give as generously as our capacity and means allow.

p. 35 *Shishya* The 'ideal student' mindfully develops the following qualities:

A healthy and stable body–mind.

An honest and sincere disposition, free from pride and with honourable intentions.

A sympathetic and open heart that shows invariable compassion to all living things.

The capacity for happiness, enjoyment and sensual pleasure, yet with the inclination to master desires and passions.

Disinterest in the trivial, material wealth or social hierarchies.

A willingness to sacrifice self-interest in the discharge of duties to parents, family, partners and teachers.

A willingness to explore possibilities beyond the obvious or ordinary.

A genuine desire for liberation from detrimental self-limitation.

p. 51 Purushartha The four Aims of Life, considered the most effective path to wisdom:

1. Dharma (p. 52) Expansion of consciousness through the fulfilment of moral duty.

Think, say and do nothing to our own or another's detriment. Determine our true nature and then live fully and happily in accordance with it. Honour our families, ancestors, teachers. Show benevolence to all, without judgement or condition.

2. Artha (p. 61) Expansion of consciousness through the fulfilment of social responsibility.

Diligently and honourably support ourselves and provide for those for whom we are responsible. Do our part to maintain a balanced society in which even the least able can flourish according to their own natures. Acquire beneficial knowledge and nurture friendships.

3. Kama (p. 63) Expansion of consciousness through the fulfilment of sensual pleasures that do not diminish the quality of our consciousness.

Mindfully embrace, heighten and explore our senses, not only through sight, taste, sound, smell and touch, but through art, music, dance and food; play, work, *sadhana*, love and breath; family and friends; and by attending to the well-being, and thereby the happiness, of others.

4. Moksha (p. 68) Expansion of consciousness by learning to perceive the essential interconnection, the

indivisibility, that underlies what might initially appear to be difference and separation.

Develop greater empathy, expressed through effective, dynamic compassion. Become of ever greater benefit both to ourselves and others.

p. 113 *Yamas* The Six Restraints in Personal Conduct, applied to our relationship with the world, guiding us to develop respect for ourselves and all those with whom we come in contact.

1. *Ahimsa* (p. 115)   The wisdom gained by learning to avoid causing harm to ourselves or others, in either thought, or word or action.

2. *Alobha* (p. 118)   The wisdom gained by learning to live without selfish ambition. It is not by taking from others, but in giving of ourselves that we truly gain the most.

3. *Asteya* (p. 120)   The wisdom gained by learning to extinguish the desire to possess that which belongs to another, whether their property, relationships, social rank, talents, employment, reputation or appearance.

4. *Brahmacharya* (p. 122)   The wisdom learnt by seeking to understand and thereby embrace and live according to our true nature.

5. *Tyaga* (p. 125)   The wisdom gained by learning to release our self-identification with material possessions. Learn to acquire only that which is necessary to live healthily and freely.

6. *Shaucha* (p. 127)   The wisdom gained by learning to maintain internal and external cleanliness. Develop purity/clarity of thought, speech, action (*ahimsa*) and intention (*bhavana*). Learn to live without prejudice, enmity or resistance.

p. 133 *Niyamas* The Five Observances of Personal Conduct, applied to our relationship with ourselves, guiding us to reduce the conflict between our internal perspective – our thoughts and conscience – and our external action.

1. *Santosha* (p. 135) The wisdom learnt by choosing to be content with the necessities of a healthy, fulfilled life: food and warmth; purposeful, rewarding work and mental stimulation; human intimacy and meaningful friendships.

2. *Dana* (p. 137) The wisdom gained by learning to give of ourselves without thought of reward. Live by a love that is fearless, impersonal, dynamic, unfailingly humane and without condition.

3. *Tapa* (p. 139) The wisdom learnt through developing the self-discipline and willpower, the physical, emotional and mental endurance required to overcome self-defeating habits.

4. *Svadhyaya* (p. 142) The wisdom gained by remaining open to new learning without prejudice or inhibition. Expand awareness through personal enquiry, contemplation, mindful listening and *sadhana*.

5. *Pranidhana* (p. 144) The wisdom learnt through applied endeavour and focused attention. This includes the three-part tantric practice of self-mastery, *ulto sadhana*: mastery of the breath, mastery of sexual response and mastery of the mind. These can only be learnt directly from an authentic teacher of the Tradition.

p. 149 *Tin Gunharu* The three qualities keepers of the Tradition are mindful to develop:

Dedication (p. 150) – commitment to the process of liberating ourselves from detrimental thought, word and behaviour.

Concentration (p. 151) – living with honest awareness and constructive purpose.

Discretion (p. 153) – making no show of our learning, whilst applying our knowledge and insights to the benefit of others, rather than for our own profit.

p. 157 *Guru* A 'dispeller of darkness', one who routs ignorance by offering guidance and comfort gained from personal experience, with no thought of personal reward or notice.

Avoid any system founded upon any notion of 'spiritual hierarchy'.

p. 164 *Divyachara* 'Going by daylight' – enlightenment: perception beyond mere mental conditioning; beyond the ordinary, all-consuming preoccupation with our physical, emotional and sexual responses to external stimuli.

Seek an understanding free from the distortions of our own self-interest by learning to apply the principles of *bhavana*, the four Purushartha, the three *Gunharu*, the eleven *yamas* and *niyamas*.

p. 171 *Nama* The essence of who and what we are; our 'inner nature'.

p. 171 *Rupa* The external, material form; our 'outer life'.

When our *Rupa* is not a true reflection of our *Nama* we will find ourselves in perpetual conflict. Only when they are in harmony can we live and love healthily and to our full capacity. We would do well to examine the learnt labels and roles by which we live.

p. 209 *Samskaras* Acquired ideas and beliefs determined by our own biography; the emotional responses we have gathered by attachment to the past, and through which we unwittingly identify ourselves and thereby experience the external world, until we no longer see life as it is, but rather only as *we* are.

Learn to release self-identification through outdated responses and attachments. Mindfully seek uplifting, enlightening memories with which to replace the adverse and the obsolete.

p. 321 *Shava-sadhana* Contemplation on – traditionally, confrontation with – our mortality.

Re-evaluate the absurdity of wasting a brief and precious life on judgement and prejudice; attachment to appearance, memories, possessions or reputation; self-interested acts of either aggrandisement or disparagement; or our obsessions with detrimental conformity and habit.

Choose to keep thoughts, words and actions benevolent, never underestimating the difference each one of them can make, both to others and ourselves.

Stay curious, seeking out wisdom wherever and with whomever we may be.

Restore balance, bring peace – always starting with ourselves.

Live and love so fully, so joyfully that there is no time, no mind for fear.

Engage with every day as though it were both our very first and very last.

Choose always to be happy.

ACKNOWLEDGEMENTS

There are many without whose encouragement and support this book could not have been written.

My special thanks must go to Mario, a remarkable friend who so generously provided me with the time and a roof-top view of Vancouver's North Shore Mountains to write *Limitless Sky*.

Lynne and Joanna for the invaluable insights their friendships and years of dedication as students of the Tradition have afforded me. Sarah and Emma for their enthusiasm for and their patience with the faltering process that has brought this book to fruition. Manoj, whose ever grateful and perceptive heart never ceases to inspire.

Uncles Ananda, Shiva and Sishir; cousins Josiah, Clifford and Demetrius for all their practical assistance, cultural insights and help with translations.

My agent, Sheila Ableman, for her determination and guidance. Judith Kendra, Susan Lascelles and the team at Rider/Random House for their confidence and expertise.

And of course Bernard, a companion beyond compare.

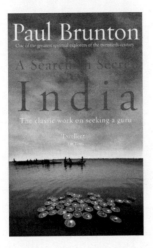

India: the Road Ahead

Mark Tully

As former Chief of Bureau for the BBC in India, Mark Tully draws upon a lifetime's knowledge of this most diverse of countries to consider an emerging superpower at a pivotal moment in history. There are many unanswered questions about the sustainability of such growth and its effect on the stability of the nation. In search of answers, Tully meets industrialists and farmers, spiritual leaders and bandits, politicians and untouchables, capturing the voices of the nation at a time of great change.

'Superb' *TLS*

ISBN 9781846041624

Order this title direct from www.riderbooks.co.uk

In the Valley of Mist

One Family's Extraordinary Story:
from Peace to War in Kashmir

Justine Hardy

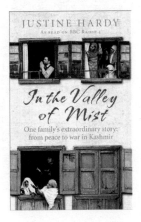

Mohammed Dar and his three brothers were born on a houseboat in Kashmir, a place of exquisite beauty that was to become a war zone. This Himalayan valley of water, mist and mountains was once one of India's greatest tourist draws. In 1989, it exploded into insurgency, and Mohammed Dar and his family found themselves living in a country riven by violence.

Justine Hardy has stayed with the Dar family for many years and shares their extraordinary story of family survival at the heart of a conflict within and beyond the Muslim world.

ISBN 9781846041518

Order this title direct from www.riderbooks.co.uk

Last Seen in Lhasa

The Story of an Extraordinary Friendship in Modern Tibet

Claire Scobie

Some go to Tibet seeking inspiration, others for adventure. Award-winning journalist Claire Scobie found both when she left London for the Himalayas. Her search for a rare red lily took her to Pemako, where the myth of Shangri-la was born. It was here she became friends with Ani, the rosy-cheeked Tibetan nun who was to change her life.

Claire chronicles a rapidly changing world – where monks talk on mobiles and Lhasa's sex industry thrives. By turns tragic and humorous, *Last Seen in Lhasa* is a compelling story of friendship, insight and adventure.

'Laced with gentle humour and great affection … Required reading for the traveller interested in understanding the paradoxes of contemporary Tibet' – *Sunday Telegraph*

ISBN 9781846040061

Order this title direct from www.riderbooks.co.uk

JOIN THE RIDER COMMUNITY

Visit us online for competitions, free books, special offers, film clips and interviews, author events and the latest news about our books and authors:

www.riderbooks.co.uk

Rider Books on Facebook

@Rider_Books

riderbooks.tumblr.com

RIDER BOOKS, 20 VAUXHALL BRIDGE ROAD, LONDON SW1V 2SA
E: INFO@RIDERBOOKS.CO.UK